After centuries of neglect the life and works of Lucius Annaeus *c*. 4 BCE–65 CE). At one time a and his political career came to a later plot to kill the capricious and murderous emperor and compelled to commit suicide. Discredited through collusion, or at least association, with a notorious and tyrannical regime, Seneca's ideas were for a time also considered derivative of Greek Stoicism and thus inferior to the real thing. In this first in-depth introduction to be published for many years, Christopher Star shows what a remarkable statesman, dramatist and philosopher his subject actually was. Seneca's original contributions to political philosophy and the philosophy of the emotions were considerable. He was a favourite authority for many early Christian authors, and he is a key figure in the history of ideas and the Renaissance, as well as in literature and drama. This new survey does full justice to his significance.

CHRISTOPHER STAR is Associate Professor of Classics at Middlebury College, Vermont. He is the author of *The Empire of the Self: Self-Command and Political Speech in Seneca and Petronius* (2012).

UNDERSTANDING CLASSICS

EDITOR: RICHARD STONEMAN (UNIVERSITY OF EXETER)

When the great Roman poets of the Augustan Age – Ovid, Virgil and Horace – composed their odes, love poetry and lyrical verse, could they have imagined that their works would one day form a cornerstone of Western civilization, or serve as the basis of study for generations of schoolchildren learning Latin? Could Aeschylus or Euripides have envisaged the remarkable popularity of contemporary stagings of their tragedies? The legacy and continuing resonance of Homer's *Iliad* and *Odyssey* – Greek poetical epics written many millennia ago – again testify to the capacity of the classics to cross the divide of thousands of years and speak powerfully and relevantly to audiences quite different from those to which they were originally addressed.

Understanding Classics is a specially commissioned series which aims to introduce the outstanding authors and thinkers of antiquity to a wide audience of appreciative modern readers, whether undergraduate students of classics, literature, philosophy and ancient history or generalists interested in the classical world. Each volume – written by leading figures internationally – will examine the historical significance of the writer or writers in question; their social, political and cultural contexts; their use of language, literature and mythology; extracts from their major works; and their reception in later European literature, art, music and culture. *Understanding Classics* will build a library of readable, authoritative introductions offering fresh and elegant surveys of the greatest literatures, philosophies and poetries of the ancient world.

UNDERSTANDING CLASSICS

Archimedes	CHRIS RORRES *Drexel University, Pennsylvania*
Aristophanes and Greek Comedy	JEFFREY S. RUSTEN *Cornell University*
Augustine	DENNIS E. TROUT *Tufts University*
Cicero	GESINE MANUWALD *University College London*
Euripides	ISABELLE TORRANCE *University of Notre Dame*
Eusebius	AARON P. JOHNSON *Lee University, Tennessee*
Homer	JONATHAN S. BURGESS *University of Toronto*
Horace	PAUL ALLEN MILLER *University of South Carolina*
Latin Love Poetry	DENISE MCCOSKEY & ZARA TORLONE *Miami University, Ohio*
Martial	LINDSAY C. WATSON & PATRICIA WATSON *University of Sydney*
Ovid	CAROLE E. NEWLANDS *University of Wisconsin, Madison*
Pindar	RICHARD STONEMAN *University of Exeter*
Plutarch	MARK A. BECK *University of North Carolina, Chapel Hill*
The Poets of Alexandria	SUSAN A. STEPHENS *Stanford University*
Roman Comedy	DAVID CHRISTENSON *University of Arizona*
Sappho	PAGE DUBOIS *University of California, San Diego*
Seneca	CHRISTOPHER STAR *Middlebury College, Vermont*
Sophocles	STEPHEN ESPOSITO *Boston University*
Tacitus	VICTORIA EMMA PAGÁN *University of Florida*
Virgil	ALISON KEITH *University of Toronto*

SENECA

Christopher Star

UNDERSTANDING CLASSICS SERIES EDITOR:
RICHARD STONEMAN

Published in 2017 by
I.B.Tauris & Co. Ltd
London · New York
www.ibtauris.com

Copyright © 2017 Christopher Star

The right of Christopher Star to be identified as the author of this work has been asserted by the author in accordance with the Copyright, Designs and Patents Act 1988.

All rights reserved. Except for brief quotations in a review, this book, or any part thereof, may not be reproduced, stored in or introduced into a retrieval system, or transmitted, in any form or by any means, electronic, mechanical, photocopying, recording or otherwise, without the prior written permission of the publisher.

References to websites were correct at the time of writing.

ISBN: 978 1 84885 889 3 (HB)
         978 1 84885 890 9 (PB)
eISBN: 978 1 78672 038 2
ePDF: 978 1 78673 038 1

A full CIP record for this book is available from the British Library
A full CIP record is available from the Library of Congress

Library of Congress Catalog Card Number: available

Text designed and typeset by Tetragon, London
Printed and bound in Great Britain by T.J. International, Padstow, Cornwall

Contents

Acknowledgements	ix
Introduction	1
I · Seneca's Philosophy	25
II · Seneca's Tragedies	67
III · Reception	117
Notes	171
Select Translations, Commentaries and Collections of Essays	177
Bibliography	181
Index	191

Acknowledgements

SEVERAL FRIENDS, family members and colleagues have helped me during the writing of this book. It is with profound gratitude that I acknowledge only a few of them here. Alex Wright, Richard Stoneman and Susanna Braund first suggested this project to me and continued to offer assistance in a variety of forms throughout the time I worked on it. I am grateful to Sara Magness, Melanie Marshall and Alex Billington for helping to see this book smoothly through production. My colleagues in the Middlebury College department of Classics, Jane Chaplin, Randall Ganiban, Pavlos Sfyroeras, Ian Sutherland and Marc Witkin, provided a stimulating atmosphere in which to work on this and other projects. I was also fortunate to have the help of several outstanding student research assistants: Margaret Clark, Sophia Hagen, Rebecca Goodman and Hailey Culhane. My greatest debt is owed to my family, especially my wife, Sarah. Our son, Jeremiah, was born during the early stages of my work on this book. He can now identify different pictures of Seneca and ask me when I will be done working with 'old books'. I dedicate this 'new book' to him.

Introduction

Overview

THIS BOOK OFFERS AN INTRODUCTION to the life, works and legacy of Lucius Annaeus Seneca Minor, better known today as Seneca the Younger, or simply Seneca. Seneca lived during some of the most momentous and horrifying years of Roman history: the establishment and consolidation of the principate, or one-man rule, over the Roman Empire by Augustus and his successors, Tiberius, Caligula, Claudius and Nero. The loss of the Republic deeply affected the Roman psyche. According to tradition, Romulus initiated a line of kings at Rome in 753 BCE, which ended with the establishment of liberty and the Republic in 509 BCE. In theory, the Senate and the People of Rome (SPQR) guided the Roman Republic. In reality, the Republic was an oligarchy, but it was also one of the most successful empire-building machines ever known. After conquering much of the Mediterranean, the Romans directed their aggressive impulses at each other. After decades of civil war in the first century BCE between powerful generals, Julius Caesar's nephew, heir and adopted son, Octavian, was left as the last man standing. As a means to forget the past, Octavian was granted the honorific title Augustus, and handed back power to the Senate and People of Rome. Augustus fashioned himself as the *princeps*, the first citizen among equals. In reality, he inaugurated the age of the Roman emperors, which would only end in the West in 476 CE.

In many ways, the writings of Seneca shape and are shaped by difficulties the Roman elite experienced in coming to grips with this new balance of power and political system. Seneca was at the centre of this transition. He lived under all of the Julio-Claudian emperors; Nero, the last, only survived Seneca by three years. Seneca was also close to the royal family, at least from the time of Caligula (37–41 CE). He suffered both the deep despair of exile and the heights of political power at their hands. He eventually became Nero's tutor, speech writer, advisor and, finally, one of his many victims.

During his lifetime, Seneca wrote a wide array of works in both prose (philosophy) and poetry (tragedy) and also wrote a satire that combines both (*Apocolocyntosis*). Given his long life and prolific literary output, Seneca is a crucial figure who bridges the gap from what has traditionally been seen as the Golden Age of literature under Augustus (Virgil, Horace and Ovid) to the decline and decadence of Silver Latin under Nero. He was a follower of the Stoic school of philosophy, which began in Athens in 300 BCE, and thus is an important source for documenting how this philosophy was practised during the Roman period. In Seneca's hands, philosophy becomes a road map for both the emperor and his subjects to learn how to live and die well. His tragedies are based on stories from Greek myth, but also relate to Seneca's world of empire and autocracy.

Constructing Seneca's biography is a difficult task. In fact, it was not until comparatively recently that we knew how many Senecas there were. The fifth-century poet, Sidonius Apollinaris, writes of two, one who wrote philosophy and the other who wrote tragedy (*Carm* 9.232–236). This mistake is in some ways understandable, given the fact that Seneca's two main bodies of work can seem mutually irreconcilable. There were in fact two Senecas: Seneca the philosopher and tragedian, who is the subject of this book, and his father, typically known today as Seneca the Elder or Seneca Rhetor, as he was the author of two books on rhetoric, the *Controversiae* and the *Suasoriae*. During the late Middle Ages and early modern period the father and son were often meshed into one person. Thus, it was thought that Seneca had lived to be over 100 years old and had seen the end of the Republic and all, save three years, of the Julio-Claudian dynasty that followed.[1] While the works of the father have been separated from those of the son, and scholars remain fairly certain that the two plays attached to Seneca the Younger's name, *Octavia* and *Hercules Oetaeus*, are by a later imitator, writing a biography of Seneca's life is nevertheless a difficult task. Seneca rarely discusses events from his life in his writings. Scholars must rely primarily on the works of two historians, Tacitus's *Annals* and Cassius Dio's *Roman History*. Suetonius also provides a few interesting pieces of information about Seneca in his biographies of Caligula and Nero. All three are writing well after Seneca's death. Tacitus's and Suetonius's works can be dated to the early decades of the second century. Dio, who wrote in Greek, can be dated to the early third century. Further complicating matters is the fact that we no longer have the actual text of Dio's history for the period during which Seneca lived. Rather, what survives is a redacted account, often called the 'epitome', by the eleventh-century Byzantine scholar, Xiphilinus. Both Tacitus and Dio only bring Seneca into their narrative once he has made a name for himself in Rome. Thus, they offer no information about Seneca's early life. In addition, each provides strikingly different portraits of Seneca. Tacitus is primarily sympathetic, whereas Dio is hostile.

Our Seneca was born around the year 4 BCE, although some put the date as late as 1 CE in Corduba, a city in the Roman province of Hispania (modern Córdoba, Spain). He died by his own hand, yet paradoxically following the emperor Nero's death sentence, at his suburban villa, which was located a few miles from Rome, surrounded by his wife, Paulina, friends and slaves on an evening in April of 65 CE. Over the course of the 60 plus years of his life, Seneca became known as one of the leading intellectual figures of his day, and attained some of the highest political offices, both official, as consul, and unofficial, as tutor, speech writer and 'friend' of the young emperor Nero. In the more than 2,000 years since his forced suicide, Seneca's works have served as an important source of Stoic philosophy and as a model for tragedy. Given what we know about his life, however, it is painfully clear that Seneca did not achieve his fame without making radical compromises. For many, Seneca is a hypocrite who preached Stoic austerity in his philosophy while living in the lap of luxury at Rome and in his many villas. His two main bodies of work, philosophy and tragedy, also suggest that Seneca was never fully reconciled himself with the Stoic world view. The hopeless, violent and passion-fuelled world of his tragedies seems to contradict the celebration of Stoic reason and divine providence of his philosophy to such a degree that when viewed in tandem, Seneca can come across as an author who holds two mutually irreconcilable visions of humanity, politics and the cosmos. Finally, the most damning condemnation of Seneca's inability to put his philosophy into practice stems from his failure to shape Nero into a philosopher-king, or a decent ruler, at the very least. Today, some may see Nero as a misunderstood genius, but typically his name is a catchword for tyranny, and he is even seen as the Antichrist of the Book of Revelation (13:18).[2] Given his close connection to Nero, it seems fair to ask whether Seneca was simply an ineffectual, but good-intentioned, advisor or did in fact teach Nero how to become a tyrant, as Dio claims (61.10.2)?[3]

The study of Seneca is a study in contradictions, paradoxes and antitheses that do not give way to easy resolutions or syntheses. Seneca's philosophical works champion using Stoicism as a guide to life, a way for learning how to live and die. Yet, as we have noted, we know very little about Seneca's own life from his writings, and virtually nothing about his political life. This reticence about himself in his own works reveals a further paradox hindering the writing of Seneca's biography. Over the past few decades, Seneca has come to be seen as one of the central figures in the development of the concept of the individual. Yet Seneca's own self is rarely revealed in his works. If it were not for Tacitus and Dio, we would know next to nothing about Seneca's life in politics.[4] In fact, many of Seneca's works that were likely written at the height of his power in Nero's court strongly advocate a life of philosophical retirement away from politics. The ideal life presented in these texts is very different from what we know of the 'real' life Seneca lived. Nevertheless, Seneca's biography frequently colours the way we judge his philosophy. This fact is rare among ancient philosophers. Readers generally do not worry about Plato's and Aristotle's personal histories when approaching their works. When we come to Seneca, however, we happily apply the 'biographical fallacy', and ignore Roland Barthes's famous statement that 'the birth of the reader must come at the cost of the death of the author'.[5] In fact, Seneca's death, as narrated by Tacitus, strongly affects how Seneca has been read. Seneca might have been happy with this connection, but as noted earlier, in his own writing he seems to wish to detach his true self from his works.

To continue the paradoxes, throughout his philosophy Seneca advocates self-consistency: always being the same person. Even leaving aside the question of whether Seneca's own life was consistent with what he wrote, the Senecan corpus itself is wildly inconsistent. It is polyphonic and multigeneric, encompassing philosophy, tragedy and satire. One of the key questions of Senecan scholarship is how his two main bodies of work, philosophy and tragedy, fit together – if they do at all. This question already limits what Seneca wrote into a simple dichotomy of philosophy versus tragedy. Seneca also wrote the *Apocolocyntosis*, a satire on the death and deification of Claudius, which is our only complete example of the genre of Menippean satire. Like Seneca's overall corpus, this brief work alternates between prose and poetry, and subsumes within a dizzying array of genres including epic, tragedy, history, philosophy, panegyric, oratory, biography and official reports of the acts of the Senate. In addition, a good deal of Seneca's works have not survived, such as a biography of his father, a work on the geography and religions of Egypt, all of his speeches, and a treatise on moral philosophy, which he was working on at the end of his life. After he died, several works were attached to his name, such as the plays *Octavia*, the sole extant example of Roman historical drama (*tragoedia praetexta*), and *Hercules Oetaeus*. Several epigrams in the *Anthologia Latina* are said to be by Seneca; very few, if any, were likely written by him. By the late fourth century an apocryphal correspondence between Seneca and St Paul was written. Thus, soon after his death, Seneca came to be seen as a model for tragedy. For later Christian writers, Seneca was a moral authority who lived at the time of Jesus and the Apostles and who witnessed the first persecutions of Christians. Tracing Seneca's complicated legacy is the topic of the final chapter.

After giving an account of Seneca's life and death in this introduction, in the first chapter we will investigate Seneca's philosophical works, as well as the *Apocolocyntosis*. In many ways this work may seem the outlier in Seneca's corpus. Despite the Saturnalian laughter that characterises this piece, it also does important political work for the start of Nero's reign, and can be read in tandem with Seneca's only work of political theory, *On Mercy*. The majority of Seneca's philosophy can be classified as moral philosophy. Seneca's main concern is to help his readers, and himself, learn how to live well and die well. For a Stoic like Seneca, this entails living a life that follows reason and moral virtue, and is free from the emotions, such as sorrow and anger. One should meet death happily and without fear, whenever it comes. In fact, one of the main methods for living a good life according to Seneca is to continually think about the fact that death can come at any time, to any person: 'We die each day', as Seneca notes in the first letter of his *Moral Epistles* (1.3). Despite the fact that Seneca is concerned with his own moral progress and development in his writings, as we have already noted, his philosophy is rarely autobiographical. Instead, it presents an idealised portrait of a Stoic *proficiens* trying to help himself and others make progress down the path to perfection – all the time knowing that this ideal will never be attained. The fact that the Stoic project of self-perfection is ultimately doomed to fail perhaps accounts for the importance of forgiveness and making allowances for human frailty that we see in Seneca's philosophy. Miriam Griffin, author of the best biography of Seneca, succinctly sums up one of the key tensions at the core of Seneca's Stoicism: 'morbid asceticism' coupled with 'realistic humanity'.[6] Seneca's moral philosophy often cannot escape from the tyranny of his biography. Taken on its own, we might praise and admire his wisdom. But does its value change when we remember that Seneca advocated for poverty, the private life and self-control while reaping the monetary and social rewards of his closeness to imperial power? Is Seneca simply a hypocrite? At the very least, Seneca's philosophy causes us to question the origins of moral and philosophical authority. Does the character and biography of the speaker mar the message?

Chapter II looks at Seneca's tragedies. As with his biography, these plays constitute a threat to Seneca's Stoic philosophy. Centuries before Seneca, Plato had already outlined the danger of tragedy and the 'ancient quarrel between poetry and philosophy' (*Resp.* 607b). Seneca's younger contemporary and fellow Stoic, Epictetus, easily deflates tragedy's power as 'the suffering of humans who have been wonderstruck by chance events' (*Diss.* 1.4.26). Several questions surround Seneca's plays. We do not even know the original performance context. Were they written for full-scale performance on the stage, or recitation? Given the problematic relationship between tragedy and philosophy, we must wonder why Seneca wrote plays rather than simply critiquing existing ones, as most philosophers in the ancient world did. Seneca's reasons remain a mystery. He never mentions his plays in his prose works. Although the *Apocolocyntosis* likely alludes to his *Hercules*, Seneca did not write a lengthy treatise on poetry or drama, nor can a picture of Senecan poetics be gleaned from his philosophy that can definitively guide us in the interpretation of his plays.[7] Did Seneca write his plays to extend his philosophical lessons? Do they show the consequences of not being a Stoic? Did Seneca use his plays to explore some of Stoicism's darker possibilities? Or do they give the lie to the Stoic vision of the world and of humanity? On the other hand, are philosophical questions best ignored and are Seneca's plays to be considered as literary works of art? Do they have nothing to do with his philosophy and serve as an example of Seneca trying to add to his fame as writer by tackling yet another genre? While Seneca's plays demand such questions, they do not supply definitive answers.

Chapter III treats the history of Seneca's reception. This is the story of scholars, poets and artists coming to grips with Seneca and using his life and works to develop their own original creations over the past two millennia. In fact, the reception of Seneca likely started while he was still alive. It can be seen in the humour and satire of Petronius's *Satyricon* as well as the portrayal of fate, Roman politics and Seneca's hero, Cato, in the epic poem, *Civil War*, by Seneca's nephew, Lucan. Soon after his death, Seneca's life, death and works were explored, critiqued and pillaged by poets and historians. In the centuries that followed, Christian writers debated Seneca's value as a moral guide to life, and by the late Middle Ages his supporters had invented the myth of his conversion to Christianity. By the Renaissance, Seneca had become a central figure supplying (not uncontested) models for proper Latin, advice to rulers, and drama in both Latin and modern languages. In the eighteenth and nineteenth centuries, Seneca became a less central figure. Much of the controversies died out, as judgement of his philosophy and poetry were decidedly negative (although this simplifies things, as the final chapter will show). By the late twentieth century, Seneca's fortunes had taken a turn for the better and a new revival has been underway for several decades. Today, scholars, artists, students and general readers alike continue to grapple with the complexity of Seneca's life and works. It is my hope that this book will continue this trend and aid readers in their own engagement with Seneca, as we seek in the following pages to understand his biography, writings and how they have been reinterpreted and reimagined for over 2,000 years.

Seneca's Biography

The precise date of Seneca's birth in Corduba cannot be fixed. Scholars have presented options ranging from 4 BCE to 1 CE. An earlier date is generally favoured. The region of Spain from which Seneca's family came had long since been Romanised and the Annaei may have originally been Roman settlers.[8] The majority of our information about Seneca's family and early life comes from Seneca's consolation to his mother (*Consolation to Helvia*), a few of his *Moral Epistles*, and from the works of Seneca's father.

Seneca's father had political ambitions for Seneca and his two brothers that life in the provinces could not fulfil. The family moved to Rome when Seneca was very young, carried in his aunt's arms, as he writes in his consolation to his mother (*Helv.* 19.2). Seneca's brother Novatus most closely followed his father's wishes. In order to advance his career, he was adopted into a leading family in Rome and took the name L. Junius Gallio Annaeanus. He was the addressee of several of Seneca's works, most notably *On Anger*. Seneca's brother served as governor of the Greek province of Achaea and is most widely remembered by his adopted name, Gallio. He appears in the Christian book of Acts of the Apostles when Paul is brought before him by a group of Jews who are hostile to Paul's teaching. Gallio refuses to render a judgement in the matter (Acts 18:12–17).

The youngest brother, Mela, declined to enter the Senate and spent his life as an equestrian. This enabled him to actively engage in business, which was forbidden to senators. He is most famous for his son, Marcus Annaeus Lucanus, known today as the poet Lucan. Born in 39 CE, Lucan's talents were recognised by Nero, who brought him into his circle of literary luminaries. According to his biography, Lucan sung Nero's praises at the *Neronia*, the games celebrated in the young emperor's honour in 60 CE. Nero eventually grew jealous and banned Lucan from publishing his epic on the civil war that was fought between Julius Caesar at Gnaeus Pompey Magnus in 49–8 BCE. Lucan's possibly unfinished *Civil War* opens with fulsome, and possibly ironic, praise of Nero. Yet the poem's complex portrayal of Julius Caesar and the portrayal of Caesar's defeated enemies, Pompey and Cato the Younger, suggest that the *Civil War* takes an intentionally problematic and even contradictory view of the death of the Republican freedom and the advent of autocracy. Whatever the poem's views on Caesarism may be, Lucan was implicated in the Pisonian conspiracy against Nero and, like his uncle, was forced to commit suicide in 65 CE.

In his letters, Seneca offers some insight into his early philosophical education at Rome. By about 19 CE he was studying under Quintus Sextius, who developed a form of Stoicism that incorporated neo-Pythagorean elements (*Ep.* 91.13, 108.13–23). He was also a student of Sotion (*Ep.* 49.2, 108.17), Papirius Fabianus (*Ep.* 100.12) and Attalus (*Ep.* 108.3). Certain tenets of Pythagoreanism must have made a strong impression on Seneca, as he writes that he became a vegetarian for a year. He only gave up the practice at the urging of his father because under Tiberius any type of activity deemed 'unRoman' endangered one's life (*Ep.* 108.22). As a young man, Seneca left Rome at some point in the early or middle 20s CE to travel to Egypt to join his uncle, Gaius Galerius, who was prefect there. He may have left the city in part because of health reasons, hoping that the drier climate would help with the respiratory ailments that would afflict him throughout his life. We know next to nothing about his time there, except that he wrote a work on Egypt. His interests in the area would remain throughout his life, both intellectually and financially. In *Natural Questions* Seneca writes about the mysteries of the Nile's regular flooding (*Quest. Nat.* 4a). He mentions his estates in Egypt in *Moral Epistles* 77. Papyri fragments found in the Egyptian sands contain evidence of Seneca's property holdings there.[9]

In 31 CE, Seneca had to return to Rome with his family. Seneca's uncle died on the return voyage. In his consolation to his mother, Seneca vividly recounts how his aunt bravely saved her husband's body from the shipwreck (*Helv.* 19.4). It is unknown why the prefect had to leave Egypt so abruptly, but it has been suggested that Seneca's family may have owed their advancement to their ties to Sejanus, the powerful head of Tiberius's royal guard at Rome. His sudden fall from power and execution may have signalled the end of Seneca's uncle's time in Egypt. This is only speculation, but it is of note that Seneca's earliest surviving work, the *Consolation to Marcia*, celebrates her father, the historian Aulus Cremutius Cordus, who was an enemy of Sejanus and was forced to burn his works and then committed suicide. With this consolation Seneca may have been attempting to win favour with Marcia's family, whose power was on the rise after the fall of Sejanus.[10]

After Seneca's return, his aunt helped him and his brother with their political careers in Rome. Seneca does not appear to have been in a great rush to seek elected office. His father notes in the *Controversiae*, which he was likely working on during the last years of his life in the mid-30s CE, that his two sons are only preparing for public life and elected offices (*Contr.* 2. pref. 4). Seneca served as quaestor for the year 37, and may have been as old as 40 when he finally entered the Senate. While his political influence may have been slight, he became increasingly famous for his intellectual and oratorical skills and gained entrance into the Julio-Claudian court. He was likely on close terms with members of the imperial family, in particular the emperor Caligula's sisters, Julia Livilla and Agrippina, perhaps even having adulterous affairs with one or both (Tacitus *Ann.* 13.42, Dio 61.10.1). Seneca's oratorical skills and his relationship with his sisters attracted the wrath of Caligula. The emperor not only criticised Seneca's pointed style of speech as 'sand without lime' (Suet. *Cal.* 53.2), but also reportedly wished to execute Seneca, simply because he argued a case well in the Senate while he was present (Dio 59.19.7). According to the soap-opera-like account preserved by Dio, Seneca was only spared from this capital sentence by one of Caligula's lovers. She claimed that due to his ill health, Seneca was going to die soon anyway (59.19.8). Seneca of course survived to see the assassination of Caligula, but sickness, respiratory ailments in particular, attended him throughout his life, a topic that Seneca discusses often in his later works. It is doubtful that Seneca had a hand in the conspiracy, but he was not sorry to see Caligula go. He praises the acts of the assassins at the end of book one of *On Anger* and in *On the Constancy of the Wiseman* (18.1–5).

Introduction

Seneca's good fortune of escaping the anger of Caligula did not last long. Upon the ascension of Caligula's old uncle Claudius, Seneca was banished to Corsica in 41 CE for his alleged adultery with Caligula's sister, Julia Livilla. Seneca spent eight miserable years there. Nevertheless, he was careful to ensure that his literary reputation was remembered in Rome. He published two separate works of consolation, each of which give decidedly different takes on his exile. One was addressed to Claudius's influential freedman, Polybius, to console him after the death of his brother. Seneca used this event as a means to reach the emperor's ear. In his praise of the emperor's sense of mercy, Seneca demonstrates that he is not above fawning and flattery. Scholars have been troubled by Seneca's praise of Claudius in this treatise, especially in light of Seneca's merciless condemnation of the emperor after his death in the *Apocolocyntosis*. While this text may be a key example of Seneca's hypocrisy, if we look closely at the *Consolation to Polybius* we can gain insight into Seneca's rhetorical technique. Several of the laudatory themes in the consolation, in particular the focus on the emperor's mercy and power of his speech, reappear as attributes of Nero in *On Mercy*.

Seneca's consolation to his mother Helvia takes a more philosophical tone concerning his exile. In the opening, Seneca celebrates the uniqueness of the text he is writing. He states that he is the first to write a consolation while being the source of his addressee's grief (*Helv.* 1.2). In contrast to his *Consolation to Polybius*, where Seneca begs to be recalled to Rome, here Seneca declares that exile is not an evil, but rather the state of humanity and of nature. The planets and stars continually change their place. The human race does not remain sedentary; no city can claim that it is inhabited solely by people who sprang from the earth and have lived there since time immemorial. This fact is particularly true of Rome, since it was founded by Aeneas, a Trojan exile. Seneca is happy in exile, he assures his mother, because he is free to study the wonders of nature. Despite the different tones of Seneca's two consolations, one goal bound them together: to keep him and his literary abilities in the minds of the Romans. Like Ovid's exile poems sent back to the city from Tomis, Seneca's consolations are tools of self-propaganda. Unlike Ovid, however, Seneca was successful.

Although it is unclear what the specific nature of Seneca's connection with Caligula's sister Agrippina was before his exile, it is clear that she did not forget him during his years in Corsica. After the execution of his third wife, Messalina, Claudius took the unprecedented step of marrying his niece Agrippina. The Romans viewed this union as incestuous. Soon after their marriage, Agrippina was able to convince Claudius to reverse his decree and recall Seneca to Rome in 49 CE. Agrippina did not act out of simple kindness. She had a son by her first marriage to Gnaeus Domitius Ahenobarbus. This young boy was older than Claudius's and Messalina's son Britannicus. Agrippina wanted to ensure that young Domitius was seen as the favourite for the throne. Recalling Seneca to have her son taught by the most famous intellectual of the age was only part of her plan. She also had her son adopted by Claudius and take the Julio-Claudian name Tiberius Claudius Nero Caesar. In 53 CE Agrippina secured Nero's marriage to Claudius's daughter, Octavia. When Claudius voiced his regret at favouring his adopted son over his natural-born one, Agrippina killed him by serving him poison mushrooms, according to one story (Suet. *Claud.* 43–4).

Agrippina's 'favour' of recalling Seneca at once set him on the path to achieving his greatest political influence and plunged him into the world of court intrigue. About his early years as Nero's tutor we know very little. He was appointed praetor at Rome upon his return. Thus he was, at least in theory, further indebted to and dependent upon the influence of Agrippina. We have two anecdotes about Seneca's reactions to his recall. One source states that Seneca initially hoped to avoid Rome and travel to Athens to study philosophy.[11] Suetonius claims that Seneca dreamt that he would tutor another Caligula (*Nero* 7.1). These stories may be inventions, but they are important for shedding light on the tradition of the perception and interpretation of Seneca's return. Suetonius also supplies us with two interesting details about Nero's curriculum. Agrippina did not allow Seneca to teach Nero philosophy, claiming that the subject was incompatible for someone who was going to rule (*Nero* 52.1). Suetonius also claims that Seneca did not allow Nero to read any early authors, so that Nero would adopt Seneca's 'modern' style (*Nero* 52.1). According to Tacitus, Nero's interests did not lie in rhetorical training, or in crafting his own oratorical style. From his

Introduction

early youth, Nero preferred other endeavours, such as painting, poetry and chariot racing (*Ann.* 13.3). Nero's lack of public speaking skills were such that when he was elevated to the throne in the autumn of 54 CE, he was the first emperor who needed 'the eloquence of another', to use Tacitus's memorable phrase (*Ann.* 13.3). Upon Nero's succession Seneca gained a new job description: imperial speech writer. He also gained a new designation, *amicus principis*, friend of the *princeps*. Seneca's father's political ambitions were realised as his two sons were granted the highest office. Gallio was designated consul suffect for 55, and Seneca for 56 CE.

In his writings, Seneca offers few specific details about his political life. Tacitus's *Annals* provide us with the most information about Seneca's role in imperial politics. The historian does not give us a running commentary. Rather, Seneca appears at a few specific moments in Tacitus's narrative. According to Tacitus, Seneca was the architect of one of Nero's first public acts as *princeps*. He wrote the young emperor's funeral eulogy for his adopted father. Tacitus's account offers significant insights into the audience's reaction to Nero's speech. Tacitus claims that the older members of the audience noted that Nero was the first emperor who did not possess his own eloquence and did not compose his own speeches. This comment is likely Tacitus's creation, but it is important because it both highlights the significance of Seneca's position and demonstrates the suspicion with which its unprecedented nature was viewed. Tacitus suggests that Nero severs the link between innate oratorical ability and imperial power. Nero's use of borrowed eloquence foreshadows the end of the Julio-Claudian line. According to Tacitus, beginning with Julius Caesar, all of the rulers before Nero were powerful orators, even the mad Caligula and the stuttering Claudius.

Tacitus also comments on the style and content of Nero's speech. He notes that it was carefully written by Seneca and expertly crafted to suit the tastes of the time. When Nero spoke of Claudius's ancestry and military accomplishments, the audience listened intently. When the speech discussed the deceased's 'wisdom and foresight', no one could restrain their laughter. This laughter may have been an unintended consequence of Seneca's carefully constructed speech (*Ann.* 13.3). On the other hand, Seneca may have intentionally mocked the dead emperor. This laughter could have been used to exclude Claudius and create a new community of good feeling around Nero, to say nothing of Seneca possibly venting some of his personal animosity at the man who banished him.[12] This use of laughter to both degrade Claudius and elevate Nero is precisely the strategy employed in the *Apocolocyntosis*, which Seneca most likely completed a few months after this speech.

Soon after Claudius's funeral Nero entered the Senate and gave another speech, likely composed by Seneca, in which he outlined the plan for his rule and the models he would follow (*Ann.* 13.4). Nero promised that the Senate would retain its ancient powers, and offered specific assurances that he would discontinue Claudius's imperial monopoly on the court system and check the power of the imperial freedmen. Tacitus notes that Nero was true to his word, stating that many things were decided according to the decisions of the Senate (*Ann.* 13.5). Seneca was not the only advisor guiding the new emperor. Sextus Afranius Burrus, the head of the palace guard, the praetorian prefect, was Seneca's partner in power. Tacitus praises their early influence over Nero.

> These men were the controllers of the young emperor and they did so in harmony – a rare thing when power is shared. They were equally powerful by different means. Burrus used his life as a soldier and severity of character and Seneca used his teaching of eloquence and his gentlemanly affability. They aided each other in turn so that they might restrain more easily the dangerous years of the emperor's youth. And if he should spurn virtue, they would restrain him by allowing certain pleasures. Both had to struggle together against the ferocity of Agrippina.
>
> (*ANN.* 13.2)

Agrippina did not intend to fade silently into the background now that her son had become emperor. According to Tacitus, Agrippina planned the first murder of the new principate without Nero's knowledge (*Ann.* 13.1). She would have continued her purges had Seneca and Burrus not stopped her (*Ann.* 13.2). Agrippina also attempted to upstage Nero and publicly display her power as equal with her son. This was also stopped by the discretion of Seneca. As Tacitus writes:

Introduction

> When legates from Armenia had come and were pleading on behalf of their people before Nero, Agrippina was preparing to ascend onto his platform and preside over the meeting along with the emperor. And she would have done so, if Seneca, while everyone else was standing still with fear, had not urged Nero to step down and meet his mother. Thus, with the appearance of familial love, disgrace was averted.
>
> (*Ann.* 13.5)

During the next year (55 CE), a campaign began for demonstrating Nero's mercy. He restored Plautius Lateranus to the Senate, who had been expelled because of his adultery with Messalina. Tacitus states that Nero assured the Senate of his mercy 'in a number of speeches' (*Ann.* 13.11). This claim also likely refers to the publication of Seneca's *On Mercy*. Yet these public declarations hid the darker reality of the imperial household. Agrippina realised Nero was favouring Seneca and Burrus and that the three were attempting to deny her any power. She threatened that now that Britannicus was coming of age she would support him over Nero, claiming that they would have the backing of the army due to their blood ties to the royal house. All Nero had on his side were his two counsellors (*Ann.* 13.14). Nero quickly liquidated the treat of Britannicus by poisoning his meal during a family dinner. It is unlikely that Seneca had a hand in it, let alone knew of the plan to murder Britannicus beforehand. Nevertheless, in *On Mercy* we see Seneca portraying the official image of Nero as innocent and without guilt – claims he may have known were false, but deemed necessary to help quell any rumours about the circumstances surrounding Britannicus's untimely demise.

Soon, Nero wished to do away with his mother, and tried to enlist Burrus to bring her up on false charges (*Ann.* 13.20). By 59 CE, the emperor realised that murder was the only way that he could be free. Knowing he could not use more traditional means such as poison or the sword, Nero adopted the ingenious plan of the freedman Anicetus, who was captain of the fleet at Misenum on the Bay of Naples. He demonstrated that a ship could be constructed with a collapsible section, which could dump Agrippina overboard while on the high seas. In this way, her death would appear accidental (*Ann.* 14.3). Nevertheless, Agrippina survived the sham shipwreck and swam safely to shore. Once Nero learnt of this, he was thrown into a panic, thinking that his mother would soon take her vengeance against him. He summoned his two counsellors for advice. Tacitus surmises that they already were in on the secret (*Ann.* 14.7).

After arriving, all three remained silent for a time. Seneca spoke first, and suggested to Burrus that the military should be given the order to kill Agrippina. Burrus refused to implicate the praetorians, claiming that they had sworn their loyalty to protect the entire house of the Caesars. Anicetus must finish the job, a commission that he eagerly took up. After he left with his chosen retinue, Agrippina's freedmen, Agermus, arrived to announce the 'joyful' news that Nero's mother had survived the shipwreck. Not to be outdone by this dissimulation of happiness, Nero set the stage for the execution of his mother on a charge of treason. While Agermus was delivering his message, Nero threw a sword at his feet and had him arrested for attempted assassination. In Tacitus's account the histrionics culminated in Agrippina's murder. As a centurion approached her with drawn sword, she offered her womb to the blow and exclaimed, 'Strike my belly!' (*Ann.* 14.8).

Seneca tried to pawn off the responsibility for the murder on his colleague Burrus. However, he himself became implicated in the cover-up that followed. Nero was fearful about returning to Rome, so Seneca scripted a letter to the Senate outlining the events surrounding his mother's death. In doing so, the people's odium fell on him. Tacitus writes: 'Nero was not the victim of hostile rumours – his cruelty went beyond what all could complain about. Rather, the victim was Seneca, because by composing such an oration he had written a confession.' (*Ann.* 14.11). Quintilian preserves a brief passage from the letter. He does not condemn the passage for the nefarious circumstances under which it was written. Ever the professor of oratory, Quintilian censures Seneca for his weak rhetorical technique:

> Simple repetition makes a certain type of aphorism, as that of Seneca in the letter which Nero sent to the Senate after his mother had been killed, when he wanted to make it seem like he had been in danger, 'That I am still alive I neither believe nor rejoice'.
>
> (*INST.* 8.5.18)

INTRODUCTION

After the murder of Agrippina, Seneca fades from Tacitus's narrative. It is only after the death of Burrus in 62 CE, perhaps another victim of Nero, that Seneca reappears, attempting to extricate himself from Nero's service.

Although inaugurated by the poisoning of the emperor Claudius and his son, the first years of Nero's principate were seen as years of good rule. Yet the exact number of these good years is a matter of debate. It would seem natural to assume that the murder of Agrippina ushered in Nero the tyrant. Yet the portrait that Tacitus gives us suggests that Nero did not fully transform until after the death of Burrus in 62 CE. Thus for Tacitus, the influence of Seneca was paramount for determining the tenor of Nero's reign.

It remains unclear how great a hand Burrus and Seneca had in shaping Nero's political and legal decisions. Dio, through Xiphilinus, whose compilation of Dio's history of the reign of Nero has survived, provides evidence that Seneca and Burrus took an active role in the official affairs of the state. He writes that they abolished old laws and wrote new ones, while letting Nero indulge in his pleasures (61.4.2). Despite the credit he gives to Seneca and Burrus for Nero's good years, Tacitus is strangely silent about the direct political role they played. It does not appear that Seneca influenced any laws, decrees or edicts. Tacitus's narrative represents Seneca and Burrus working behind the scenes in order to maintain Nero's public image. This can be seen when Seneca encourages Nero to leave the dias so that Agrippina does not appear as his equal in front of the envoys from Armenia. When Nero angered his mother by taking the freedwoman Acte as his paramour, Seneca employed his friend Annaeus Serenus to pretend that he was really her lover (*Ann.* 13.13). Later, when Nero wanted to drive a four-horse chariot and sing on the stage with the lyre, Seneca and Burrus granted him the former indulgence. They allowed him to race his chariot in the relatively secluded confines of the circus, which Caligula began building in the Vatican valley (*Ann.* 14.14). Thus, Seneca may have unwittingly played a role in the future location of St Peter's Basilica. According to tradition, Peter was among the Christians whom Nero executed for allegedly starting the fire at Rome in 64 CE.[13] Peter may have been crucified and buried on the Vatican Hill.

If Tacitus does not give Seneca any direct credit for Nero's decrees, he notes that people assumed that Seneca was at work behind them. In 58 CE decrees were revived in order to punish *ex post facto* lawyers who had illegally profited under the reign of Claudius. One of the main beneficiaries of the Claudian courts was Publius Suillius. He understood these decrees as being directed specifically at him, and he launched a scathing attack on Seneca, which suggests that Suillius thought Seneca was to blame. Suillius's condemnation is worth quoting in full as it represents one of the earliest portrayals of Seneca as the hypocritical millionaire philosopher. According to Tacitus, Suillius attacked him as:

> The enemy of the friends of Claudius, under whom he had endured a most just exile. At the same time, since he was accustomed to idle studies and inexperienced youths, he did not like those who used their lively and pure eloquence to defend their fellow citizens. He had been Germanicus's quaestor; but Seneca was an adulterer in the royal house. Was obtaining a voluntary payment from a litigant for honest work to be judged more serious than defiling the beds of princesses? By what wisdom, by the teachings of what philosophers, had he within four years of royal friendship gained 300 million sesterces? At Rome the wills of the childless had been captured, as if driven into his nets; Italy and the provinces were emptied for his immeasurable profit ...
>
> (*ANN.* 13.42)

Seneca's unscrupulous economic practices are also a topic of Dio's narrative. Dio goes so far as to ascribe a portion of the blame for the revolt of the Britons led by Boudicca in 61 CE to Seneca's predatory lending practices. He states that after forcing the Britons to accept 40 million sesterces in loans from him, Seneca recalled them all at once and used force to exact the payments (62.2.1). How seriously should we take these portraits of the greedy Seneca? Should we trust Dio, and see Seneca as an imperially sanctioned loan shark, sending off thugs to collect from the Britons? We must remember that Dio's portrait of Seneca is considerably more hostile than that of Tacitus. The main critique that Tacitus writes against Seneca is put in the mouth of a man who profited under Claudius. Nevertheless, Seneca was not immune to the charges that were laid against him concerning the level of his wealth. In *On the Happy Life*, a dialogue that has been dated between 54 and 62 CE, during the height of Seneca's power under Nero, Seneca concludes with a lengthy defence against those who 'bark at' philosophers for not practising what they preach (17–28). Seneca claims to be providing a general defence and not a personal apology (17.4), but his focus on the perceived incongruity between wealth and philosophy suggests that he may have been partly motivated by attacks like that of Suillius. Seneca's defence has not won many supporters, and the criticisms of Suillius and Dio have survived to the modern era. Baron Thomas Babington Macaulay ironically summarises Seneca's hypocrisy: 'The business of a philosopher was to declaim in praise of poverty with two millions sterling out at usury.'[14] We should be wary, however, of accepting ancient invectives against wealth at face value. Furthermore, Seneca's stance on the role of wealth in society is considerably more nuanced than Suillius and Lord Macaulay give him credit for.

Attacking a personal enemy's wealth as inordinate and ill-gotten was a favourite moral and rhetorical strategy of the Romans.[15] This does not mean that the attacker is poor. Tacitus states that although Suillius's invective against Seneca proved ineffectual and he was exiled to the Balearic Islands, he 'asserted later that a life of luxury and abundance had made his seclusion not intolerable' (*Ann.* 13.43). The Romans had a particularly ambiguous attitude towards wealth. On the one hand, they celebrated the poverty and simplicity of the early days of the Republic. Paradoxically, these frugal virtues had allowed the Romans to gain their empire, which is per se a greedy and acquisitive act that brings with it the wealth and customs of the conquered. The money and luxury items that flowed into Rome were welcomed silently, but vocally condemned.

Seneca may seem like a hypocrite advising his wealthy readers to set aside days in order to practise poverty. He describes his own attempts at playing the pauper and confesses that he is uncomfortable with it (*Ep.* 87.2–4). Yet what may on the surface appear to be vain and laughable attempts to assuage the guilt of the wealthy and recapture antique Roman frugality and purity are in fact part of his larger project. Seneca does not proscribe wealth; rather, he wants to rid his readers of the fear of losing it.[16] Wealth should be a possession; it should not possess you. Although we may doubt the veracity of

Seneca's disastrous loans to the Britons, he did profitably invest his money. His vineyards at Nomentum were famous for their monetary return. In fact, economic thought is central to Seneca's philosophy. He describes the process of writing, of creating new philosophical works, as the careful managing of an inheritance. The patrimony must be increased so more can be left to the heirs (*Ep.* 64.7). The wisdom he imparts to Lucilius in the *Moral Epistles* is frequently represented in monetary terms. Seneca's *On Favours* consists of seven books on the giving and receiving of favours and the differences between monetary and gift exchange. In *On the Happy Life*, Seneca declares that wealth should not be forbidden to philosophers (23.1) and is something the Stoic wise man would welcome (26.1).

After being blamed for the murder of Agrippina, Seneca disappears from Tacitus's narrative. He reappears after the death of Burrus, perhaps poisoned by Nero, with the terse statement that his partner's demise 'broke the power of Seneca' (*Ann.* 14.52). Nero was now listening to unnamed 'inferior people' who, like Suillius, maligned Seneca for his wealth, but also accused him of eclipsing the emperor in fame and openly mocking his horse racing and singing abilities. Now that he was fully mature, so the argument went, it was time for the emperor to rid himself of his teacher (*Ann.* 14.52). Seneca would have been more than happy to oblige Nero's new advisors, and in 62 CE he attempted to retire from Nero's service. Tacitus scripts a dramatic meeting between the two in which Seneca attempts to tender his resignation. In his speech, Seneca focuses on economic concerns. He is being crushed under the inordinate wealth he has gained from the emperor's favour. In short, Seneca feels overpaid for the humble services he has provided. Tacitus's Seneca states:

> How have I been able to invite your munificence except for my studies, which, I might say, have only been brought up in the shadows? The fame that has come to them is only because I seem to have been present at the early education of your youth. This is a great reward for my service. But you have shown me limitless gratitude, and have surrounded me with incalculable wealth.
>
> (*ANN.* 14.53)

Seneca asks Nero to take back his gifts. He, a humble provincial from an equestrian background, can no longer endure his place among the wealthiest men in Rome. Seneca's only defence for accepting Nero's gifts is that he could not refuse them. This statement recalls Seneca's own claim in *On Favours*. He notes that a true gift is one that creates friendship between the giver and receiver and must be freely accepted. Otherwise the recipient is simply obeying (2.18.5).[17]

Nero responds by turning Seneca's claims on their head. Seneca's gifts, such as Nero's oratorical abilities, are eternal. All that Nero has given and can give – 'gardens, money to invest, and villas' – is transitory (*Ann.* 14.55). The emperor's gifts that Seneca finds so burdensome and excessive are only a small token of Nero's gratitude. According to Nero, the two will never be even. Tacitus's retirement scene is based on the problematic nature of exchange in general and how the system becomes even more complicated under an emperor. This connection suggests that Tacitus was working with themes from Seneca's writings when constructing this narrative. At the conclusion of their meeting, Seneca can only dissimulate his thanks to the emperor (*Ann.* 14.56). This result echoes Seneca's own advice for how to live safely in a royal court: accept insult and say thank you (*On Anger* 2.33.2). Despite this forced expression of thanks, Seneca did take steps to remove himself from the court. According to Tacitus, he acted as if he no longer had any power. He rarely came to Rome and offered sickness, or the study of philosophy, as the reason for his absence (*Ann.* 14.56).

After this dramatic meeting, Seneca only receives a few brief mentions in Tacitus's narrative (*Ann.* 14.65, 15.23). After the Great Fire, Seneca attempted to distance himself from Nero, but was again refused official retirement. Tacitus also records the claim that Seneca survived attempts to poison him by sustaining himself on a frugal diet of wild fruits and spring water (*Ann.* 15.45). Seneca's final appearance in the *Annals* is his most lengthy and most memorable: his forced suicide in the aftermath of the Pisonian conspiracy. In early 65 CE a plot was formed to assassinate Nero led by Gaius Calpurnius Piso. When the plot to kill Nero during games held in honour of the goddess Ceres (19 April) was betrayed by the freedman Milichus, one of Piso's close confidants, the equestrian Antonius Natalis, implicated

Seneca. Tacitus is unsure whether Natalis named Seneca because he had in fact served as an intermediary between him and Piso, or he did so simply to please Nero, who, according to Tacitus, was eager to do away with his former tutor (*Ann.* 15.56). When Tacitus begins the narrative of Seneca's death, he does not fully excuse him from complicity in the plot, but he notes that only Natalis implicated him. Regardless, Nero was happy to have the excuse. Tacitus notes that Seneca's 'slaughter' (*caedes*) was a 'most happy event for the *princeps*', who was glad to proceed against Seneca openly with the sword since poison had not worked (*Ann.* 15.60). The most damning evidence given against Seneca was that he was alleged to have stated that 'his own safety depended on the life of Piso' (*Ann.* 15.60).

Nero sent soldiers led by Gavius Silvanus to ask Seneca about this claim. The troops found Seneca, who had 'by chance or on purpose' (*Ann.* 15.60) returned from Campania on that day, at his suburban villa four miles from Rome. They arrived in the evening and found Seneca dining with his wife, Pompeia Paulina, and two friends. Seneca admitted that Natalis had visited him asking why he refused to see Piso. With regards to the specific charge, Seneca responded that he had no reason to value the safety of a private individual over his own. He then reminded the soldiers that he was not given to flattery, a fact that Nero himself should be aware of (*Ann.* 15.61). When the news was taken back to Nero and his two intimate counsellors, his wife Poppaea and the prefect Tigellinus, the emperor enquired whether Seneca was preparing to take his own life. When the messenger responded that the philosopher's household gave no signs of sadness, Nero ordered his death.

Seneca must have known it was a matter of time before the order was given because he had hemlock at the ready. This fact suggests that Seneca had planned to model his death on that of Socrates. Yet in Tacitus's narrative, this link is only one element of Seneca's protracted death scene. Seneca does not immediately follow his Greek exemplar. Unlike Socrates, he is concerned about economics and the bequests he will leave to his friends in his will. When the soldiers refuse to allow Seneca to amend his last testament, he declares that he will leave his friends the 'image of his life' (*Ann.* 15.62). Also unlike Socrates, who sends his wife Xanthippe brusquely away, so that the men can philosophise (*Phd.* 60a), Seneca's wife Paulina remains present.

INTRODUCTION

She resolves to die as well, and Seneca declares that her glory will be greater than his for this act. Instead of following the Athenian custom of drinking hemlock, Seneca and Paulina follow the Roman precedent of slitting their veins. Seneca's frugal lifestyle, however, does not allow him to die quickly, and he and Paulina must be separated lest their spirits waver as they witness each other's agony. When Nero learns that Paulina is prepared to die with her husband, he orders his men to bind her wounds lest further odium fall on him. Tacitus does not know if Paulina was conscious when this was done or if she was happy to be spared. Regardless, Tacitus states that she lived a few more years dutifully honouring Seneca's memory and that pallor remained in her complexion demonstrating how much of her vital spirit she had lost.

After this digression on the fate of Paulina, Tacitus returns to narrating Seneca's difficulties dying. Even after having the veins in his arms and then behind his knees cut, Seneca's eloquence remains and he dictates a long work to his scribes, which was later published (*Ann.* 15.63). Only after the removal of Paulina does Seneca drink the hemlock, which had been prepared much earlier (*Ann.* 15.64). The poison does not work fast enough, however, and Seneca is brought in to his bathhouse, where he finally expires. Tacitus cannot resist adding one final detail concerning Seneca's possible involvement in the Pisonian conspiracy. He notes that there was a rumour that after killing Nero, Subrius Flavus and the centurions planned to kill Piso and hand the empire over to Seneca. According to Tacitus, Seneca was not unaware of this plan (*Ann.* 15.65).

What are we to make of Tacitus's portrayal of Seneca's death? Does Tacitus mock him by showing how Seneca's plans were continually frustrated, and ironically suggest that Seneca's philosophical preparation for death in fact hindered it? Or do Seneca's several attempts prove his toughness and allow him to imitate the deaths of his two favourite exemplars? His first attempt at suicide through a self-inflicted knife wound references the famous death of Cato the Younger at Utica after his military defeat at the hands of Julius Caesar in 46 BCE. The drinking of hemlock places Seneca in the Socratic tradition, with Seneca's own updating to allow women to philosophise and achieve a glorious death. Finally, Seneca's actual death points to the wealth for which he has been continually criticised, as he dies in the luxury of his private bath. As James Ker has noted, Seneca's death is a literary death. As Seneca's lifeblood flows out of him, his eloquence also continues to flow from him as he dictates his final work.[18] His various attempts at death also reference the diversity of Seneca's own writings. Not content simply to write in one genre, so Seneca's death cycles through various stylistic possibilities. In addition, Seneca's death is both imitative, of Socrates and Cato, and imitated. In the final surviving book of the *Annals*, the courtier Petronius parodies Seneca's philosophical death (*Ann.* 16.18–19). The manuscript of the *Annals* breaks off with the forced suicide of Thrasea Paetus, the execution of whom Tacitus refers to as the extinguishing of virtue itself (*Ann.* 16.21). As his blood flows from his veins and sprinkles on the ground around him, Thrasea quotes Seneca and notes that he too is making his libation to Jupiter the Liberator (*Ann.* 16.35).

We will now turn to an investigation of Seneca's philosophy. As we have noted, Seneca is typically treated as a moral philosopher. His overall goal is to help himself and his readers live better lives by controlling their emotions and following reason and virtue. Yet he pursues this goal from a variety of angles. These include the study of nature (*Natural Questions*), gift exchange (*On Favours*) and politics (*On Mercy*), as well his twelve books of *Dialogues* and his *Moral Epistles*, which focus on a variety of topics. *Dialogues* is a misnomer, as they are not like the vivid dialogues written by Plato, but treatises in which the voice of the philosopher dominates, only occasionally interrupted by an interlocutor. Half of the twelve books focus on ridding the soul of the passions, specifically sadness or grief (*dolor*) in his three consolations to Marcia, Polybius and Helvia, and anger (*ira*) in his three books *On Anger*. The other six treat important issues such as fate (*On Providence*), retirement from politics (*On the Private Life*), calming the soul, (*On Tranquillity of Mind*), the ideal of the Stoic sage (*On the Constancy of the Wise Man*), the proper use of time (*On the Shortness of Life*) and the good life (*On the Happy Life*). By treating Seneca's prose first, I am not suggesting that his philosophy should be granted pride of place in the Senecan corpus or that it holds the key to his tragedies. It will be helpful, however, to have a basic understanding of Stoic philosophy and what Seneca wrote in prose before turning to his poetry. This will help to tackle the question of the extent to which Seneca's two bodies of work may be related.

I

SENECA'S PHILOSOPHY

IN THE PAST, SENECA'S PHILOSOPHY was devalued for a variety of reasons. We have already dealt with the charges of hypocrisy. Intellectually, the philosophy of the Roman period has been seen as dilettantish and eclectic. It was believed that the only value in studying Seneca's philosophy was to mine it for kernels of authentic wisdom from the earlier Greek Stoics. True, Seneca was not a teacher of philosophy or the head of a school. He is indeed knowledgeable and complimentary of other schools of thought, and he is not a Stoic simply out of blind adherence to the doctrine. In fact, he often praises Epicurus, whose ideas are often judged to be the antithesis of Stoicism. Although a self-confessed Stoic, Seneca grants himself the freedom to choose the ideas and doctrines that he finds to be true and most applicable to leading a good life. As Seneca says, the truth is not the sole property of one philosophical sect; it is the possession of the entire human race (*Ep.* 21.9). Stoicism was a school that allowed for innovation and did not uncritically accept the views of its founder, Zeno of Citium, as infallible. Epicureans were unambiguously the followers of Epicurus. The Stoics were not named after Zeno, but took their title from where the school was based in Athens – at the Stoa Poikile, or painted colonnade in the Agora. In fact, Stoicism is credited with having two founders, Zeno and then Chrysippus. The latter was head of the school from c.230–206 BCE and is viewed as the most important thinker the school produced.[1]

It was not simply the philosophy written during the Roman period that has been devalued and understudied in the past. The Greek philosophical schools, Stoicism, Epicureanism, Scepticism and Cynicism, which developed during the Hellenistic period (323 BCE–27 BCE), have in the past not been seen as important schools of philosophy in their own right. In the nineteenth and early twentieth centuries in particular, scholars preferred to study Plato, Aristotle and the Presocratics as 'real' philosophers and expressions of 'true' Hellenism. Hellenistic philosophy was seen as the debased product of a hybrid world. It is true that the philosophies that developed after the death of Alexander the Great in 323 BCE are different from their classical forebears. Abstract intellectual enquiry is still important, but its significance is subsumed to the ultimate goal of living a good life. In general, Hellenistic philosophy focuses on creating a unified system of logic, physics and ethics in order to achieve this goal. Elitist elements are minimised. In Stoic thought in particular, women and slaves were seen as being able to live lives of virtue and study philosophy. This is not to suggest that Plato and Aristotle were not read and critiqued by the Stoics or that the two philosophical giants did not have their adherents during the Hellenistic and Roman periods. Stoicism itself underwent a 'Platonising period' under the influence of Panaetius (head of the school 129–110 BCE) and Posidonius (c.135–51 BCE), two Stoics who in turn influenced Roman thinkers during the late Republic.[2] Although Cicero looked favourably on the Stoics, he considered himself an academic sceptic. He was a follower of Plato, whose school was called the academy; but he also incorporated the newer sceptical ideas that developed out of Platonism during the Hellenistic period. Throughout *On Anger* Seneca critiques the Aristotelian idea that anger is necessary and that it should be allowed in the soul rather than excluded from it.

As a Stoic, Seneca was heir to a more than 300-year-old philosophical tradition. Founded by Zeno of Citium (a city on Cyprus) in Athens around the year 300 BCE, Stoicism became one of the most dominant modes of thought in the ancient world until the rise of Neoplatonism and Christianity. Although a 'new' philosophy compared to the famous schools established by Plato and Aristotle, the Academy and the Lyceum respectively, Stoicism had a revivalist aspect. The school sought to get back to the 'original' Socrates and cut through what they saw to be the impractical and false ideas that had been attached to his name by Plato and others. More than any specific philosophical theories, Socrates's life and death came to be the model for the Stoics on how one should conduct oneself in the world and leave it. We need only think of Seneca's death, or that of Cato the Younger, who read the *Phaedo*, Plato's account of Socrates's final hours, to see what a powerful model Socrates was for the Roman Stoics. For the Stoics, and for their Hellenistic brethren, the Epicureans, the purpose of philosophy was not to get lost in abstract enquiries or metaphysical questions; nor was it to gain knowledge simply for the sake of gaining knowledge. Rather, philosophy came to be viewed as a guide to life. Picking one school over another was not simply an intellectual move, but also one that shaped one's entire way of living and interpreting the cosmos. In many ways, philosophy could play the same role in one's life that religion does today.

A medical metaphor structures both Epicurean and Stoic thought. As Seneca notes, he is not a doctor administering to patients, but rather one of the sick (*Ep.* 8.2). He hopes his writings will treat himself and his fellow human beings who are afflicted by the same illness. What was this illness that philosophy sought to cure? The answer is ignorance; specifically, ignorance about the working of the cosmos, one's place in it, how one should live and what is to be considered the highest good. Each philosophy developed its own answers to these questions. The Epicureans believed that atoms and void made up the universe. All things were created by the chance coming together and eventual dissolution of atoms. The gods exist, but being perfectly happy and self-sufficient, they never are troubled nor trouble humans. Thus, the Epicurean ideal was defined as *ataraxia*, freedom from disturbance. This was to be achieved by refusing the call to political life, or living a life 'in secret', as Epicurus put it, recognising that the gods have no control over this world or the next, and that death was an inevitable dispersal of atoms after which we will have no sensation or care. Life must be led in pursuit of pleasure. The stereotype of Epicureans as libertine hedonists has been around almost as long as the school itself. Epicurus and his followers made it clear, however, that the pleasure to be pursued in life is small-scale and passive. The active, or 'kinetic' pleasures such as eating, drinking and sex were not necessary for achieving true pleasure. Excessive attachment to such pleasures would prohibit one from achieving *ataraxia*, and would cause life to be the 'hell on earth' that the Roman Epicurean poet Lucretius claims is the fate of the unenlightened masses.[3]

Although both philosophies share the belief that the study of philosophy provides the only route to happiness and the good life, Stoicism is in many ways the polar opposite of Epicureanism. Like the Epicureans, the Stoics also desired to live a tranquil life, and the Stoics focused particularly on the psychological aspects of this tranquillity. The Stoics defined one of their goals as *apatheia*, freedom from the passions. Yet this goal is not to be sought in a secluded Epicurean garden. As evidenced by the career of Seneca, the Stoics encouraged the political life and active service to one's community and fellow human beings. Nevertheless, a major tension throughout Seneca's writings concerns how this service is best accomplished: through the traditional routes of political and military endeavour or through the more detached contemplative life of the philosopher. We shall treat this conflict in Seneca's thought in more detail in the pages that follow. For now let us continue to outline the core tenets of Stoicism.

Both the Stoics and Epicureans looked to the human baby as 'proof' of what goals and tendencies properly structure human life. The Epicureans argued that the baby's primary impulses were towards pleasure and safety. The Stoics would look at the same child and proffer the opposite argument. They noted that toddlers will continue to try to walk despite the pain of falling. For the Stoics, this was the prime example of how humans innately strive to fulfil their potential and engage with the outside world regardless of painful setbacks.[4] This tendency forms the core of the Stoic concept of *oikeiôsis*, or appropriation (literally 'making one's own'). As humans develop, this process of appropriation extends beyond our own personal development to encompass family, friends, citizens and ultimately all human beings as well as the divine controller of the universe.

Unlike the Epicureans, who argued that the primary constituents of the universe were void and atoms ceaselessly and randomly swerving together, the

Stoics believed that the core element of the universe was fire. This is not the everyday fire with which you might cook your food, but rather divine, rational fire that guides the universe. A piece of this fire inhabits our soul and may survive death to return to the heavens. The universe will eventually be destroyed and return to this primal fire – an event that the Stoics called the *ekpyrosis* – and then be reconstituted in exactly the same way. The lives we have lived have already happened and will happen again after the *ekpyrosis*. The divine rational fire that guides the universe, which may commonly be called Zeus or Jupiter, can also be equated with fate and nature. Zeno of Citium enigmatically said that the Stoic was to live 'in agreement', by which he likely meant 'in agreement with nature'. Our lives must remain in harmony with the events that happen to us, because these events were fated by divine providence. Zeno's successor Cleanthes encapsulated the Stoic view of fate in his 'Hymn to Zeus', part of which survives thanks to Seneca's translation from the original Greek:

> Lead, O father and master of the high heavens,
> Wherever you have decided. There will be no delay in my obedience.
> I am present and ready. Even if I should be unwilling, and follow lamenting my fate,
> I will suffer as a bad man, what was permitted for me to accomplish as a good man.
> The fates lead the willing and drag the unwilling.
>
> (EP. 107.11 = CLEANTHES, FRAG. 527 VON ARNIM)

Human life was likened to a dog tied to a cart: you can either be led along, or dragged along, but follow you must.

The centrality of fate to the Stoic system had significant consequences for their ethics. If everything is fated and guided by divine providence, what is the use in trying? The Stoics avoided being passively dependent upon fate by actively following it, as Cleanthes's hymn makes clear. Living life in harmony with nature means accepting all events that happen, both good and bad, as part of the unavoidable chain of fate. These events are entirely beyond our control. What does remain in our control is our reaction to these events. This claim is supported by Stoic theories of psychology and epistemology. Unlike Plato and Aristotle, who divided the soul into rational and irrational parts that struggled against each other, the Stoics argued that the soul was entirely rational. They did believe that the soul was divided into eight parts, which included the five senses, speech, reproduction and a central 'command centre' (*hegemonikon*), which controls everything.[5] But ultimately the core of our soul is a piece of the divine reason that controls the universe. According to this theory, human beings are entirely rational creatures. When we go wrong we cannot attribute it to an inherent, irrational and emotional part of our soul. Rather, when we act wrongly we do so ultimately out of a disobedience to or rejection of reason. This rejection of reason occurs not because reason has been defeated by the irrational or emotional part of our soul, but because of our false beliefs and judgements about the value of things.

For the Stoics, virtue is the sole good and vice the only evil. Everything else is classified as an indifferent. Indifferents were further broken down into 'preferred', such as health and family and 'dispreferred', such as sickness and death of loved ones.[6] Humans are entirely self-sufficient for achieving happiness, which consists in the exercise of right reason in the pursuit of virtue. Health, wealth and family are unnecessary. As the Stoics morbidly noted, the wise man is happy on the rack. We go astray when we wrongly assign high value to things that are beyond our control. Thus, we react in sadness when a loved one dies because we falsely judged that person to be irreplaceable and necessary to our happiness. We react in anger when someone insults us because we believe that our public reputation is central to defining who we are.

According to the Stoics, there are only four emotions, which can be grouped into commonly held positive or negative feelings about the present and future.[7] Pleasure and pain characterise our emotional responses to what is at hand. We can look forward to what is to come with either desire or fear. All of the other emotions that make up our world are subspecies of these four according to the Stoics. Thus, what we call anger is really the pain we feel in the present for the perceived wrong done to us and the fear we have about what will happen if it is not avenged. These emotional reactions are the products of our false beliefs, which corrupt the proper, rational functioning of our soul, hence the Stoic call for the extirpation of all emotions. While the Stoics defined their ideal as *apatheia*, freedom from the passions, they also claimed that there were three 'good emotions', or *eupatheiai*, that characterised the psychology of the wise man. They were joy for the present, and volition and caution for preferred or 'dispreferred' events in the future. Note the absence of pain in the present. As we have already noted, the Stoic wise man is happy on the rack and can smile when being tortured (See *Ep.* 78.18–19).

Based on their premise that the soul is fully rational, the Stoics argue that the extirpation of the passions felt by those of us who have not achieved the perfection of the wise man – which of course means the entire human race – is not only possible but also necessary for us to try to live a life that does not deny our core humanity. This premise also reveals the intellectualism that underlies Stoic psychological theory. Like Socrates, the Stoics argued that no one does wrong willingly. *Akrasia*, weakness of will, which is often summarised as 'knowing the better path but following the worse' was considered by the Stoics to be an impossibility.[8] The Stoics claimed that psychological wavering between two courses of action was not the result of rational and irrational parts of the soul in conflict with each other, but rather the rapid succession of the entire soul adopting different judgements about what to do. According to this line of argument, one must learn how to judge properly the stimuli that one receives. Here we come to the three-step process of Stoic epistemology and action. The soul receives an impression (*phantasia* in the original Greek), to which it is able to grant assent (*synkatathesis*) or withhold it. Assent automatically leads to the impulse (*horme*) to act.

These are the basic tenets that undergird Seneca's thought. Aside from his detailed discussion of the origin of anger in *On Anger*, Seneca rarely focuses on technical discussions or debates. He does not provide a primer or outline of basic Stoic theories. Seneca expects that his readers will already have a general knowledge of Stoicism and what separates it from other philosophical schools. Seneca's main goal is to help his readers live a good life, which can be achieved by following the key Stoic axioms that the world is ruled by divine providence, that reason can and should triumph over emotion and that virtue is the only good. As noted in the previous chapter, Miriam Griffin has aptly summed up the two poles that structure Seneca's thought: 'morbid asceticism' and 'understanding humanity'.[9] At first glance, these poles may seem to be contradictory and an example of the unsystematic mode of thought for which Seneca has been accused. They may also seem to be an example of his hypocrisy as well. Seneca wants it both ways: the hard and world-renouncing road of the philosopher combined with easy forgiveness for backsliding. Yet on closer inspection, this startling combination of seemingly antithetical impulses may be combined to serve a higher philosophical and therapeutic purpose. Seneca sets the bar high for his readers. The goal for the Stoic should be the self-perfection of the *sapiens*, the wise man, impervious to the passions and the blows of fortune, whom the Stoics admit is a nigh impossible ideal. Hence the importance of 'understanding humanity'. When one falls short of one's goal, as inevitably will happen in daily life, one must forgive one's own failures as well as those of others. Seneca vividly depicts this dichotomy in *On Anger* 3.36. In his example of his nightly practice of self-investigation in order to help extirpate the emotion of anger, Seneca first castigates himself for reacting angrily during the day. He then forgives himself for doing so. Seneca admits that the writing of philosophy may make it seem that he is a physician of his readers' souls and vices. In fact, he is a patient as well, lying in the sickbed along with everybody else. In short, Seneca's philosophy can be seen as an honest look at the paradoxes and compromises that people may make while living a life of political and literary ambition but also striving for intellectual peace, equanimity and personal, moral growth.

When seen in this light, the out-of-hand dismissals of Seneca as a hypocrite or second-rate philosopher have been replaced by a renewed focus on what his philosophy has to offer us, both for understanding life in Julio-Claudian Rome and for seeing Seneca as a key representative of an intellectual movement during the Roman imperial period that places a focus on living one's philosophy (however imperfectly in practice) and on personal development, or 'the care of the self', to use Michel Foucault's famous phrase.[10] These themes sparked the renewed interest in Seneca the philosopher, so it is to Seneca's moral philosophy and focus on the individual and the emotions to which we now turn.

Michel Foucault's evaluation of the development of the self in the philosophy of the imperial period has justly been subject to critique and refinement by classicists, philosophers and other scholars since the publication of volumes two and three, which focus on the Greek and Roman periods respectively, of his three-volume *The History of Sexuality* in the early 1980s. Nevertheless, his discussion of Seneca's focus on and specifically his innovative vocabulary for 'the care of the self' can serve as a starting point. On this topic Foucault writes:

> This 'cultivation of the self' can be briefly characterised by the fact that in this case the art of existence – the *techne tou biou* in its different forms – is dominated by the principle that one must 'take care of oneself.'
> ... it is to this activity according to him [Seneca] that a man must devote himself, to the exclusion of other occupations. He will thus be able to make himself vacant for himself (*sibi vacare*). But this 'vacation' takes the form of a varied activity that demands that one lose no time and spare no effort in order to 'develop oneself', 'transform oneself', 'return to oneself'. *Se formare, sibi vindicare, se facere, se ad studia revocare, sibi applicare, suum fieri, in se recedere, ad se recurrere, secum morari* – Seneca commands a whole vocabulary for designating the different forms that ought to be taken by the care of the self and the haste with which one seeks to reunite with oneself (*ad se properare*).[11]

The maxim 'know yourself' (*gnothi seauton*) was inscribed, along with 'nothing in excess' (*meden agan*), on the Temple of Apollo at Delphi, in which the god's priestess rendered his oracles, and was a goal at the heart of classical civilisation. Yet a variety of options for how one comes to 'know oneself' presented themselves, ranging from divine revelation, as suggested by the location of the inscription, to tragic self-recognition, as suggested by the stories of Oedipus and Narcissus, in which divine oracles play a significant role. The philosophers also claimed that study of the self and the soul could lead to fulfilment of this maxim without divine aid and without the terrible endings experienced by Oedipus or Narcissus. The practice of philosophy itself came to be not only a process of self-discovery, but also a continual process of therapy and self-creation. For the Stoics, philosophy was not simply confined to the lecture halls, but a lived experience. As Seneca notes, it is not simply enough to quote what others have said, or even to write one's own treatises; philosophy must be put into practice each day.

Therapy of the Emotions: Dolor *and* Ira

The Stoics are (in)famous for their belief that the emotions must be extirpated from our souls in order to live the good life. Seneca fully supported this tenet. Two emotions that particularly concerned him were sadness (*dolor*) and anger (*ira*). His three earliest surviving works are all consolations that aim to cure the recipient of their *dolor*. The Latin word means more than simply 'sadness'. It also can encompass 'pain', for example the physical and emotional pain that can accompany the extreme sorrow and grief caused by the loss of a loved one. We have already considered the self-promoting aspects of Seneca's two consolations written from exile, to Polybius after the death of his brother, and to his mother Helvia, to console her during her son's exile. With his earliest surviving work, *Consolation to Marcia*, likely written under Caligula (37–41 CE), he may also have hoped to gain the favour of an important political family. Along with the self-serving politicking, Seneca also offers advice on how to conquer sorrow. The seemingly insurmountable grief caused by the loss of a family member was a particularly difficult test for ancient philosophy's promise of equanimity and the ability to withstand the blows of fortune. After the death of his daughter Tullia in the February of 45 BCE, Cicero became acutely aware of this point and put philosophy to the test. He wrote a now lost consolation to help relieve his sorrow for the death of his daughter. Although in his *Consolation to Helvia* Seneca states that his son died 20 days before he was exiled, Seneca does not dwell on his personal grief and prefers to show himself as able to help others, even when afflicted by exile (*Helv.* 2.5).

Two of Seneca's consolations are addressed to women. From these two works we can see that Seneca has confidence in these women's intellectual abilities, but also that he feels that these abilities are limited. Seneca also adopts the standard misogynistic viewpoint that the vast majority of women are ruled by their emotions. Only a select few, such as Marcia and his mother, can benefit from Seneca's advice. Marcia had two sons and two daughters, but she lost both her boys. Seneca's treatise comes after the death of her second son. Seneca opens this work noting that he would not even have bothered trying to cure Marcia's grief if he did not know that she was 'as far removed from the weakness that characterises a woman's soul as she was from all other vices' (*Marc.* 1.1).

With his mother, Seneca adopts his beloved military comparisons. He declares that her grief has 'not simply broken the skin, but torn apart her breast and guts' (*Helv.* 3.1). Yet Seneca has faith that his mother can endure the therapy he will set before her in this treatise. She is not like a newly recruited soldier who is more afraid of the surgeon's knife than swords in battle. Rather, Helvia ought to be like a veteran soldier, who patiently and without uttering a groan submits to his treatment (3.1). The link between the military and philosophy is a key theme for Seneca. Philosophy is ultimately shown to be superior. The wars that are waged within ourselves with the passions, such as grief and anger, are more difficult and of more consequence than any of the battles fought by military leaders. These internal wars and the destructive power that erupts once one has succumbed to the passions comes out most clearly in Seneca's three book treatise *On Anger*.

A secure date cannot be attached to this work. It was certainly written after the assassination of Caligula in 41 CE, which Seneca celebrates at the end of book one. Scholars surmise that the first two books may have been written during Seneca's exile, and that the work was completed and published soon after his return in 49 CE, most likely before 52 CE.[12] *On Anger* is part of a long tradition of philosophical treatises on anger and the emotions, dating back at least to Xenocrates's and Aristotle's lost works *On the Passions* (*peri pathon*). The Stoics Zeno and Chrysippus also reportedly wrote similarly titled works. Closer to Seneca's time, Posidonius wrote an *On the Passions* and an *On Anger*, which survive in fragments.[13] Seneca's treatise is one of the few, and likely the earliest, to survive intact.[14] As far as we know, it is the only one written in Latin during the classical period. Each of the three books has a particular thematic focus. Book one seeks to define anger and looks at the horrors caused by this emotion from a general standpoint. Book two opens with a technical discussion of the origins of anger and begins the formal process of therapy. The therapy continues in book three as more methods of eradicating or suppressing anger are provided throughout.

We have already noted that Seneca's *On Anger* is part of a long tradition of philosophical investigation of the origins of the emotions. This concern was neither limited to nor did it begin with the philosophers. The poets beat them to it. *Menis*, the divine anger of Achilles, is the first word of the *Iliad*, and a key theme of the entire epic. Later in the poem Achilles offers his own insights on the perverse pleasure of anger and how the wrath he felt against Agamemnon led him to sit out from the battle and let his companions be slaughtered by the Trojans (*Iliad* 18.107–11).[15] Anger, *ira*, is central to the Roman foundation myths. Writing during the Augustan period, Livy tells of how Romulus killed his brother Remus in anger (1.7.2). Virgil makes this theme central to the *Aeneid*. Aeneas is buffeted on land and sea because of the 'mindful anger of cruel Juno' (1.4). At the poem's famously problematic end, when Aeneas kills the suppliant Turnus, he is described as 'on fire with fury and terrible with his anger' (12.946–7). Given the centrality of anger for defining who the Romans were in their national myths, we can see that Seneca was in a particularly difficult situation. In fact, this emotion was considered to be so engrained in the human psyche that the Latin word for soul (*animus*) could also mean anger. This lexical phenomenon partly survives in English in the words animus, meaning anger, or ill-will and animosity.

As we have seen, the Stoics believed that the soul was entirely guided by reason. There is no natural place for anger in the soul, as anger, and all of the emotions, reject reason. For the Stoics, anger is irrational and equivalent to a brief period of madness. One succumbs to anger only through a rejection of reason. Since it is such a dangerous emotion, it must be fully extirpated. Throughout this treatise, Seneca's interlocutor frequently takes up an Aristotelian position that a moderate amount of anger is sometimes necessary to fight, avenge wrongs or argue cases in the forum. Seneca rejects this claim of the Aristotelian mean, claiming that anger cannot be controlled. Once it is let into the soul it will drive out reason and take over. One will not be in control of one's actions and risks acting either excessively or not enough, since the passion of anger typically dissipates quickly. Seneca compares the onset of anger to falling off a cliff (1.7). Yet since it is the product of judgement, not simply a natural or uncontrollable impulse, it can be eradicated by judgement and reason. It is the goal of Seneca's treatise to teach his readers the truth about anger, its origins and how it can be extirpated from the soul. But what are we to do in situations when a response is called for and anger seems justified? Seneca's interlocutor asks, '"What then? The good man does not get angry as he sees his father killed and his mother raped?"' Seneca's answer appeals to one of the core virtues by which the Romans defined themselves, *pietas*, or duty: 'He will not be angry, but he will avenge them, and he will protect them. Why then are you afraid that familial duty (*pietas*) without anger will not be enough of a stimulus for that man?' (1.12.1). In other words, Seneca is not forbidding violent revenge, and we should not turn the other cheek in every situation. The point is that we do not need anger, which defies reason, to do what must be done. We should act out of our duty to our family (*pietas*).

The question then becomes, why must anger not be allowed to affect us even after witnessing the murder of our father and rape of our mother? On this point, Seneca would give two main answers. One is more technical. Anger is a vice and *pietas* is a virtue; the two should not be mixed. The second we may find a bit more convincing or at least as offering a deeper consideration of the nature of anger. Seneca disagrees with the argument, notably put forward by Aristotle, that anger can be useful and even necessary, but it must be moderated and kept within certain limitations. Seneca counters that it is easier to simply exclude the passions than to rule them. Because, according to the Stoics, the soul is fully rational, once anger is allowed in, it takes over the soul and drives out reason (1.7.1–3). It is a form of brief insanity. Thus, if we avenge our parents out of anger, not only will we act in a subhuman manner by denying our defining capacity for reason, but we also risk acting excessively. Since our actions will be devoid of reason, we cannot be sure that our punishment will be appropriate. Or worse, because the passions are by their nature short-lived, if we seek revenge out of anger we might not punish enough, because our fit of anger has left us too quickly.

Thus, anger has several marks against it. By putting reason to flight it denies our humanity. Paradoxically, anger is only present in humans because it ultimately springs from reason and our (misguided) judgements. Seneca notes that animals do not feel anger because they do not possess reason. Secondly, acting out of anger means that our actions will be either excessive or deficient; we will punish either too much or too little. Finally, Seneca also appeals to his readers' sense of decorum – their vision of themselves as ideally calm, cool and collected at all times. Because anger defeats reason and is a form of insanity, we also will look and act like maniacs. Seneca notes:

> Anger has this evil: it does not wish to be ruled. It rages against the truth itself, if it appears contrary to its desire; with shouts and tumults and with a shaking of the entire body, it pursues those whom it has marked out, adding curses and insults.
>
> (1.19.1)

Seneca is not calling on the Romans to live without violence; he is only advising them to use reason to support their violent actions. He notes:

> Reason does not do any of these things [described above]; but if it is necessary, silently and quietly, reason destroys entire households from the bottom up; and families who are plagues to the republic along with wives and children it destroys; it pulls down roofs and makes them equal to the ground and extirpates names that are enemies of liberty.
>
> (1.19.2)

In order to support these points, Seneca looks back at military history and notes that several famous Roman generals, such as Quintus Fabius Maximus and the two Scipios, conquered their own anger before defeating their enemies (1.11.5–7). Others, such as Hannibal (2.5.4) and Alexander the Great (3.7.1–2), are condemned for being slaves to their passions. Roman leaders are not immune, however, and Seneca criticises tyrants from Rome's more distant past (Marius and Sulla 3.18.1), and recent memory (Caligula 3.18.3). In this treatise, Julius Caesar and Pompey the Great are briefly praised for their restraint (2.23.4), but later in his letters Seneca links the two Roman generals with the same passionate madness that drove Alexander the Great's conquests (*Ep.* 94.62–7).

How then are we to avoid anger? Seneca offers a theoretical explanation of how the emotions spring from reason. In the opening of book two of *On Anger*, Seneca gives a possibly innovative version of the Stoic three-step process of emotion:

> In order that you may know how the passions begin and grow and are carried away, there is a first movement that is not voluntary, as if a preparation for emotion and a type of threat. The second is voluntary but not defiant, as if asking whether it is right for me to be avenged when I have been harmed, or whether it is right for someone to be punished when he committed a crime. The third movement is already out of control. It wants revenge not if it is right, but at all costs. It completely conquers reason.
>
> (2.4.1)

The concept of the first, non-voluntary movement, or 'preliminary preludes' to emotion, has attracted particular attention from scholars. This concept is likely present in earlier Stoic theory, but it is unclear how much development and focus it was accorded.[16] What is interesting in Seneca's account is his stressing of the pre-rational, uncontrollable nature of the first movements. Seneca would return to this topic much later. In his *Epistles* (57.3–4) Seneca notes that even the perfect Stoic wise man cannot eradicate these reactions.[17] Furthermore, Seneca's discussion of the first movements also provides an important buttress to Stoic psychological theory and therapy. We might imagine a critique running something like this: If the Stoics advocate the extirpation of the passions and argue that the passions spring from reason, how can they explain blushing or shivering or hairs standing on end? The theory of the first movements denies that such reactions are really emotions. We are not truly feeling shame or anger simply because our face turns red. Nor do we shiver in 'fear' or furrow our brow in 'sadness' when hearing a story or watching a play. These are simply pre-rational reactions. They are not emotions. It can be easily seen how they can lead to emotion. If we know the truth about these uncontrollable bodily reactions, we will not let them get the best of us and mistakenly judge that because of them we are actually feeling fear, or anger or sadness.

For the Stoics, following reason at all times and in all situations would enable one to live an ideal life of virtue. It is necessary to unpack the etymological meaning of the Latin word, *virtus*. In current English, 'virtue' often connotes ideas of 'Christian virtue' and morality. For the Romans the key root of this word is contained in the first three letters 'vir', which in Latin means man. Thus, *virtus* literally means the qualities of being a man, manliness or manly courage. There is indeed a 'tough guy' mentality at the core of Seneca's conception of Stoic virtue. In fact, a distinctive aspect of Seneca's Stoicism is the military ideals and metaphors that it employs.[18] We have seen how Seneca defines military prowess as the ability of generals to conquer their emotions. This focus on the military is part of Seneca's 'Romanisation' of Stoicism in order to appeal to his audience. The crux of the matter can be found in one of Seneca's pithy aphorisms, 'to live is to be a soldier' (*vivere ... militare est Ep.* 96.5). The life of a philosopher, however, is even more demanding than the life of a soldier. One is never free from the threat of the emotions. Lifelong therapy and study is necessary. Nevertheless, we will inevitably fail to live up to our ideals; hence we must submit ourselves to daily self-study and self-introspection. What form does this take? To answer this question we can turn to one of the most discussed passages in Seneca's philosophy.

In *On Anger* 3.36 Seneca provides an extended account of his daily practice of philosophy, the *meditatio*. As scholars have noted, this sort of spiritual exercise of self-review was likely invented by other philosophical schools, but became a central aspect of Stoic practice.[19] Seneca states that he learnt this technique from his teacher Sextius, who used to question his soul at the end of each day, 'Which of your evils have you cured today? Which vice have you hindered? In which part are you better?' (3.36.1). Seneca then expands upon Sextius's basic questions. Using a series of judicial metaphors, Seneca notes that each day the soul must be called into court and give an account of itself. Seneca notes that anger will stop or at least become more moderate if it is called each day before a judge. He even declares that a 'tranquil', 'deep' and 'free' sleep follows this method of self-investigation and self-censorship (3.36.2). Seneca then offers his own example of his daily self-investigation:

> I use this power and each day I argue my case within myself. When the lights have been taken away from my view and my wife, now long aware of my practice, has fallen silent, I scrutinize my entire day and reflect upon my words and deeds. I hide nothing from myself. I pass

over nothing in silence. Why should I fear any of my errors, when I am able to say to myself:

'See that you don't do this again; I forgive you now. In that argument you spoke too combatively. From now on don't spend time with the ignorant. Those who have never learnt anything, do not wish to learn. You offered advice to that man more bluntly than you should have, and so you did not correct him, but rather insulted him. In the future, see to it that you do not only speak the truth, but that the man to whom you are speaking is able to handle the truth.'

(3.36.3–4)

Several points are significant in this passage. First, it should be noted how mundane the examples Seneca gives are. Some of Seneca's most memorable passages in this treatise vividly illustrate the violent and extreme effects of anger. Cities are laid low by the emotion; tyrants, both foreign and Roman, order outrageous punishments for their subjects, or murder their friends. Yet this text does not simply present sensational images of anger; it covers the full spectrum of the emotion and attempts to offer day-to-day advice on how to eradicate it. In book two, for example, Seneca offers advice on how to raise children who do not get angry, but still retain a competitive, aristocratic spirit (2.19.1–2.21.11). With Seneca's example of his *meditatio*, we are clearly back in the mundane, domestic sphere. This fact is made clear when Seneca notes that he investigates himself each night after his wife has fallen asleep. The examples he gives of his occasions for anger are far from sensational, but rather address the daily annoyances that we all must face: speaking 'too pugnaciously' in an argument, admonishing someone too strongly. Later he brings in the example of his reaction after being insulted by people at a party (3.37.1).

Seneca's examples also situate us squarely in the quotidian world of Rome and reveal Seneca's own class consciousness. Seneca imagines himself getting angry with a doorkeeper who turned away one of his friends. He then chastises himself for getting angry at this 'lowest of slaves' who is simply 'a chained dog', which will stop barking once some food is thrown at it (3.37.2). Seneca's solution to this insult to his and his friend's status is to 'walk far away and laugh' (3.37.3). Seneca's opinion of slaves has received much attention from scholars.[20] Here, Seneca admits the servile baseness of slaves, but he does not advocate violently responding to their insults or mistakes. Earlier in the treatise, Seneca recommends not punishing slaves when angry at them. He offers two suggestions for what to do in this case. First, he notes that when Socrates was angry he did not physically punish a slave (1.15.3). Later, he states that when angry, Plato asked his brother to punish his slave for him (3.12.6–7). In general, Seneca only advocates for somewhat more humane treatment of slaves by their masters. He famously declares in one of his letters that 'slaves are people' (*Ep.* 47.1). He does not, however, call for an end to slavery or seem to have the faintest idea that the institution is per se dehumanising.

Politics and Society

We know that Seneca lived an active political life. If many of his works reveal the challenges and reservations he faced in leading this life, we cannot overlook the political and social aspects of his philosophy. Admittedly, his two main political works, the *Apocolocyntosis* and *On Mercy*, can be dated to the start of Nero's reign. Thus, we can see something of a progression in Seneca's philosophy in favouring the private life, which culminates in his *Natural Questions* and *Moral Epistles*, works that can be securely dated post 62 CE. Yet for a brief period at the start of Nero's principate, Seneca had a chance not only to interpret the world but also to change it for the better, to adapt Karl Marx's famous critique of philosophers. Although Seneca ultimately failed and was judged by the historian Dio to have been the 'tyrant's teacher', with *On Mercy*, Seneca can at least be credited with outlining a theoretical justification of autocracy in Rome. If this text did not serve its immediate purpose, it did come to serve as an important text for political theory during the Middle Ages and Renaissance.[21]

Surprisingly, Seneca's first method for shaping Nero and the public's perception of him seems to have been through the use of humour and political satire. The role of satire in Seneca's political programme is not simply confined to the *Apocolocyntosis*. As we have noted, according to Tacitus,

Nero's first public act as the new emperor was to deliver the funeral eulogy for Claudius, a speech that Seneca wrote. Tacitus notes that all listened intently and decorously while Nero praised certain aspects of his stepfather's reign and character, but when he mentioned his intelligence, no one could restrain their laughter (*Ann.* 13.3). This humour may have been unintended on Seneca's part, but it also may have been part of Seneca's plan – a possibility that becomes more attractive when we consider the *Apocolocyntosis*.

To say that the *Apocolocyntosis* is a problematic work would be to put the case mildly. In the past, scholars have not agreed on the meaning of the title, the date of the work, its intended audience and even if Seneca in fact wrote it. Thankfully, since the publication of P. T. Eden's excellent edition of the text (Cambridge 1984), there has been more consensus. Today few would question whether the work is genuinely Senecan. The *Apocolocyntosis* is our only complete surviving example of the genre of Menippean satire, a hybrid of prose and poetry credited to the Cynic philosopher Menippus of Gadara. The genre was developed in Latin before Seneca by the late Republican polymath, Varro. For the most part, only titles of his satires survive, but some of them use outlandish Greek words, which suggest a political reference, for example 'The Three-Horned Beast' (*Trikaranos*), which may refer to the First Triumvirate of 60 BCE.[22] Seneca's title is most likely a pun on the Greek *apotheosis*, or deification, and means something like the deification of an empty gourd (that is, the fool-king Claudius), or the pumpkinification of Claudius. As for the dating of the work, a time soon after Claudius's death would make the most sense as his reign would be freshest in people's minds and the humour would have the most bite. The text itself makes several references to Saturnalia, which suggests that the *Apocolocyntosis* was composed for the December holiday of 54, during which, according to Tacitus, Nero served as master of revels. Thus, the text was out only two months after Claudius's death. We do not know the intended audience. This text may have simply been Seneca's private venting against the emperor who exiled him, or it was intended only for a very small circle of intimates. It may also be the case that the *Apocolocyntosis* was intended for a wide audience and that along with Nero's speeches, it was part of Seneca's early political propaganda, which culminated in the publication of *On Mercy*.

The *Apocolocyntosis* is characterised by aggressive and damning political satire that focuses on the supposed physical and mental defects of Claudius. Seneca portrays the recently deceased and deified emperor as subhuman. He relentlessly draws our attention to Claudius's ugliness, his limping gait, his twitches, his speech impediment, his stupidity and absent-mindedness. The narrative of the text tells the story of Claudius's failed attempt – despite the Senatorial decree and having Hercules serve as his champion – to gain admittance to Olympus. Thanks to the speech of the deified Augustus, who speaks for the first time in the Olympian Senate since his apotheosis, Claudius is driven from above to Hades. In the Underworld, the emperor meets with several of his victims who bring him before the judge Aeacus. The emperor is unable to have his case heard, and is first sentenced to eternal dice-rolling with a cup that has no bottom – a fitting Sisyphean task for a man who was supposedly addicted to gambling. The sentence is changed on the advice of Caligula, to whom he is granted as a slave. He in turn hands Claudius over to his legal secretary. Thus, the emperor who spent much of his life capriciously domineering the legal courts of Rome will eternally but powerlessly serve as a slave to a slave in the Underworld.

Several points for comment present themselves. First, the damning of Claudius is unexpectedly shocking when we consider the praise that Seneca bestows upon the emperor from exile in the *Consolation to Polybius*. Here is a prime example of Seneca's political opportunism. He knows how to flatter those in power. Why then would he risk appearing like a hypocrite and also mock the official decree of the Senate divinising Claudius? While Seneca did take several risks with this satire, we must remember that political insult and satire lie at the heart of the Roman tradition – if considerably muted with the rise of autocracy. We must also consider the political effects of the laughter that Seneca hopes to arouse at Claudius's expense. At the time, the true cause of Claudius's death was likely unknown by the public and there had to have been rumours that Agrippina was responsible. The *Apocolocyntosis* presents the 'official' version. The laughter at Claudius's expense, which we have to remember was also occasioned by Seneca at the emperor's funeral, serves to create a new community around Nero. If, and this is the risk Seneca is taking, people laugh at the dead emperor, he is excluded from Nero's new 'in' group.²³ Furthermore, Nero is able to have has cake and eat it too, politically speaking. He can play the dutiful son and honour his stepfather with a divinisation, plus he can lay claim to the title that only Augustus before him had, 'son of a god'. At the same time, Nero can also ridicule and denigrate his predecessor, and thus make himself look even more appealing.

The humour and insult of the *Apocolocyntosis* also maps itself onto traditional Roman modes of political invective. The metaphor of the body politic plays a central role in this text. As Claudius cannot control himself, a point graphically realised by his final act in this world, defecating over himself, so he is unfit to rule Rome. Nero only appears briefly in this text, but when he does it is in the context of the song of Apollo as the Fates spin out a new Golden Age for the emperor and for Rome. His decorous, youthful and Apolline beauty and singing ability are stressed, which stands in stark contrast to the bestial, aged, limping and stuttering Claudius. Thus, Seneca presents a standard piece of autocratic political theory: the physical condition of the ruler determines the state of the empire. Yet Seneca's point goes deeper than this bit of sympathy between ruler and ruled. Claudius's actions during his reign, specifically his monopolisation of the Roman judicial system, serve as an important negative example for Nero. By extension, Seneca offers a hopeful promise to his wider audience that Nero will not be a capricious and cruel judge in the mode of Claudius. These two key points, the sympathy between ruler and ruled and the judgement of the emperor, both in the sense of the judgements he passes and the subsequent judgement of him by his subjects, make up the crux of Seneca's subsequent work, *On Mercy*.²⁴

If the date of December of 54 CE is accepted for the *Apocolocyntosis*, it becomes clear that this work served as a precursor for the more serious work of Seneca's treatise on clemency, specifically addressed to Nero himself. Once again, we run into problems of dating. Seneca states that he is writing this work during Nero's 19th year, which if we accept the traditional dating of Nero's birth as 15 December 37 CE would mean that the composition of *On Mercy* took place from December of 55 to December of 56 CE (1.9.1). This date has been criticised by some based on Seneca's statement within the text that Nero has not shed a drop of blood (1.11.3).²⁵ How could Seneca have made such a patently false statement, when Nero poisoned his stepbrother

Britannicus in February of 55 CE? It is patently false to us, who have the benefit of Tacitus's and Suetonius's accounts of the murder of Britannicus, written decades after the event. At the time of his death, as with that of Claudius only a few months earlier, the public would only have access to rumours. As in the *Apocolocyntosis*, so in *On Mercy*, Seneca does his best to move suspicion away from strife within the royal family and clear Nero's name. While *On Mercy* is a prime example of the hypocrisy that Seneca has so often been accused of, it also offers insight into the Faustian bargain he made by accepting Agrippina's invitation to return from exile.

The surviving text of *On Mercy* is fragmentary. Internal evidence suggests that Seneca may have intended the work to encompass three books, but only the first is complete and the text breaks off soon after the start of the second. The tone of the two books is also incongruous. The first is more general, while the second delves into more technical, Stoic aspects of mercy and its relationship to other virtues and vices. Yet *On Anger* follows a similar scheme, with book one offering general thoughts on anger, before moving into a technical discussion of the origins of the emotion at the start of book two. The choice of the topic is significant for political reasons that run to the heart of Julio-Claudian ideology. Julius Caesar claimed that mercy was one of his chief attributes, hence the pardoning of those who fought against him in the civil war. This mercy backfired, as many of the people he forgave, most notably Brutus, turned into Caesar's assassins. In his early years, Octavian learnt from this misstep, and started his triumvirate with proscriptions of his enemies. Yet after his defeat of Antony and Cleopatra, which signalled the conclusion of Rome's decades of civil wars, Octavian, now granted the honorific title Augustus by the Senate, was also awarded a golden shield, which praised the *princeps*'s virtue, clemency, justice and dutifulness.

Similar to the *Apocolocyntosis*, Augustus plays an important role in *On Mercy*. Yet Seneca makes it clear that Augustus is not to be held up as the ideal *princeps* by Nero, nor by his subjects. According to Seneca, people no longer remember the good old days under Augustus or the early years of Tiberius; Nero is to look to himself as an exemplar. In fact, Seneca gives the lie to Augustan 'clemency'. He reminds his readers of the violent and cruel early life of Octavian and notes that mercy was only a policy he adopted late in life, which came not of his own prompting, but from the suggestion of his wife, Livia. As Seneca tells it, Augustus was on the point of suicide as the result of his inability to stop the assassination attempts against him. Livia's advice is to publicly forgive the latest would-be assassin (1.9). This solution works, but Seneca does not judge Augustus to be truly merciful; rather, his policy of lenience was the result of 'worn-out cruelty' (1.11.2).

If aggressive humour is the key rhetorical technique of the *Apocolocyntosis*, flattery, despite Seneca's protests to the contrary, is one of the core methods of persuasion in *On Mercy*. This flattery is self-referential and mirror-like. Nero does not need to look to any past examples; he only needs to look to himself. Seneca makes this point of self-observation clear in the opening passage of the text. He states that this treatise will serve as a mirror showing Nero's greatness and merciful nature to himself (1.1.1). Possibly alluding to Nero's love of the theatre, Seneca notes that Nero's mercy is not a mask worn in order to placate the people and that eventually his true nature will be revealed (1.1.6). Yet, the mask of the merciful prince is exactly what Seneca is hoping to place upon Nero.[26] The over-the-top flattery, telling Nero how merciful and godlike he is, is Seneca's means to construct Nero into this ideal. One cannot simply tell an autocrat what to do. As *On Mercy* makes clear, a safer and hopefully more successful route is to praise the ruler as already having the traits you are trying to instil. Thus, Nero will come to the self-realisation of his own nature; his decision to act mercifully will seem to come from within, rather than being the product of his advisor.

At the same time, *On Mercy* also works as a powerful piece of propaganda and reveals to the public Nero's true nature. This tactic of revealing the private life of Nero is best seen in the opening of both books. Book one opens with Seneca imagining Nero talking to himself about his supreme, divinely granted power and all the times in the past he has forgiven people. Book two opens with Seneca making public Nero's brief and impromptu statement, which he actually said before signing the death warrant of two criminals, 'I wish I never learnt how to write!' (2.1.2). Seneca notes that Nero's exclamation was one of the chief reasons he was moved to write this treatise. Seneca's inclusion of this statement by Nero serves several purposes. It reveals the private Nero to the public and lets them know that even under a merciful emperor, the people should not think that they can get away with everything. Executions of criminals will still take place. Yet perhaps most importantly for Seneca, Nero's statement reveals that his mercy springs from his inborn character; it is the job of this treatise to make this character trait part of Nero's rational, fixed judgement. Thus, Nero is shown to be the opposite of Claudius, who, as in the *Apocolocyntosis*, is portrayed in *On Mercy* as a cruel and capricious judge (1.23).

There are also elements of cleverly interposed political theory in this treatise. Seneca quashes any thoughts of a return to the Republic and notes that this form of government died long ago at the hands of Julius Caesar (1.4.3). Seneca also attempts to do away with the niceties of Roman political terminology by equating kings with the *princeps* (1.4.3). Seneca is only willing to go so far, however. He never calls Nero a king. Seneca also notes that Nero does not need any constitutional authority to justify his position. In the opening of the text he has already made it clear that Nero is granted his position by divine right and he acts as regent of the gods on earth (1.1.2). In this opening monologue, Seneca also subtly makes it clear that Nero is not bound by any laws, but he will act *as if* he is (1.1.5). This statement starts an important dialectic of freedom and slavery for Nero. On the one hand, according to the realpolitik of the principate, Nero is in fact free to do what he wishes. Yet on the other, Seneca tries to guide Nero away from exercising this license first by having Nero say that he freely chooses to submit himself to the laws. Later, after outlining the uniquely public life and constrained life that Nero must lead by virtue of his position as emperor, Seneca imagines Nero declaring in disbelief, "'This is servitude, not imperial power'" (1.8.1). According to Seneca, however, the way for Nero to be free is to act in accordance with mercy. It grants Nero 'liberty of judgment' (2.7.3). Mercy also allows Nero to demonstrate his ultimate dominance over the laws and the rest of humanity. As Seneca once again imagines Nero saying, "'Everyone can kill contrary to the law, no one can save a person except me'" (1.5.4).

Finally, Seneca also seeks to establish a sympathetic relationship between Nero and his subjects. As Claudius's physical ugliness and lack of bodily control manifested his political inabilities in the *Apocolocyntosis*, so Seneca argues in *On Mercy* that the kind and mild state of Nero's soul will gradually diffuse itself through the body of the empire (2.2.1). According to Seneca, Nero is the soul of the empire and the people are his body. By sparing his subjects, Nero is in fact sparing himself. The people will in turn love their ruler and seek to protect him en masse, as the body protects its soul. This body/soul relationship is not one of absolute authority, but rather of reciprocity. As the people protect a merciful king, they will be driven to rebellion against a cruel one (1.8.6–7, 1.12.4, 1.26.1). Thus, perhaps the ultimate trump card for Seneca is Nero's fear for his safety. If driven by the excessive cruelty of a tyrant, the people will rebel and destroy him. As Seneca notes, the life of a tyrant is short and hateful both to himself and to his subjects. If the ruler does not act properly, political rebellion and tyrannicide are justified, according to Seneca. Harking back to Plato's famous claims in the *Gorgias* and the *Republic*, Seneca argues that the tyrant is the most *un*free person of all. Once he starts along the path of cruelty he loses all bonds with humanity and is forced to continue acting with ever-increasing cruelty because he wrongly believes that this is the only assurance of his safety.

Seneca's two political works offer us an important glimpse into the ideology and grim realities of autocracy at Rome. His treatise *On Favours*, also likely written under Nero and before 62 CE, offers a unique take on the social world. Roman life was dependent upon the giving and receiving of favours. We can see a physical representation of this ideal of reciprocity in the images of the three intertwined Graces, who, according to Seneca and other philosophers, represent the eternal flow of giving, receiving and giving back. This process bound the elite of ancient society together, who would give consulships, money, priesthoods or provinces, as Seneca notes. This unequal exchange of goods and services seems like the height of political and social corruption, but as Seneca notes it is the glue that holds society together (1.4.2). How is this so, and how does the exchange of favours differ from the exchange of money? Seneca discusses the social significance of both in this treatise. Favours are unequal and not equivalent. By doing a favour for someone, you do not expect to get the same thing back in return. Furthermore, favours create bonds of friendship and also mark that the receiver is in your debt until the favour has been repaid. Thus, by accepting a favour one acknowledges the temporary superiority of the giver. Hence, the process is competitive, and the return of a favour can be something greater and more valuable than the thing given in order to fully restore one's status. Seneca portrays this system as one of harmonious competition as one tries to outdo the other with their gifts (1.4.2–4).

The exchange of money works in precisely the opposite fashion. Money is a universal equivalent; we can use it to purchase any number of things. Once we purchase something, or pay off a loan, we are no longer obligated to the seller or lender. No ties of friendship are formed. Of course, both systems of exchange were at work simultaneously in Seneca's Rome, and Seneca makes it clear that the exchange of money frees us from being indebted and becoming friends with less desirable members of society (2.21.1–2). The giving and receiving of favours requires careful attention. We must be certain the person upon whom we bestow a favour is worthy of being admitted into our circle and that when we accept a favour we are willing to be in the giver's debt and lower our status in comparison. The centrality and importance of this practice for the functioning of society and the delicate matters of status at work are part of the reason that Seneca devotes so much time to the topic. Consisting of seven books, along with the *Moral Epistles* and the *Natural Questions*, it is one of Seneca's longest surviving works. He opens *On Favours* noting how all of the many other works on the topic, even that of the second founder of Stoicism, Chrysippus, are lost in pointless and overly subtle arguments, such as allegorical explanations of the Graces (1.2.1–1.4.1). They fail to teach us properly how to give, receive and return favours. From this opening, and Seneca's portrayal of the great and public competition of gift exchange, we are led to expect a treatise that will focus on the social aspects of gift exchange. Seneca quickly moves away from the public world to the psychological, however.

Immediately after enjoining his readers to embark on this great aristocratic competition, Seneca notes that 'money, consulships, priesthoods, and provinces' are simply the marks of the benefits that have been bestowed, not the benefits themselves: 'A benefit cannot be touched by the hand; the exchange takes place in the soul' (1.5.1–2). Here we come to the problem of *On Favours*: the social world quickly disappears as Seneca looks at the psychological mechanisms of gift exchange. Seneca sums up the crux of the work: 'to accept a favour gladly is to have repaid it' (2.30.2). Seneca admits that this is one of the famous paradoxes of the Stoics. But unlike their claims that all men save the wise man are fools and slaves, and that all sins are equal, Seneca states that the paradox of gift-giving is the easiest to accept. This core aspect of Seneca's treatise had led to claims that it is useless as a social document and lost in the world of Stoic paradoxes and idealism.[27] Indeed, Seneca is mainly interested in the psychological realities of gift-giving and the concepts of gratitude and ingratitude. But he also shows that the psychology of gift-giving is one of its most problematic aspects. Seneca notes that while ingratitude is one of the greatest crimes and most destructive to society, it is a very hard psychological state to determine. A person who repays a favour may not do so out of kindness and a feeling of gratitude (*gratia*); and a person who fails to return a favour may in fact be truly thankful for it.

Recently, *On Favours* has received a good deal of scholarly attention ranging from considerations of Seneca's re-evaluation of the concept of gratitude, to the treatise's usefulness for elites living under an autocrat.[28] Indeed, this work addresses and attempts to solve some of the problems affecting the Roman elite living in a new world of one-man rule. In the ideal system all members of the upper class would be part of this system of exchange, but as Seneca notes, the emperor refuses to take full part. Not only does he typically refuse to accept gifts, because doing so would diminish his status and place him in the debt of one of his subjects, but also according to the examples Seneca gives of imperial largesse, emperors often give gifts in order to humiliate the recipient (2.7.1 on Tiberius, 2.12 on Caligula). Emperors further problematise the system in that one cannot say no to an emperor's gift without risking his life. Gifts must be freely given, received and returned in order to qualify as such. In fact, according to Tacitus, Seneca himself was a victim of this situation. When he tried to give Nero's excessive gifts back and retire to the simple life, Tacitus's Seneca claims that he only accepted the gifts because he could not refuse them (*Ann.* 14.52–6).

Thus, Seneca's treatise is not simply concerned with the social exchanges among roughly equal elite individuals, but also focuses on the hierarchical aspects of gift exchange. Seneca argues that an inferior should be able to perform a benefit for his superior. On this point we see Seneca, contrary to the Stoic Hecton, looking down the social ladder and arguing that slaves can perform favours for their masters. Here Seneca is to be granted some credit for noting the essential humanity of slaves and that their souls remain free despite the servitude of their bodies (3.18–28). But, as we saw in *On Anger*, he only goes so far. He does not call for the abolition of the practice, although he does note that some slaves have been granted their freedom in return for their good deeds. Seneca's discussion of slaves only naturalises and possibly strengthens their subservient social position. They are expected to perform deeds beyond the requirements of their place. Masters ultimately lose no status by accepting a slave's favour and may ultimately assuage any qualms they may have about being a slave owner by doing so.

Otium

The Stoic goal of life is to 'follow nature', which means always obeying universal reason and accepting bravely all events that happen to us. Yet, the ideal Stoic is not completely without emotion and will still feel joy, caution and volition. He or she is rendered invulnerable and superior to all events, since his or her life is led not only following nature but also free from all external attachments. At the same time, however, a Stoic life is also a life of service and connection to others. According to the Stoics, all human beings are at their core fully rational; we all share the same divinely rational soul. The problem is that we all, to some degree, have been led astray by the siren songs of a corrupted and corrupting society, which teaches us to place a high and irreplaceable value upon things, such as reputation, health, wealth and family, that are ultimately beyond our control. This fact does not mean that we should run off and become hermits and renounce all the things of the world. The Stoics viewed our human nature as one of ever-expanding concentric circles of concern. The technical term is *oikeiôsis*, which literally means making things familiar, or part of one's home (*oikos* means house or home in Greek). Only the first and smallest circle concerns our self and care for our soul. The Stoics recognised that self-preservation is a basic human instinct, but also that as we grow, so does our ability to incorporate others. Thus, the second circle would include our family, a wider one friends, a still wider one our hometown or city. Ideally, this process continues until the outer circle embraces the entire cosmos, and hence all of humanity and the divine reason guiding the universe. Cosmopolitanism, or universal citizenship, is also a key point of Stoic philosophy and a problem with which Seneca wrestles throughout his writing. How much does he owe to himself, others and Rome? What is the balance between the active political life and a life of retirement and philosophical contemplation?

The claims of philosophy and the desire to spend one's time in retirement and study have a particular urgency in many of Seneca's works. The pull of the private life is of course clear in Seneca's two major works from his unofficial retirement, the *Natural Questions* and the *Moral Epistles*, but it also can be seen works of less certain dating, but likely composed before the break in 62 CE. For example, in *On the Shortness of Life*, addressed to Seneca's father-in-law, Paulinus, on his perhaps forced retirement as the head of Rome's grain supply (*praefectus annonae*), Seneca claims that the philosophical life of contemplation is the only life worth living.[29] Despite the satirical tone that may characterise this work, Seneca makes several points that concur with those made throughout his corpus. He argues that the self is our only possession and that time is our most valuable commodity. This topic becomes one of the main themes of his letters. As he does in *On Anger*, so in this dialogue as well, Seneca brings back heroes from Rome's past and uses them to fit his argument. The great political leader Cicero (5.1–3) and even Augustus regretted all the time they wasted on the public life. Seneca even alleges he has letters from Augustus to back up this claim (4.1–5).

The opening of *On Tranquillity of Mind* offers a portrait of the psychological indecision faced by a Roman philosopher about whether to lead an active or contemplative life. Seneca presents his interlocutor Serenus's complaints about how he continually flees in and out of retirement. The majority of the treatise is taken up by Seneca's advice to Serenus on how to cure his psychological restlessness and fluctuation. At the end, Seneca notes that the mind must also relax and offers examples of how great men from the past would relax. He notes that Socrates played with children,

Cato the Younger would drink, and Scipio would dance. Seneca is careful to describe the type of dance the great general performed. He did not dance in the modern style that descends below 'feminine softness', but rather in the ancient and 'manly style' (17.4). It seems that Seneca sides with Cato's method. The treatise ends by noting that sometimes the best solution for curing the soul's ills is drunken revelry. Philosophy, reason and politics must on occasion take a back seat to Bacchus. He concludes by citing with approval three Greek maxims. The first is from an unnamed Greek poet, 'Sometimes it is pleasing to go mad'. The second two are attributed to Plato and Aristotle respectively: 'The person who is in control of himself knocks in vain at the gates of poetry', and 'there has been no great talent without a mixture of madness' (17.10).

Leisure, or time away from business and politics (*otium*), was not simply a problem for philosophers, but one that went to the core of what it meant to be Roman. Even this 'free time' had to be spent in fruitful pursuits rather than simply doing nothing. Typically, *otium* could be used profitably in study or in the composition of poetry, with the caveat that both pursuits were seen as dangerously unRoman and possibly a corrupting waste of time and hence potentially worse than remaining idle. During the Republic, we can see these anxieties clearly in Cicero's speech in defence of the Greek poet Archias (62 BCE). Cicero confesses that he is a lover of literature but only turns to it at the end of a hard day at work and only because it helps him lead a better public life. Even the poet Catullus, who we are to imagine spent his days writing poetry and fawning over his mistress, Lesbia, notes the personally and politically destructive nature of leisure (51.13–16). Seneca takes a more positive view of *otium*, as long as it is directed towards philosophical study. In fact, in his treatise specifically on the topic, *On the Private Life* (*De otio*), he outlines how a life of philosophy in fact does more for the common good than a life of political service.

This fragmentary treatise opens with Seneca imagining the critiques thrown at him for leaving a life of public service. He has left the rigours of a life of a Stoic for the ease of an Epicurean life (1.4). Seneca admits that the two schools present radically different visions of one's duty to the state: 'Epicurus says: "The wise man will not serve the commonwealth unless something intervenes [i.e. an emergency]"; Zeno says, "He will serve the commonwealth, unless something prevents him'" (3.2). According to this line of argument, the Stoic should only retire from public life for special causes; but Seneca admits a wide definition of what these causes might be, ranging from ill health to the impossibility of helping a commonwealth that is so corrupt that it cannot be repaired. It is of course tempting to see Seneca here offering his own reasons for trying to leave Nero's court as a place beyond remedy. Indeed, according to Tacitus, after Seneca's failed attempt at retirement in 62, Seneca offered his failing health as a reason for avoiding the public, but again we must remember that we cannot date this treatise with certainty. Although it likely was composed before 62 CE, as with most of Seneca's philosophical works, we cannot be certain of the date or political context. Seneca avoids all mention of Rome; he judiciously notes that Athens and Carthage have not proved to be suitable states for the wise man. Since this is a fragmentary work, we do not know what conclusion Seneca arrives at concerning the private life.

Be that as it may, this dialogue contains some of Seneca's most detailed discussions of the value of a life of philosophical contemplation and Stoic cosmopolitanism. He points out that there are in fact two commonwealths: 'One is great and truly common, which contains humans and gods, in which we look to neither this little corner of earth or that one, but we measure the boundaries of our citizenship with the sun'; the other is simply terrestrial, such as Athens or Carthage, and has been assigned to us by an accident of birth (4.1). Seneca argues that we can serve the greater commonwealth better in retirement from public life by asking philosophical questions; the best way to live the core Stoic maxim that one must follow nature is to study her (4.2–5.1).

A life of philosophy also benefits more people, according to Seneca. Returning to his favourite trope of noting how philosophers are greater than politicians or military men, Seneca declares:

> We Stoics certainly say that Zeno and Chrysippus did greater things than if they led armies, held public office or passed laws. The laws which they passed were not for one state, but for the entire human race. Why, then, should such leisure not suit the good man? Through his leisure he

governs the future ages and does not speak among the few but among all peoples of every race, who are and who will be.

(6.4)

Yet Seneca does not simply claim that a life of philosophy is the best life; he briefly tries to prove that this is the case. He states that a life of contemplation is the best because it encompasses all other paths of life, which Seneca reduces to two: a life devoted to pleasure and a life devoted to action. In both cases, however, one must base one's actions on contemplation, and thus, according to Seneca, a life of contemplation is favoured by all (7.4).

'Retirement'

If we can believe Tacitus's account of Seneca's unsuccessful attempt to give back Nero's gifts and tender his resignation, Seneca did achieve a degree of freedom from the imperial court. He stayed out of Rome using ill health or the study of philosophy as a pretext. Seneca put his precarious *otium* and unofficial retirement from public life to good use. During the last three years of his life (62–5 CE), he composed two major works, which are mostly extant today, *Natural Questions* and the *Moral Epistles*. The latter have long been considered Seneca's philosophical masterpiece, while the former has begun to receive increasing interest and appreciation from scholars. In his letters, Seneca also notes that he is at work on *Books of Moral Philosophy*, which he states will cover the entirety of the topic. Unfortunately, these are completely lost. At first glance, working on natural and moral philosophy would appear to be a testament to Seneca's supposed eclecticism, or worse, the dilettantish nature of his philosophical study. A modern person might think there is little relationship between the study of nature and the study of morals. There was less of a gap between these two discourses in the ancient world, and in fact for the Stoics, nature and ethics were united. It is only by understanding the nature of the universe that we can lead a good life. While the majority of what survives of Seneca's philosophical corpus is concerned with ethics, psychology and self-development, he was also deeply interested in the study of nature as well. He wrote a (now entirely lost) work on the geography and religions of Egypt. Perhaps drawing on this earlier work, Seneca returns to the study of Egypt when he discusses the Nile in the *Natural Questions*. A lost work on stones is also attributed to him. Writing from exile, Seneca tells his mother how his time in Corsica has enabled him to study the wonders of nature more fully (*Helv.* 6.7–8). In his later work, *On the Private Life*, Seneca outlines how the Stoic goal to live in accordance with nature also requires that nature itself be studied (5.1). He then notes that nature has created us for this very purpose. She has given us a curious mind, placed us at the centre of her works and, unlike all the other animals

> she has not only made man stand upright, but also has made him able to contemplate her works. In order that he might follow the movements of the stars from rising to setting and turn his face to look upon everything, she has made his head atop his body and given him a pliant neck.
>
> (5.3–5)

As this passage suggests, nature, which the Stoics also identified as god or divine providence, has created the world for the exclusive enjoyment of human beings. Yet as in the world of human beings, so in the natural world many events happen that suggest this is not the case. How can we explain earthquakes or other natural disasters? Thus, the study of nature not only sets out to assuage human fears about such events, but also serves to justify the core Stoic theory that all events, even those that appear to be tragedies, happen according to the guiding hand of nature and divine reason.

The study of nature is a study of the rational causes of phenomena on the earth and in the heavens, but Seneca also admits that the creator only reveals his secrets gradually. As such, Seneca sees his work in a long series of philosophical investigations that of necessity will continue after him (7.30.5). Seneca states in the preface to book one that the study of nature is the most elevated branch of philosophy, because it deals with the divine and often leads to pure contemplation of the workings of the earth and cosmos.[30] Nevertheless, the knowledge we gain from the study of nature can help us in our daily lives. By focusing on the greater commonwealth that is the universe, we can abstract ourselves from being caught up in the minutiae of our daily lives. Not only do we learn the ultimate insignificance of ourselves and our actions but also the insignificance of all human creations. Seneca's goal in this work is to help us gain this 'cosmic viewpoint'. In the preface to book one, he illustrates this ideal.[31] As the soul studies the universe, it is able to journey up into the heavens from whence it came and be granted a view of the vanity of human pursuits. From this perspective, even the expanse of the Roman Empire is reduced to insignificance and is likened to ants moving across a small space (1 Pref. 10).

The vanity of Roman politics is illustrated with full force again to Seneca's addressee, Lucilius Junior. As Seneca was writing this work, Lucilius, also the addressee of the *Moral Epistles*, was serving as governor of Sicily. Seneca wants to ensure that Lucilius does not become overly pleased with his political accomplishments. Thus, at the start of book 4a, Seneca promises to lead Lucilius away from Sicily and take him along as he investigates the mysteries of the Nile. Yet on this point we can illustrate one of the key tensions at the core of this text. While Seneca seeks to abstract himself and Lucilius from the political world of Rome, this world also structures the text. For example, when Seneca imagines the soul gaining its view from above at the opening of book one, this view still focuses precisely on the borders that shape the Roman Empire.[32] Questions about the Nile were common in the ancient world, and its source remained a mystery for centuries after Seneca. During the reign of Nero there was heightened interest in the river. Seneca's nephew Lucan provides an extended excursus on the Nile in his *Civil War* (10.172–333), on which he was likely working during the period of Seneca's composition of the *Natural Questions*. In addition, Seneca's up-to-date knowledge about the river was provided thanks to Nero. Aside from the *Apocolocyntosis* and *On Mercy*, *Natural Questions* is the only other work in which Seneca mentions Nero by name. As in the two earlier works, here Seneca praises the emperor. According to Seneca, Nero is 'a great lover of all the virtues, and especially the truth' (6.7.3), because he sent two centurions to discover the Nile's source. Seneca notes that he questioned the soldiers about their discovery, but remains unsure whether they truly found it (6.8.3–5). Pliny the Elder is less charitable in giving Nero's reasons for sending the expedition. Rather than simply wishing to discover the truth, he states that Nero was planning an expedition against Ethiopia (*HN* 6.181).

Another contemporary event is discussed in book six. This book opens with Seneca's discussion of the devastating earthquake that recently struck Lucilius's hometown of Pompeii. This event either took place in February of 62 or 63 CE. Here we can see Seneca's therapy at work. Before turning to debates about the (ultimately unknown) causes of earthquakes that make up the majority of this book, Seneca looks at this occurrence with great sympathy. He offers a brief account of the local destruction and notes that earthquakes in particular are great sources of fear. The earth seems to lose its essential quality, stability. There are ways to hide from many other natural disasters, but earthquakes can swallow up entire homes, and Seneca notes that many feel that this is a particularly terrible way to die (6.1.1–8). Seneca offers cold comfort, but comfort that is typical of his philosophy. We should not blame nature for the death and destruction caused by earthquakes. Nature is in fact fair in that death levels all. What does it matter if we are killed by a single rock or buried by a mountain (6.1.9)? He continues:

> Therefore, let us take up great courage against this disaster which can neither be avoided or predicted and let us stop listening to those who have renounced Campania and who have emigrated after this event and say that they will never return to the region. Who promises them that they will stand on better foundations on this or that ground?
>
> (6.1.10)

We have to accept the fact that earthquakes, although rare, are an inescapable phenomenon. The best way to assuage our fear of them is to seek to understand their causes and accept their universality.

While the study of nature may help us to accept rationally its terrors and marvel at its wonders, we must also understand that we are ultimately powerless before it. Towards the end of book three's discussion of terrestrial waters, Seneca admits that the human race will one day be destroyed by a flood and describes the universal destruction at length (3.27.1–30.8). Seneca notes the fragility of humanity and its dependence upon the current state of nature; any deviation will cause the human race to become extinct (3.27.3). Yet this catastrophe will not be the result of random events; the universal flood was decreed at the creation of the earth (3.30.1). Thus, the core goal of the *Natural Questions* is twofold. We are to move from the particular and individual to the universal. As we do so, we are to gain an understanding of the order that underlies all things. These processes should help us to understand ourselves, the workings of the universe, our place in it and ultimately free us from irrational fears.

Composed at roughly the same time and to the same addressee, Seneca's *Moral Epistles* exhibit important connections to the *Natural Questions*.[33] Seneca continues to urge Lucilius not to put too much stake in politics, and advises him to seek out the private life. At first glance, the focus of these letters may seem to be squarely on the particular, both in terms of the mundane events Seneca reports and in terms of the focus on the relationship between Seneca and Lucilius. Yet we should not think of these letters as one unadulterated half of a correspondence between the two. Seneca states that these letters are not like those of Cicero, who simply writes about whatever comes into his mind (*Ep.* 118.1). Seneca stresses the literary fame that will be granted to Lucilius because of his inclusion in the letters (*Ep.* 21.5). Thus, we must think of these letters as conscious literary and philosophical constructions, which give the illusion of the everyday. Seneca talks about what he is doing, or reading, or refers to the content of a previous letter sent by Lucilius. Yet in every instance, the mundane and particular is turned into an occasion for philosophising about the universal significance of apparently insignificant events. Furthermore, despite the apparent autobiographical nature of these letters, we learn very little about Seneca himself. These letters are a form of self-investigation, but ultimately they are also universalised into a philosophical practice that can benefit others. They are not simply for Seneca and Lucilius. Thus, these letters have a multifaceted quality. On the one hand, we learn of Seneca's readings, travels and bouts of illness; yet on the other, we learn very little about contemporary historical events, and nothing about Rome or Nero. While Lucilius Junior was likely a genuine person and slightly younger contemporary of Seneca, the significance of his name should also be noted. Lucilius is the diminutive of Seneca's *praenomen*, Lucius. Thus, we also have a sense that this 'little, young Lucius' is serving as a foil for Seneca to look at himself and back on his past life.[34] Indeed, Seneca at times makes us aware of his old age and sickly body and even offers some rare pieces of information about his early life and philosophical training. These letters are both enjoyable and a challenge to read. They offer an example of the daily practice of philosophy and along with Seneca's daily *mediatio*, outlined in *On Anger* 3.36, represent a key example of Stoic spiritual exercises.

Divided up into 20 books, 124 letters survive. We know that more were originally composed, as Aulus Gellius (*NA* 12.2.2–13) preserves a fragment from the 22nd book. As we have noted, the letters contain a fascinating combination of the particular and the universal. On the one hand, the sheer mass of the corpus (three Loeb volumes) treats a wide range of topics, which ideally should be read in order. We can see the path of Lucilius's and Seneca's progress. The first three books (letters 1–29) are typically brief as the philosophical ascent begins. Seneca's overall style is epigrammatic and lends itself to quotation. Frequently in the early letters Seneca offers Lucilius a 'payment' of a memorable maxim from his reading. Surprisingly, these quotes are often from Epicurus, and the debate with Stoicism's rival is carried on throughout the letters. At first, Seneca takes a particularly charitable view of the philosophy, noting that Epicurus himself could almost be seen as a model, and his maxims are worthy of internalisation. Rather, as Seneca notes elsewhere, it is his followers, the contemporary Epicureans, who have given the philosophy such a bad name (*On the Happy Life* 13.1–3). As in his other works, Seneca demonstrates his intellectual independence. He will not reject the good aspects of Epicureanism simply on principle. He notes that the truth is not the property of a single school. He describes his technique of philosophical composition as starting with a wide-ranging programme or reading, which he combines, digests and makes his own as he writes. Yet after the initial quotations from Epicurus, Seneca does advise Lucilius not to spend his time learning maxims, but to move on to the fuller ideas of the Stoics. At the same time, however, Seneca does not want Lucilius simply to quote what he has read. He does not wish for his pupil to go around spouting 'Zeno said this; Cleanthes said that' (*Ep.* 33.7). Instead, Seneca advises: 'Take command and say something that can be handed over to posterity. Offer something from your own stock' (*Ep.* 33.8). This advice is ostensibly directed at Lucilius, and in other letters Seneca praises the writings of Lucilius, both in prose and in verse. This command can also be directed at Seneca himself and taken as a metaliterary statement referring to Seneca's own process of composition. By the very act of writing these letters, which represent the birth of the philosophical letter in Latin, Seneca is also following his own advice to 'hand something over to posterity'.

As the collection proceeds the letters grow in length, and they treat more complicated philosophical topics, such as Plato's concept of the forms (*Ep.* 58), whether precepts or doctrine on their own are sufficient for philosophical progress (*Ep.* 94 and 95, the two longest letters to survive), critiques of the Stoic theory of corporality (*Ep.* 113), or the central tenet of Epicureanism that pleasure is the goal of life (*Ep.* 124). Although Seneca never refers to Rome or Nero directly, throughout the letters he critiques the contemporary love of money and luxury (for example *Ep.* 114.24–7). He advises Lucilius to pick days in which he practises poverty to prove to himself that he is not attached to his possessions and can live with little, as nature intends us to do. Seneca himself tries at times to live beneath his station and admits that it is hard for him, especially when others see him attempting to do so (*Ep.* 87.2–4). While these points may seem to be the prime example of Seneca the hypocrite, praising poverty while being one of the richest men in Rome, we must remember that Seneca does not condemn wealth per se. Rather, his critique is directed against the improper use of money and attachment to it. He wants his readers to be unafraid of losing their wealth and to realise that they can lead just as happy and virtuous a life without it. There are of course many romanticisations of poverty: the poor are happier than the rich (*Ep.* 80.6); Rome was poor when it was great (*Ep.* 87.41), but Seneca seems to be trying to come to grips with the fact that both he and Rome have become fabulously wealthy. There is no way to undo this fact, so rather than simply decry Rome's decadence and lament the passing of the good old days (which of course Seneca does), we should try to find a way to live virtuously in the midst of luxury.

Although specific details about contemporary Rome are conspicuously absent from these letters, there are two groups of letters that relate Seneca's exploits travelling around Campania and the Bay of Naples (*Ep.* 49–57, 70–87), as well as Seneca's travels to his villas and vineyards (*Ep.* 104, 123). One of the few datable contemporary references concerns a fire at Lyons (*Ep.* 91). Latin literature is a frequent topic. There are several analyses of lines from Virgil, Ovid and Maecenas. There is also a great deal of self-reflexivity and questioning about the value of philosophy and liberal learning (*Ep.* 88 and 108), the proper style for writing philosophy and how one's writing reveals one's soul (*Ep.* 84, 114, 115). Seneca also revisits several topics he treated in earlier works, such as the exchange of favours (*Ep.* 81), the proper use of philosophical retirement (*otium*), the suppression of the passions and the nature of the soul.

The use of one's time and thinking upon death are also central motifs and give these letters a valetudinary quality, as if Seneca knew that they would be among his final compositions. Of course, this quality could be the product of hindsight for us, as we know that Seneca would continue to work on these letters right up until his death. While death is of course a common theme throughout Seneca's philosophy, in the rare instances where these letters do turn autobiographical, we are given a glimpse of an aged man who has struggled with sickness all his life and feels that his body is crumbling like the stones in one of his villas (*Ep.* 64). Yet these complaints about his body can be contrasted with the vigour of Seneca's soul as he continues to read and write philosophy. Seneca's complaints about his physical ailments ring hollow when we consider the narration of his travels around Italy, which included a forced swim from his ship to the shore to relieve seasickness (*Ep.* 53).

We can gain a sense of how these letters have benefited the philosophical progress of both Lucilius and Seneca. In an early letter Seneca notes how he is being transformed by this exchange (*Ep.* 6). While it is simply an accident of transmission, in the last letter to survive, Seneca focuses on the Stoic scale of beings:

> There are four natures, that of the tree, the animal, the human and of god; these final two, which are rational, have the same nature, and are only different because one is immortal and the other is mortal.
>
> (*EP.* 124.14)

This final surviving letter concludes with a succinct statement of the goal of Stoicism: realising that we are rational animals and that the only good is perfect reason. If only we can achieve this we will rise above humanity and become a rival of god (*Ep.* 124.23).

Of course, the ascent to this knowledge is arduous and must be practised every day, but if we continually strive for the goal of self-perfection we will achieve a form of self-divinisation. This does not mean we will be granted eternal life once we realise the divinity within us. We should not think in Christian terms. Seneca makes it clear in this letter that we are mortal (*Ep.* 124.14). In an earlier letter he talks about the survival of the soul after death (*Ep.* 57), but he is not speaking in terms of individual immortality. Our soul is a piece of the divine fire that guides the universe – after it leaves our body it will return to its heavenly origin. This is the best we can hope for. As the final surviving letter also makes clear, our mortality is our defining characteristic, one that ultimately separates us from god (*Ep.* 124.14). We should not even count on having a long life during which to make progress. One day should be enough. Here we come to the particular nature of each letter. Although we should ideally read the entire collection, reading one letter should also benefit our progress. Hence each letter can serve as a microcosm of the whole collection and Seneca's very epigrammatic style enables us to take whatever pieces we find helpful. In order to illustrate the philosophical movement of the individual letter, let us conclude this chapter by starting where Seneca intends us to start reading his final work. Below is a translation and brief analysis of *Moral Epistles* 1.

> Seneca to his friend Lucilius, greetings.
>
> Act in this way, my Lucilius: free yourself for yourself. Time, which until now was being carried off, or stolen, or fell away, collect and save. Persuade yourself that what I write is true: certain periods of time are ripped from us, others are secretly led away and others flow by. But the most shameful loss it that which comes about by negligence. And if you should think about it, a great part of our lives slips way while we are acting wrongly, the greatest part while we are doing nothing, and all of it while we are doing something other than we should. Whom

can you show me who puts any price on his time, who values his days, and who knows that he dies each day? On this point we are mistaken, that we look towards death: a great part of death has already passed by; whatever part of our life is behind us, death holds.

Therefore, my Lucilius, do that which you write you are doing. Embrace all your hours. You will value tomorrow less, if you place your hand upon today. While life is put off, it runs past us. Everything, Lucilius, belongs to another. Only time is ours. Nature has given us possession of this one fleeting and uncertain thing. Anyone who wishes can take it away from us. Such is the stupidity of mortals that they allow those things which are of the least importance and the cheapest and the easiest to be replaced to be placed in their accounts, once they have acquired them. No one judges himself to be in debt when he is granted time. All the while this is the one thing that even a grateful man cannot repay.

You may perhaps ask what I am doing, I who advise you about these things. I will confess openly: my accounts are balanced, as happens for one who is generous but also careful. I am not able to say that I waste nothing, but I can say what I waste, and why and how. I can recount the causes of my poverty. But what happens to many who are reduced to poverty through no fault of their own has happened to me. Everyone forgives, but no one offers help.

Why is this the case? I do not think he is a poor man for whom whatever remains is enough. But I want you to keep your possessions, and begin to do so now. As our ancestors thought, parsimony comes too late at the bottom of the barrel. Not only does the smallest amount remain there, but also the worst.

Farewell.

Seneca gives the impression that the opening of the collection begins *in medias res*. The focus on the precious commodity of time is familiar from other texts, in particular *On the Shortness of Life*, but Seneca has made his point more urgently and concludes his opening paragraph with a paradoxical description of life and death. We do not live each day, but rather die each day; death is not in front of us, but behind us, relentlessly claiming the days we have spent.

The urgency of Seneca's advice is shown by the frequent use of imperatives. Of note is Seneca's second imperative, which I have translated as 'free yourself for yourself'. Here we see Seneca's characteristic and dizzying use of reflexive language, which can often be difficult to capture in English. Furthermore, the Latin for 'free yourself' is *vindica te tibi*. The verb (*vindico*) has a wide range of meanings that are crucial to Seneca's thought. The verb can refer to asserting one's right over property that is in the possession of another (*OLD vindico* 1). It can also be used for asserting the freedom of a person who has been wrongfully enslaved (*OLD vindico* 3).[35] A related word, *vindicta*, is used to refer to the manumission of slaves. Seneca takes language from the everyday marketplace and uses it to describe the care of the self. This language also illustrates the point that many of us, although legally free, are in fact slaves to other things. Only the philosopher is free.

The second paragraph begins with the same imperative that opens the letter (*fac*), and also makes bold use of the language of commodities. Seneca advises Lucilius to place his hand upon today. The Latin *manum inieceris* is used for claiming a slave, or other possession, as one's own (*OLD inicio* 6 b). Seneca continues on with one of his master tropes, the commodification of time. It is our only possession (1.3).

The penultimate paragraph focuses on Seneca's use of time. He assures Lucilius that he practises what he preaches, but only with great effort and care. With another economics metaphor, Seneca notes that the accounts of his expenditures of time are balanced (1.4). He concludes with a re-evaluation of poverty and notes that a person is never poor if happy with what he has. He ends with an epigrammatic maxim, taken from Hesiod's *Works and Days* (369), thus putting his some of the radical ideas of his philosophy on the firm ground of traditional wisdom.

Given Seneca's focus on giving a daily account of his actions and how he has spent his time, we may wonder how he would justify the time he spent writing his tragedies. It is to these complex and challenging works that we now turn.

II

SENECA'S TRAGEDIES

AS WE CONCLUDED OUR INVESTIGATION of Seneca's philosophy with an uplifting passage from the letters, let us open our discussion of Seneca's tragedies with a particularly gruesome passage from his *Thyestes*. Some scholars believe that this was one of the final plays that Seneca wrote and that he may have composed it during his 'retirement', at the same time that he was writing his *Moral Epistles*. As Atreus develops his plan for revenge against his brother, Thyestes, he declares:

> Something greater and larger than usual and beyond the bounds of human custom swells in my soul and presses on my sluggish hands. What it is I do not know, but it is something great! Let it be. Seize this, my soul. It is a crime fitting for Thyestes and fitting for Atreus: what each would perform. The Odrysian house saw an unspeakable feast – I confess it is a great crime, but already taken: my pain must find something greater than this. Inspire my soul, Daulian mother and sister; the cause is similar: aid and drive on my hand. Let the greedy father delight as he tears apart his children and eats his own

limbs. It is good, it is enough: this measure of revenge is pleasing – for now.

Where is he? Why is Atreus innocent for so long? The full image of the slaughter passes before my eyes, loss of children thrust in the father's face – my soul, why are you afraid again and subside before the deed? It must be dared, come: Thyestes himself will commit the chief outrage in this crime.

(268–86)

Here we have *in nuce* many of the defining qualities of Senecan tragedy. In a lengthy monologue, Atreus describes his psychological state. This monologue incorporates aspects from the literary tradition as well as from Seneca's philosophy. First, we can note how Atreus uses techniques from Seneca's therapy of the passions, such as self-address and self-command. Rather than using these techniques to quell his passions or to steel his resolve to live a life of virtue, Atreus addresses and commands his soul in order to stir up his anger and do away with any qualms he has about killing Thyestes's children and serving them to him to eat.

Atreus's desire 'to do something greater' than has been done in the past is also one of the defining tropes of Senecan tragedy. It also alludes to Seneca's position as a poet who comes late in the literary tradition. He must surpass his predecessors. Seneca uses Atreus to demonstrate his knowledge of literary history. His language echoes Ovid's Medea at the conclusion of *Heroides* 12. It also trumps Atreus's model for inspiration, Ovid's Procne, who avenged the rape and mutilation of her sister, Philomela, by her husband, Tereus. She did so by killing their child, Itys, and serving him to Tereus. As Procne develops her plan for revenge, she states, 'I have prepared something great, what it is, I do not yet know' (*Met.* 6.618–19).

Atreus also marks his connection to this story in highly allusive terms. The 'Odrysian feast' refers to the infanticide and cannibal feast of Procne, Philomela and Tereus. While Atreus sees this story as a fitting model, it is only as a base for his crime. He cannot simply repeat it, however. Atreus must surpass these crimes. Again, with another piece of mythological allusiveness, he calls on the Daulian parent and sister (Procne and Philomela) to inspire him and guide his actions. He will go beyond their crime by killing three children instead of only one child. But even this is only satisfying for now, suggesting that Atreus will try to develop even more terrible forms of revenge, as he in fact does at the end of the play.

Political readings of the play also present themselves. As *Thyestes* may have been written when Seneca was attempting to distance himself from the court, it is tempting to see Atreus as representing Nero. It is true that both had problematic relationships with their brothers. While Atreus makes no attempt to behave like a good ruler, and Nero's reign has come to be a synonym for tyranny, direct references to Nero or any of the other emperors are not unambiguously clear in the play. The plays are, however, in a general manner deeply concerned with imperial power and the problems of autocracy.

Senecan tragedy is a difficult experience for the audience on several levels. Not only must one have a strong stomach for excessive violence and rhetoric, but one must also be knowledgeable of the literary and mythological precedents that shape his stories. If we bring in our knowledge of Seneca's philosophy, as well as his biography and involvement with Roman politics, the demands upon Seneca's audience become even more complex. What are we to make of these connections? Is Seneca showing his disillusionment with Stoicism? Have his experiences in the world of politics led him to expose the realities of autocracy through the figure of Atreus? Or is Seneca simply delighting in poetic creation, a world free from the constraints of Stoicism and politics? Each of these options seems to offer plausible interpretations of this passage from Thyestes. Yet the complexity of Senecan drama suggests that we should not simply see one line of interpretation as the definitive reading. Literary history, political history and philosophy combine in Seneca's plays to produce some of the earliest manifestations of megalomaniacal and titanic characters, many of whom take great delight and pleasure in evil.

Our investigation of the plays in this chapter is divided into two parts. The first offers overall thematic considerations of the plays, which are focused on some of the main scholarly debates. We will treat the plays' relationship to literary history and metatheatrical qualities, questions of performance, the plays' relationship to Roman politics, and finally, their relationship to

Seneca's philosophy. The second half provides discussions of each of the plays and focuses on plot, mythological backstory and key issues.

The eight tragedies composed by Seneca, and the two attached to his name, are our only surviving complete examples of Roman tragedy. The titles and order commonly attributed to the plays are as follows: *Hercules* (*Furens*, or *Hercules Insane*), *Troades* (or *Trojan Women*), *Phoenissae* (or *Phoenician Women*), *Medea*, *Phaedra*, *Oedipus*, *Agamemnon* and *Thyestes*. As noted earlier, two other works, *Hercules Oetaeus* (*Hercules on Mt. Oeta*) and *Octavia*, our only surviving example of Roman historical drama, *tragoedia praetexta*, have been ascribed to Seneca. Today it is generally accepted that both plays are by an imitator, rather than by Seneca himself. Scholarly debate does continue about the author of *Hercules Oetaeus*.[1] Given the likelihood that these plays represent some of the earliest literary receptions of Seneca, they will be treated at the start of the following chapter.

Along with the time he spent in the uplifting company of philosophers, Seneca also explored the depths of human tragedy via Greek mythology. All of the plays that can be ascribed to Seneca tell well-known stories from Greek myth. There are of course Roman elements, some might say anachronisms, in Seneca's plays, and some have even argued that his plays are to be seen as coded allusions to the crimes of the Julio-Claudians.[2] Such direct references are best avoided, as tempting as they may be. When it comes to the dating of Seneca's plays, we are on even less stable ground than the dating of his philosophical works. They could have been written under any of the emperors from Tiberius to Nero. A generally accepted relative chronology has been developed that groups Seneca's plays into three periods of early (*Agamemnon*, *Phaedra* and *Oedipus*), middle (*Medea*, *Troades* and *Hercules Furens*) and late (*Thyestes* and the possibly unfinished – as it lacks a chorus – *Phoenissae*).[3] How these specific periods can be dated is difficult to say. Only *Hercules Furens* provides a clue. As the Hercules of the *Apocolocyntosis* parodies the play's tragic diction, scholars have accepted late 54 CE as the *terminus ante quem* for the play.[4] Yet even this dating is problematic, as it requires us to accept that the *Apocolocyntosis* was composed in the immediate months after Claudius's death and that Seneca had in fact already composed *Hercules*. It has also been argued that *Thyestes* was written late in Seneca's life, during his period of retirement, and that in this play Seneca looks back on his failed political life under Nero and deconstructs many of the ideals of *On Mercy*.[5] The *Phoenissae* could have been left unfinished at the time of Seneca's death, although some scholars have argued that it is not incomplete, but rather is an experimental play.[6] There is one example of a Hellenistic Greek play without a chorus, the *Exagoge* of Ezekiel, which does not recount a story from Greek mythology but rather narrates events from the life of Moses.

Along with questions of dating, there are several crucial aspects of Senecan drama about which we would like to know more. Were they written for full-scale performance or recitation? Were scenes only intended to be performed or were the plays simply tucked away in Seneca's desk, written for his own amusement? What is their relationship to other literary models? What is their relationship to Senecan philosophy? In this chapter we will address questions of literary precedents, contemporary relevance, performance and the role of philosophy. Each of these directions can be fruitfully explored on their own, and indeed a defining aspect of Senecan drama is its multifaceted nature.

Let us start with the question of literary history, as those familiar with Greek drama may already be wondering about the connections between Seneca's plays and Athenian tragedy by virtue of the similarity of their respective titles. Indeed, simply going by that evidence, we can see that Seneca's plays reference the *Agamemnon* of Aeschylus and the *Oedipus* of Sophocles, while the remainder, save *Thyestes*, have Euripidean parallels. The fact that *Thyestes* does not have an extant classical Greek parallel has in the past been taken as evidence that the story's 'unpleasantly sanguinary' quality – it is perhaps the most violent and bloodiest of a dramatic corpus full of horrors – did not appeal to the more decorous tragedy of the Greeks.[7] Yet the fact that we do not have a Greek *Thyestes* is simply an accident of the transmission of texts from the ancient world. Sophocles and Euripides, along with several other Greek tragedians, wrote plays on this myth. It was also a popular topic with Roman dramatists, but again only notices of publication and a few fragments survive. Here we come to one of the cruxes of the analysis of Senecan drama from the standpoint of literary history. The synonymous dramas of the great fifth-century Athenian playwrights are only one model among many for Seneca's plays. We must remember that over 400 years elapsed from the deaths of Euripides and Sophocles at the end of the fifth century BCE to Seneca's day. During that time, Greek drama developed further and Roman drama was born in 240 BCE according to the traditional dating. In fact, as Richard Tarrant (1978) has demonstrated, many of the dramatic conventions of Seneca's plays, such as five-act structure, the detachable choral odes, the use of asides and stage directions, have no direct parallels in classical Athenian drama, but can be seen in later Greek and Roman comedies.

Thus, Seneca wrote his plays with a different idea of dramatic possibilities, and we should not simply look to Aeschylus, Sophocles and Euripides as Seneca's main or even primary influences. In the past, this has been the case. Frequently, Seneca's plays were judged to be inferior and best used to help reconstruct lost plays by the Athenians. For example, Euripides's (now lost) first production of *Hippolytus* apparently had a more aggressive Phaedra, and scholars believe that Seneca based his heroine in part on this version. This may well have been the case, and there is no reason to think that Seneca did not have the Athenian dramatists at his side when he composed his plays. It is also crucial to remember that centuries of literary history elapsed between Seneca and Euripides – a history that for us is almost entirely lost. It is only an unfortunate coincidence that Seneca remains our only extant example of classical tragedy after Euripides, and our only extant example of Roman tragedy. We can glean important parallels from the fragments of Roman tragedy that do survive. Comparing the fragments of Accius's *Atreus* and Seneca's *Thyestes* reveals that Seneca followed the Republican play to some extent. Yet what relationship Seneca's *Thyestes* had to the play of the same name written by Varius at the request of Augustus for his Triple Triumph of 29 BCE, or Seneca's *Medea* had to Ovid's lost tragedy *Medea*, we can only guess. Seneca also turned to non-dramatic works for models, especially Virgil and Ovid. On this point we are considerably more fortunate, as we can trace Seneca's engagement and rivalry with the great poets of the Augustan age. Indeed, the weight of literary history, 'the anxiety of influence' felt by Seneca and even by some of his characters, is one of the defining characteristics of Senecan drama.

Intertextuality and Metatheatre

While the role of politics in Seneca's plays is presented in general terms and cannot be seen as specifically commenting on an individual ruler, when we consider literary history we can see clearly Seneca's competitive engagement with his poetic rivals, particularly the Augustan poets.[8] Seneca's self-conscious relationship to his predecessors reveals itself in several ways throughout his plays. The complicated family struggles of brother against brother, father against son and nature turning back upon itself are not simply aesthetic devices that shape the horrific nature of Senecan drama; they can also be seen as metaphors for Seneca's struggles as a poet, ranging back over the past, taking pieces from various genres and predecessors, and assembling them into something new and terrifying.

If we start with the opening lines of *Hercules* – the first play as transmitted in the oldest manuscript – we immediately see Seneca's complicated engagement with the poetic predecessors of the Augustan age. Euripides's *Heracles* opens with a brief monologue from Heracles's mortal stepfather, Amphitryon, who in typical Euripidean fashion gives the backstory for the play. Seneca's play opens with a lengthy (124 lines) monologue of Juno, who angrily complains about the infidelities of Jupiter. Hercules was conceived as the result of one of Jupiter's many rapes of mortal women. In this case, Jupiter came to Alcmene disguised as her husband.

> Sister of the Thunderer (for only this name remains for me), I, a widow, have deserted Jupiter, who is always another's, and the temples of the highest aether. And having been expelled, I have given my place in the sky to mistresses; I must dwell on earth for Jupiter's mistresses hold the sky.
>
> (1–5)

Seneca's focus on the wrath of Juno takes us to the world of Roman epic, most notably the opening of Virgil's *Aeneid*. Aeneas is hounded by land and sea on account of the 'mindful anger of cruel Juno' (1.4). Juno speaks the first words in the epic. She outlines to herself the reasons for her wrath against Trojans (1.37–49). She refers to herself with the honorific epithet that goes back to Homer, 'sister and wife of Jupiter' (1.46–7). Seneca changes the focus of Juno's speech. In the *Aeneid* she worries that humans will not honour her if the Trojans succeed, and is angered that she has not been allowed to punish her enemies as Pallas has. In contrast, Seneca looks at Juno's conjugal life. She is angry at Jupiter's infidelity and the subsequent honours he has given to the mortal women who are his victims. Assuming that the audience will know her official title as 'sister and wife' of Jupiter, Juno states that she can only properly be called the god's sister. This focus on the loves of Jupiter moves us from the world of Virgil's epic to Ovid's *Metamorphoses*. The opening books of this Augustan epic tell of Jupiter's many sexual encounters on earth and Juno's unsuccessful attempts to thwart them. Juno's anger at the heavenly honours decreed for Jupiter's lovers in *Hercules* refers in part to Callisto, who in book two of the *Metamorphoses* was turned into a bear by Juno, but then turned into the Great Bear (Ursa Major) constellation by Jupiter along with her son, Arcas (Ursa Minor). In a lengthy speech, which outlines her anger that one of Jupiter's mistresses has been granted a place in heaven, Juno demands from the sea-goddess Tethys that the constellations not be allowed to 'rest' and set beneath the sea (2.512–30). In book three, Juno rages against Jupiter's lover Semele and notes that she is 'Jupiter's wife and sister, but certainly his sister' (3.265–6). In the first line of his play, Seneca alludes to Juno's indignation at the unsuitability of her title in Ovid.

Seneca's Juno plans to destroy Hercules by calling up the Furies from the Underworld to drive the hero mad. This plan is strongly reminiscent of Virgil's Juno's monologue in book seven of the *Aeneid*. In Virgil's epic the goddess declares that she will use the powers below to destroy the peace between the Trojans and the Italians (7.293–322). She then calls on the Fury Alecto to accomplish this task (7.331–40). Instead of inciting the madness of war, Seneca's Juno sees the madness generated by the Furies as war against the self. She declares that Hercules will 'wage war with himself' (85). The self-directed nature of madness is made clear by Juno's personification of Furor, 'who is always armed against himself' (98). This fact is further illustrated by Juno's declaration that she must be driven mad by the Furies before they incite Hercules's madness:

In order that Alcides's soul may be captured and he may be driven on and incited by great madness, we must be driven mad first: Juno, why do you not yet rage? Me, sisters, overturn me first and cast down my mind, if I am to plan anything that is worthy of a stepmother. My wishes are changed: let the father return and see his children unharmed and let him come back with a strong hand. I have found the day in which the hated virtue of Hercules will help us. He has conquered me? Let him conquer himself and wish to die and go back to the gods below.

(107–17)

In this opening monologue we can outline several key themes of Senecan tragedy. Seneca takes pieces from various Augustan texts and reassembles them in a new, dramatic context.[9] In this lengthy monologue of plotting revenge, madness, internal and external motivation, as well as the divide between rational and irrational acts are problematised. Juno commands the Furies to 'overturn' her mind. Medea, for example, also opens her breast to the Furies before she kills her first child (965–6). This madness is also inspirational, as after her surrender Juno is able to perfect her plan. We have already seen how Atreus looks to the poetic tradition of infanticide for inspiration. Characters like Atreus, Medea and Juno seem to mirror the 'poetic furor' that is necessary to inspire Seneca to write his plays.[10]

The poetics and aesthetics of Senecan tragedy can be summed up with the words 'greater than' (*maiora*). The use of this adjective defines the goals of Seneca's characters and, by extension, Seneca's goals as a tragic poet. Like Atreus, Medea wishes to commit 'greater crimes' than she did in the past (50). One way Seneca accomplishes this goal is by having Medea kill both her children onstage. The second is murdered as part of a play-within-a-play. Medea kills her child as Jason and the Corinthians look on. In Euripides's play, the children are killed offstage. In his lengthy retelling of the Medea myth in the *Metamorphoses*, Ovid relegates the infanticide to one line (7.396). In Ovid's *Heroides* 12, Medea concludes her letter to Jason still unsure of what form her revenge will take. Yet she does know that her mind is conceiving of 'something very great' (*nescio quid certe mens mea maius agit* 12.212). Seneca's play graphically portrays the result of Medea's previous Ovidian plotting.[11]

Along with the goal of outdoing the horrors of the past, and producing something greater than his predecessors, Seneca's tragedies also gruesomely turn metaphors for describing literary composition into physical reality. Seneca takes apart the 'bodies' of past literary texts and assembles them into something new.[12] We can see Seneca self-consciously playing with this trope at the conclusion of *Phaedra*. As he tries to reassemble Hippolytus's dismembered body, Theseus address and commands himself, 'The scattered limbs, father, of the mangled body, set in order and restore the scattered parts to their place' (1256–8). These lines reference Horace's famous discussion of 'the scattered limbs of the poet' (*Sat*. 1.4.62). In this satire, Horace discusses how his satires are not truly poetry; one could easily take away the metre and break apart the words to produce regular, everyday speech, whereas if one scatters the limbs of a line written by a true poet, the poetry still remains. At the end of *Phaedra*, Seneca is actualising this metaphor from literary discourse. Much as we today speak about the 'metrical feet' of a poem, the Romans also used the metaphor of a poem's 'limbs' (*membra*).

Yet it is not only Augustan literary theory that Seneca turns into a reality in this passage from *Phaedra*. Theseus's attempts to collect and reassemble Hippolytus also present a gruesome realisation of Seneca's own theory of composition. In *Epistle* 84, Seneca notes that as writers we must imitate the bees, which fly about the fields and take nectar from various flowers to create their honey. A writer must assemble different pieces from his reading to create a new body (*Ep*. 84.3–8). Theseus's ultimate inability to reassemble Hippolytus's body, which is scattered across the field, into a complete whole, offers both a gruesome and pessimistic take on Seneca's own theory.

Seneca also squarely focuses on the process of character-building and dramaturgy. Seneca's characters look to past examples to create something new and greater. Many of Seneca's plays dramatise how his characters become who they are. As they enter the play they can appear old and tired, as if aware of how many times they have played their role before. Medea opens by stirring up her soul and calling on it to take up its ancient vigour (40–2). Atreus's opening words castigate himself for being lazy, inert and simply an angry Atreus. At times, characters seem to forget who they are.

In the *Troades*, after being too easily convinced by Andromache's claims that Astyanax is dead, in an aside Ulysses commands himself to get back into character (605–18). For a brief moment, Seneca's play almost takes a mythologically impossible direction. Astyanax is saved by his mother, who out-tricks the master trickster, Ulysses. Yet Ulysses himself realises the potential turn this play is taking and that by too easily believing Andromache he is not playing his proper role. In a lengthy aside he turns himself into the 'complete Ulysses' (614) and the play continues on to its inexorable conclusion.

Seneca's *Oedipus* presents self-construction in another light. Oedipus thinks he knows who he is. In a rare moment of confidence he declares that he can solve the oracle's unclear response about the cause of the Theban plague by self-referentially declaring, 'Tell it, although its meaning is doubtful: knowing ambiguities is given to Oedipus alone' (215–16). After he learns the truth and blinds himself as punishment for his crimes, Oedipus re-evaluates who he is, stating:

> The task is well done: I have paid what is justly owed to my father. I delight in my darkness. What god, at last well-disposed to me, has poured a black cloud over my head? Who has forgiven my crimes? I have escaped the witnessing day. You owe nothing, parricide, to your right hand: the light has fled from you. A face that is fitting for Oedipus.
>
> (998–1003)

Spectatorship within the plays themselves is another recurrent topos of Senecan drama.[13] The crimes of the play that are witnessed or read by the external audience are also frequently witnessed by the characters themselves, thus creating a play-within-a-play. As we have already briefly noted, at the play's conclusion, once Medea has become Medea, she takes on the role of dramaturge. She kills her first child in private, as she has visions of the Furies and the ghost of her brother. Once she hears the noises of the oncoming Corinthians, she declares to herself that she will perform the second murder publicly atop the burning palace: 'Now do this my soul: your virtue must not be lost in hiding, let the people approve the work of your hands' (976–7).

Although she actively invites the applause of the assembled Corinthians, her main goal is to be sure that Jason witnesses the culmination of her vengeance. From the palace rooftop, Medea describes the pleasure that has come over her and grows as she prepares to kill her last child. But she also notes, 'This one thing is lacking for me, that spectator. I judge that I have accomplished nothing as yet: whatever crime we have committed without him as a witness is lost' (991–4). After the slaughter, she then metatheatrically calls upon Jason to look up and recognise her (1020–1). She actively creates the play's recognition scene.

Aristotle famously noted that the best tragedies combine recognition (*anagnoresis*) with reversal (*peripetiea*). According to Aristotle, Sophocles's *Oedipus* provides the finest combination of these two themes. At the very moment that Oedipus recognises who he truly is, his fortune is reversed. Aristotle's *Poetics* has had a profound influence on the interpretation of drama since the early modern period. Yet it remains a matter of debate whether Seneca was aware of this work.[14] Regardless, recognition scenes were seen as a key part of Roman drama. Already at the end of Terence's *The Mother-in-Law*, which was performed in the 160s BCE, we can see a critique of the typical ending of comedies, where the truth is revealed to all. Recognition (*agnoscere* in Latin) is a key aspect of Seneca's plays. After being rebuked by the chorus for complaining when he should be collecting the parts of Hippolytus's body for burial, Theseus orders his son's remains to be brought to him. As he looks at the broken body he asks, 'Is this Hippolytus? I recognize my crime' (1249). When Atreus reveals the remains of Thyestes's children to his brother he asks, 'Do you recognize your children at all?' To which Thyestes responds, 'I recognize my brother' (1005–6).

For Seneca, recognition may have had deeper resonance than simply being a key piece of dramatic poetics. Recognition is also a significant aspect of Seneca's philosophy, particularly in his letters. For example, Seneca notes that through the process of philosophical epistolary exchange he recognises Lucilius. In another letter, Seneca notes that the goal of life is to play one person throughout our lives, 'so that we may be praised, or at least recognized' (*Ep.* 120.22). The importance of this Latin verb (*agnoscere*) for both Senecan drama and philosophy must be noted. This connection highlights the dramatic nature of Seneca's Stoicism. Like the characters from Seneca's plays, the life of a Stoic *proficiens* is also a performance that strives for recognition.

Performance

How were Seneca's plays originally experienced? At first, this may seem like a foolish question to ask. We know that the Attic tragedians' plays were performed on the stage, as were the Roman Republican comedies by Plautus and Terence. Yet for Seneca's plays we lack sufficient evidence to declare that his plays were ever performed during his lifetime, or at all during the classical period. As far as we know today, Senecan tragedy only began to be performed on stage during the fifteenth century. More recently, they have been performed in Latin and translated into modern languages with some frequency over the past several decades.

The original performance history of Seneca's plays still remains a matter of considerable scholarly debate. This fact is one of the great ironies of history, both because we can relatively securely date the original performances of the other dramas that have survived intact from Greece and Rome, and because the age in which Seneca lived is typically seen as a period in which the world of theatre spilt over into reality.[15] This second point can be seen on several levels. Beginning during the late Republic and Augustan period, Romans frequently decorated their houses with paintings that represented stages or scenes from drama. Indeed, one of the ways that we can reconstruct the appearance of Roman stages is from the frescos that have survived portraying stages and masks in Pompeii and elsewhere.[16] Although the Romans had invited drama into their homes by the late Republican period, there was also a strong tendency to keep actors and acting at a distance. It would not be until several centuries after the deaths of Sophocles and Euripides at the end of the fifth century that the Romans would perform a play.

The 'origin' of Roman drama is typically dated to 240 BCE with the performance of a Greek play translated by Livius Andronicus during the Roman Games in celebration of Jupiter Optimus Maximus. Andronicus likely was a freed slave from Greek-speaking southern Italy, *Magna Graecia*, who became attached to the household of the noble Roman general Livius Salinator after Rome's successful wars in the south of the peninsula. Andronicus is also credited with translating the *Odyssey* into Latin. The key point to remember is that literature and drama were not seen as a native tradition for the Romans; rather, they came from outsiders as part of Rome's military conquests. Indeed, the date of the performance of Livius's play is significant. In the previous year (241 BCE) Rome defeated Carthage in the first Punic War and thus gained the first territories outside of the peninsula, as Sicily became a Roman province. Military conquest, empire and the development of Roman culture went hand in hand.

Over the next decades a variety of public festivals were added, during which dramas would be performed alongside other forms of entertainment. Plays could also be performed as part of other celebrations, such as the funeral of the general Lucius Aemilius Paullus in 160 BCE, during which two comedies of Terence were performed. Nevertheless, the Roman authorities remained wary of performances. Although playwrights had an element of prestige from early on and eventually many elite Romans tried their hand at writing plays, the first permanent theatre in Rome, the Theatre of Pompey, was not completed until 55 BCE. Soon after two more followed, the theatres of Balbus and Marcellus. Yet actors were typically not Roman citizens, a fact that Seneca reminds us in *Epistle* 80.7–8. During the Julio-Claudian period this line was crossed. Caligula planned to appear on stage, but was executed before he could do so. Nero of course did perform in a variety of roles, which led Pliny the Younger to condemn him as the 'actor emperor' (*Pan.* 46.4). The Romans tried to keep the elite world of politics and the low, servile world of acting separate. Nero was not alone in blending the two, however. As we noted in the opening chapter, after giving his account of Seneca's death in the aftermath of the discovery of the Pisonian conspiracy, Tacitus tells us that if Nero had been deposed, Piso would have been quickly removed from power and the empire would have been handed over to Seneca. Piso could not succeed Nero, because, according to Tacitus, he shared Nero's love of performance and had been an actor in tragedies (*tragoedus Ann.* 15.65).

Paradoxically, we do not know how Seneca's plays fit into this theatricalised world. We do have two tantalising, but inconclusive pieces of evidence. Writing a few decades after Seneca's death, the orator Quintilian gives us our only picture of Seneca the tragedian. In his discussion of whether it is appropriate to create new words in Latin, he offers this reminiscence: 'I remember when I was quite young there was a debate between Pomponius and Seneca in their prefaces whether "he takes his steps out of the threshold" ought to be said in tragedies' (8.3.31). A few words of explanation are necessary. Although we cannot be sure given Quintilian's imprecise reference to his age, scholars have argued that this debate may have taken place in the early 50s CE.[17] The Latin phrase that was the topic of debate is *gradus eliminat*, which I have unpoetically translated earlier to convey the sense of the verb and why Seneca may have disapproved of it. *Eliminat* is an archaic verb, and is found in Republican drama. Perhaps it was revived in Pomponius's plays.[18] According to Tacitus, Pomponius did have his plays produced on the stage (*Ann.* 11.13). He was an older, likely more established playwright at the time of this debate, and perhaps Seneca was trying to make a name for himself by criticising the work of his elder contemporary.[19] Finally, in what sort of forum did this debate take place? Quintilian notes that Seneca and Pomponius debated the propriety of this sentence 'in their prefaces' (*praefationibus*). This word does not necessarily mean written prefaces to their plays, but could refer to spoken introductions given by their authors before the reading or performance of their dramas.

The other piece of ancient evidence is a graffito from Pompeii, which quotes a line from Seneca's *Agamemnon*, 'I see the groves of Ida' (730). Since the city was destroyed by the eruption of Vesuvius in 79 CE we have a *terminus ante quem* for when these words were written. Yet we have no idea how the mysterious writer of the words learnt of Seneca's play. Had there been a performance, a recitation, had the work been purchased from a bookseller? Or had the author of the graffito simply heard the words somewhere and for some reason felt it appropriate to scribble them on a wall, albeit in a manner that is quite unlike the spelling used in contemporary texts. *Idai cernu nemura* is written in Pompeii; *Idaea cerno nemora* is what modern editors print, but they must still emend the medieval manuscripts' reading of the first word.

Although Seneca's plays were performed during the Renaissance and during this period Seneca could be declared to be a greater tragedian than Euripides, by the nineteenth century scholars began to condemn Seneca's plays as inferior to his Greek predecessors. They were judged to be without dramatic life and simply not suited for performance. This mode of thought held sway throughout most of the twentieth century, and often Seneca's plays were seen to be 'closet dramas', which were not intended for performance but rather for private reading. We do know that during Seneca's time plays did not necessarily have to be fully staged in a public performance. They could be performed in small private theatres in the homes of the elite. Instead of performing the entire play, individual scenes could be staged. We also know that dramas during the imperial period were read aloud, or recited. During the latter half of the twentieth century, this possibility came to dominate, and Seneca's plays have often been considered 'recitation dramas'. Of course, we don't fully know how recitation dramas would have been recited. Would the author have read parts or all of his play in draft form for comments? Would another read it? Would there be two or more readers taking different parts? Would an actor or dancer mime the action while it was read?

The debates for and against performance often look at individual passages. The sacrifice scene in his *Oedipus* is claimed to be one of the key examples of how Seneca did not write for performance, but rather recitation. Given the way the scene is written, a full-scale performance would require the sacrifice to take place on stage. Manto cannot have been describing what happens offstage, since she draws specific attention to the fact that she uses her own hands to examine the animal's insides (354, 380). Furthermore, the description of the bull rushing from the altar could not, so the argument runs, have been staged (342–4). While we know very little about how the Romans produced effects onstage, Pliny the Elder writes that he has seen specially trained bulls that could fall, get up and allow themselves to be lifted (*HN* 8.70.182).[20] Thus, this sacrificial spectacle may not have been outside the Romans' technical abilities.

Even if we concede that the sacrifice scene in *Oedipus* could have been staged, it could still be argued that the very nature of Senecan drama, stuffed full of lengthy monologues, is evidence that they were intended for recitation, rather than full-scale performance. There is no denying that Seneca's plays are 'static' and devoted to lengthy speeches. Nevertheless, Senecan drama is not simply defined by characters who 'recite in turn'.[21] They also engage in lively dialogue. For example, the rapid-fire exchange between Medea and her Nurse can be seen as 'proof' not only of Seneca's dramatic abilities, but also of the fact that he could not have written for recitation by a single person.[22]

NURSE: A king is to be feared.
MEDEA: My father was a king.
NURSE: You don't fear weapons?
MEDEA: Not even if they come from the earth.
NURSE: You will die.
MEDEA: I desire to.
NURSE: Flee.
MEDEA: I regret my flight.
NURSE: Medea—
MEDEA: I will become.
NURSE: You are a mother.
MEDEA: You see to whom.
NURSE: You hesitate to flee?
MEDEA: I will flee, but I will get revenge first.
NURSE: An avenger will follow you.
MEDEA: Perhaps I will find a means of delay.

(168–73)

More recently, some scholars have moved away from considering solely how Seneca's plays might have been presented during his lifetime. Taking their cue from the recent revival of Seneca on the stage, scholars have focused on Seneca's plays under the lens of performance criticism. The works of Harrison (2000), Davis (2003: 24–36) and Kohn (2013) argue for the dramaturgical skill and artistry of Seneca's plays. Because Seneca's plays can be easily adapted for modern performance, so the argument goes, Seneca must have written with full-scale performance in mind.

Politics

The question of performance of Seneca's plays in contemporary Rome paradoxically gives way to visions of the histrionic world of the Julio-Claudian period, where, at least as our sources present it, the lines between reality, myth and acting were continually elided. Although they are set in the Greek world, Seneca's plays have shaped our vision of early imperial Rome. In fact, Seneca's *Oedipus* affects our reading of Roman history. The death of Seneca's Jocasta in this play has an uncanny connection to the portrayal of the death of Agrippina in Tacitus's *Annals* and the historical tragedy, *Octavia*.

In Sophocles's version of the play, Oedipus's wife and mother, Jocasta, hangs herself offstage. Once Oedipus discovers his mother's body, he blinds himself with a brooch from her cloak. A messenger decorously reports all of this bloody action to the chorus and audience. In Seneca's play, Oedipus blinds himself with his own fingers, which is reported by a messenger at the start of act five. After this speech, Oedipus enters, followed by Jocasta, who tries to convince her son that he is not guilty (1019). In a lengthy aside, she then condemns herself to die. After a brief attempt to convince Oedipus to kill her, she tells herself, in another aside, to seize his sword and concludes:

> Shall I fix the weapon in my breast or press it deep into my awaiting neck? You do not know how to choose a wound: this, my right hand, seek this capacious womb, which bore husband and children.
>
> (1036–9)

This death scene might simply seem like another example of Seneca's penchant for bloody excess in his dramas, were it not for the afterlife of Jocasta's last words.

The first choral ode of the pseudo-Senecan *Octavia* concludes by narrating the death of Nero's mother, Agrippina. She survives the shipwreck plotted by her son, only to be murdered on shore by his soldiers. The chorus states that one of Nero's ministers first cuts Agrippina's breast with his sword, but she orders that he, 'Bury the terrible sword in her womb. She says, "This, this you must strike with the sword, which bore such a monster"' (366–72).

This connection may simply be attributed to the close reading of Seneca's works that was clearly conducted by the unknown author of *Octavia*. Yet when we turn to the historian Tacitus's account of the death of Agrippina, we see that he also notes that Agrippina spoke and acted similarly. He writes: 'As the centurion was drawing his sword to kill her, she offered her womb, exclaimed, "strike my belly!" and was killed with many wounds' (*Ann.* 14.8). Did Agrippina model her death on Seneca's Jocasta? Or did Seneca model his Jocasta's death on Agrippina's already histrionic end? We cannot be sure of the direction of influence, or how reports of Agrippina's last words were made public. As with other imperial deaths there certainly must have been rumours, and, as we have noted, the Romans had a penchant for attributing dramatic flourishes when reporting the words of the Julio-Claudians. The striking similarity of Jocasta's and Agrippina's last words may serve as an example of the difficulty in drawing the line between myth and reality when studying the Julio-Claudian period and how one of Seneca's plays contributes to this difficulty.

Rather than offering specific historical parallels, Seneca's plays investigate the politics of autocracy in a general manner. They show the nature of tyranny and also point out, frequently in the choral odes, the unstable nature of royal power and offer examples of ideal kingship. But positive examples are lacking from the characters portrayed. There are no good kings in Senecan tragedy. Seneca shows how power can destroy reason and virtue. After giving up her stoicising advice to Phaedra to fight against her passions, the Nurse sets off to test Hippolytus, noting, 'One who fears the orders of a king must place aside and drive all honour from their soul; shame is a bad minister for royal commands' (428–30). Medea and Creon engage in a lengthy discussion of the nature of royal power. Echoing Seneca's advice for life under an autocrat from *On Anger*, Creon states, 'You must bear the just and unjust commands of a king' (195), to which Medea replies with advice that seems straight from *On Mercy*, 'Unjust kingdoms never remain for long' (196). Yet, instead of accepting this advice, Creon simply commands Medea to leave and complain to her own people (197). Medea does not heed this command and instead plays the role of royal advisor. She offers Creon insights from her own experiences as a ruler:

> How difficult it is for the soul to turn away from anger once it has been stirred up, and how one who has taken up the sceptre with his proud hand believes it to be regal to continue on in the direction he has begun, I have learnt in my own kingdom.
>
> (203–6)

Creon wants to be seen as a good king and argues that he is one because he has chosen Jason, an exile, for his son-in-law (252–61). He even grants Medea time to bid farewell to her children. He allows her one more day in Corinth, despite the fact that his fear urges him to deny her pleas (294–5), and he knows that she will use the time for treachery (290). Here we can see a variety of political as well as psychological questions being addressed. Creon should have followed his first impulse and have had Medea executed. By acting like a mild and merciful king, he seals his own doom and that of his daughter. In addition, we can also see an interesting twist to the problem of weakness of will. Creon's fear is in fact correct; rather than banish the emotion, he should rather listen to it. Weakness of will is turned on its head. Reason is not pointing out the better path to Creon; rather it is his fear. By not heeding this emotion, and instead assenting to Medea's 'rational' argument about how kings should suppress their anger, Creon nevertheless follows the worse path.

Tyrants loom large in the plays. Atreus enters *Thyestes* rebuking himself for his inaction and noting that the greatest insult that can be heaped on a tyrant is that he is unavenged (176–8). Even the punishment of tyrants is problematised. In *Agamemnon*, the usurper Aegisthus tries to justify his murder of Agamemnon by noting that his victory at Troy will have changed the ruler. Aegisthus corrects Clytemnestra's hope that Agamemnon will forgive her infidelity by noting, 'He was king of Mycenae, he will return a tyrant' (251–2). In *Hercules*, the hero destroys the tyrant Lycus. But after this act, Hercules in turn destroys his own family, thinking that he is killing the tyrant's children. In this play, the punishment of tyrants turns into madness and familial destruction. This play also offers a unique moment where political advice seems to be addressed directly to Seneca's contemporary audience.

After Hercules returns from the Underworld, his father, Amphitryon, asks Theseus a series of lengthy questions about the world below. At first Theseus is unwilling to recall what he witnessed, but he soon obliges with lengthy answers to the old man's questions. Amphitryon asks if it is true that people are punished for their sins and, if so, who judges them below (727–30). Theseus answers by dutifully naming the three traditional judges and notes that each person's punishment fits their crimes on earth (731–6). He then goes beyond Amphitryon's general question and notes the punishments meted out to evil rulers: 'I saw bloody rulers shut in prison and the backs of violent tyrants cut by the hands of the people' (737–9). On the other hand, whoever rules peacefully, mildly and without bloodshed will be rewarded with a long life. After death he will go to heaven above, or the Elysian Fields below, where he will become a judge (739–46). Theseus concludes his discussion of the rewards and punishments awaiting good and bad rulers with a remarkable apostrophe to the audience: 'Abstain from human blood, you who rule: your crimes are judged by a greater standard' (745–7). As John Fitch notes of these lines in his commentary, 'though formally addressed to all rulers ... [they] could scarcely avoid being taken as directed especially at the reigning emperor.'[23] It is difficult, if not impossible, however, to determine the specific ruler. Yet, as we have already noted, we do know that *Hercules* may have been written around the time of the *Apocolocyntosis*, which was likely composed soon after Claudius's death in October of 54 CE.[24] At the conclusion of this satire, we also encounter the idea that rulers should be punished below in a manner that parallels the crimes they committed above. In contrast to Theseus's warning in *Hercules*, this idea is ridiculed in the *Apocolocyntosis*. The inveterate gambler Claudius is given a mock Sisyphean task and is condemned to try to play dice with a bottomless dice box. He is then made the slave of Caligula's legal secretary. Caligula still has authority over the judges below and there is no hint that he is enduring a painful punishment.

While Seneca's comic text may undercut the seriousness of Theseus's messages, *On Mercy* also contains echoes of Theseus's words.[25] Here we see Seneca working through an idea via tragedy, comedy and philosophy. Although Theseus's description of punishments and rewards may warn rulers to be righteous and buttress the points of *On Mercy*, Seneca is not content to let this serious message stand. He mocks it in the *Apocolocyntosis*. This passage from *Hercules* aptly demonstrates the difficulty in pinning down Seneca's thought. He is not content to let an idea stand, but continues to investigate it, adding support, critique and even ridicule.

Even the darkest moment of his darkest tragedy, *Thyestes*, finds a moment for the ribald humour of the *Apocolocyntosis*, while at the same time engaging in political commentary. Atreus vividly describes his brother's unwitting cannibal feast to the audience. When Thyestes lets out an over-sated, drunken belch, Atreus declares his own apotheosis (910). Similarly, in the *Apocolocyntosis*, Claudius ascends to Olympus after an even more obscene bodily noise, 'emitting a greater sound from that part of his body with which he spoke more easily' (4.3). These scenes do not simply demonstrate Seneca's occasional fondness for crude humour; they also demonstrate how an idea can turn up in unexpected places and remain in Seneca's mind across time and genres. These obscene bodily sounds offer an important psychological, ethical and political critique. In the *Apocolocyntosis*, Claudius's inability to control his body demonstrates his inability and unfitness to rule properly. In contrast, Nero's physical and vocal beauty is stressed in Apollo's celebratory poem that immediately precedes Claudius's indecorous death (*Apocol.* 4).

In *Thyestes*, similar questions of bodily, psychological and political control are posed, but the easy answers of the *Apocolocyntosis* and *On Mercy* and the simple dichotomy between Claudius and Nero are considerably problematised. Thyestes, who once lived a secure life as an exile away from the royal court, quickly transforms into an uncontrolled and greedy ruler. Thyestes's belch demonstrates to Atreus that he has gluttonously devoured this meal of his own flesh and blood. But on another level it also demonstrates Thyestes's lack of control and unfitness for imperial power.[26] As Atreus notes before Thyestes begins his festive yet terrified song, 'he does not fully command his mind' (919). The fullness of Thyestes's belly (913) inversely correlates with his lack of full psychological power (919). On the other hand, Atreus succeeds as a ruler because he is able to control his emotions and those of others (497–511).

Writing during the Augustan period, the historian Livy remarked that as the early Roman kings declined from good rulers like Romulus and Numa to the tyranny of the Tarquins, the history of Rome became like a Greek tragedy (1.46.3). Livy also states that with the expulsion of the royal line and the establishment of the Republic in 509 BCE, the Romans were able to set their world of political freedom against the tragic world of kingship and crime. Yet the kings did return to Rome, although the Julio-Claudians scrupulously avoided the term, styling themselves as *principes*.[27] Perhaps, similar to the link that Livy makes between royal power and tragic crime, Seneca used his plays in part to think through the meaning of autocracy and empire. His plays show the links between power and tyranny. They also demonstrate how humans in power can be continually driven to transgress boundaries, take pleasure in others' pain, enjoy their crimes and sadistically impose their will upon others. The plays also illustrate the violence that rends apart royal families, how royal households continually produce 'tragic crimes' and are inevitably self-consuming. Although Seneca could only have guessed at how this last point might relate to Roman history, it is remarkable to consider that only three years after his death the Julio-Claudian line would be extinguished with Nero's suicide.

Philosophy

As we have seen, Seneca's plays are deeply concerned with the process of composition, character creation and spectatorship. This self-consciousness adds to the plays' overall retrograde and mirroring character. They frequently turn back upon themselves and reflect the poetic process. By extension, the plays invite us to consider our own place as consumers of the text. With this we come to another major problem in Senecan studies, which we have only briefly noted at other points. What is the plays' relationship to Senecan philosophy? Are they purely self-referential and part of a self-contained world of poetry? Or does the world of the plays bleed into the world of philosophy? The relationship between poetry – tragedy in particular – and philosophy is a question that has a lengthy pedigree. We can trace it back at least to Plato who in the *Republic* talks about the quarrel between poetry and philosophy as being already an old one (607b). Via Socrates, Plato points out what he takes to be the major problem with drama: it is pure imitation (392d–4d). Poets and actors pretend to be someone they are not, and they tell lies about the cruelty and passions of gods and heroes (386a–92a). For these and other reasons, Plato banned tragedy from his ideal state as socially harmful (607). Seneca never wrote a detailed account of poetry as Plato did or an analysis of tragedy, like Aristotle in his *Poetics*. Rather than simply define tragedy from a philosophical standpoint, however, Seneca choose to engage directly with the genre. One reason likely stemmed from his own literary ambition to try to leave his mark on yet another genre. He may also have used poetry as a means to reflect on philosophy and illustrate some of its problems, shortcomings and potential dangers. While his plays reflect upon themselves and the literary tradition, they also present aspects of Seneca's philosophy in a distorted way. As Seneca's characters are close readers of the literary tradition, they also are close readers of Seneca's prose works. We have already seen how Theseus's attempts to reassemble his son echo Seneca's own writing on the literary process, and how 'recognition' is a key concept in Seneca's tragedy and philosophy. Still, how we are to interpret the significance of these connections remains a matter of considerable debate.[28]

If we look to Seneca's philosophy hoping to find detailed comments on the nature of tragedy we will be disappointed. He does not comment on his plays or even allude to them directly, save for the mock-heroic lines given to Hercules in the *Apocolocyntosis*. Like his fellow Stoics, Seneca does value poetry for its didactic purposes. He translates the 'Hymn to Zeus' of the Greek Stoic Cleanthes, which succinctly encapsulates the Stoic theory of fate, 'The fates lead the willing, and drag the unwilling' (*Ep*. 107.11). In the following letter, Seneca cites with approval Cleanthes's claim that by virtue of its use of metre, poetry can be a more effectual teacher than prose (*Ep*. 108.10). He also states that poets have said many things that have been said by philosophers or should have been said by them (*Ep*. 8.8). In a detailed look at Greek tragedy, he provides an otherwise unknown story about Euripides's staging of a play in which a character praises wealth. According to Seneca, the audience rose up in protest until Euripides himself assured them that this greedy character would pay the price at the end of the play (*Ep.* 115.15). While Seneca's plays do provide many pithy and quotable philosophical statements, their efficacy is often undermined. Medea's and Phaedra's nurses, for example, make many great but ultimately ineffectual statements against the passions. Medea and Atreus often speak the language of a Stoic sage, but only in the service of the passions and to fuel their revenge. If we look for vice being punished at the end of Seneca's plays, as Seneca notes happened at the end of Euripides's play, we will again be disappointed. If there is not an obvious Senecan poetics to be gleaned from his philosophy and easily applied to his plays, we can look to significant rhetorical connections. These connections can be seen as simply coincidental. Perhaps Seneca liked specific rhetorical techniques and used them in both his prose and his poetry. On the other hand, these connections may be Seneca's way of inviting us to compare his two bodies of work.

First, let us consider the role of monologues, and specifically monologues of self-address. As we have noted, lengthy monologues are one of the defining characteristics of Senecan drama. In the past, this fact has been one of the major criticisms of Senecan style and offered as evidence that the plays are less dramas and more rhetorical exercises. This critique has lessened considerably as scholars and dramaturges alike have focused on performing the plays, rather than simply writing them off as inferior to Greek drama. We should also note that rhetoric is one of the defining characteristics of Seneca – his rhetorical abilities gave him his notoriety during his lifetime. And indeed, rhetorical 'excess' comes to characterise the post-classical aesthetic of Latin literature that we can see beginning in, for example, the many lengthy speeches in Ovid's *Metamorphoses*. Seneca and his contemporaries, Lucan and Petronius, expand upon this process of the rhetoricisation of literature. Yet it is not simply that rhetoric was 'in' in Seneca's day that makes his monologues significant. As we have also seen, his monologues are frequently the means by which his characters monitor their emotions and shape themselves. This same process is also central to Seneca's philosophy. A monologue of self-address is written by Seneca for Nero at the start of *On Mercy* in which the emperor outlines his past and shapes his future. A similar technique is at work in Seneca's *meditatio* in *On Anger* 3.36.

What should become immediately apparent is that in Seneca's philosophy, such monologues are used to control the passions and act mercifully; in the tragedies they are used to stir up the passions and seek revenge. In fact, the typical form of Seneca's tragic monologue, in which his characters address and command their souls, can be found in his philosophy.

In *On Providence*, Seneca scripts a dramatic monologue for his hero Cato the Younger, complete with self-address and command to his soul, which mirrors Seneca's tragic characters (2.10).[29] Cato's speech shows how drama influences Seneca's philosophy.[30] Indeed, after scripting Cato's speech in *On Providence*, Seneca also states that the gods enjoy watching heroically bloody performances of Stoic virtue (2.11). Why then does he write tragedies which seem to present the inversion of this ideal? Are we to applaud the performance of Medea's virtue, as she herself notes? One solution to his conundrum might be that Seneca's tragedies provide negative examples, or that they show the consequences of not leading a Stoic life. No one would find Medea or Atreus worthy models to follow. Why then subject the audience to the plays in the first place? Surely Seneca's philosophy is a better guide for how to live, and for offering models to follow and avoid.

Perhaps Seneca's plays are a test of the audience's adherence to Stoicism. If we don't identify with the plays' characters and remain unaffected by their passions, we pass. As Martha Nussbaum has demonstrated, this anti-Aristotelian ideal of a disengaged, critical audience has a parallel in modern theatre.[31] The German playwright Bertolt Brecht sought to create an 'epic theatre' which alienated the audience from identification with the world of the play. This critical distance would hopefully encourage the audience not to accept the events presented in the play as immutable truths. By not accepting the world of the play, the audience would not accept the current social structure as natural and unchangeable. While Brecht's ultimate goal was to use theatre to inspire social change, perhaps Seneca used theatre to inspire individual change and reflection. As Seneca himself notes, poetry can cause people to applaud and delight in seeing their own vices condemned and can lead them to a 'confession of the truth' about themselves (*Ep.* 108.10, 12). Nussbaum argues that Seneca's plays encourage this sort of alienation and critical spectatorship. It seems possible that Seneca himself did not believe in the inherent emotional power of drama. When discussing the three stages of emotion in *On Anger*, Seneca notes that our responses to drama are to be classified as the first, non-rational 'preliminary preludes' to emotion. Thus, what we feel is not really pity and fear, to use Aristotle's tragic emotions, but is simply something uncontrollable and no different from blushing, shivering or our hair standing on end (2.2.1–2.4.2). While critical spectatorship may be a way to relate Seneca's plays to the therapeutic project that undergirds his philosophy, this theory may also deny the power of Seneca's plays.[32]

This debate often boils down to an aesthetic versus a didactic reading of Seneca's plays. Yet this is too simple a dichotomy, as if Seneca is just a poet when he writes tragedy and a teacher when he writes philosophy. There is no reason to think that Seneca could not combine ethics with aesthetics. Furthermore, we also must keep in mind the full complexity of Seneca's corpus. Seneca also wrote satire. Although it is typically marginalised, the world of the *Apocolocyntosis* must also colour our readings of the 'serious' message of his political theory, philosophy and tragedy. Senecan tragedy remains only one voice within Seneca's multifaceted corpus. Like the laughter of satire, the horrors of his plays encourage us to question the cool rationalism and enlightenment of his philosophy.

The Plays

Hercules narrates events that occurred after Hercules completed the final and most difficult of his twelve labours: bringing back the three-headed dog, Cerberus, from the Underworld. The play opens with Juno giving a long monologue in which she describes how her anger at Hercules has proved ineffectual. The labours imposed on Hercules by Eurystheus have not defeated the hero. Juno devises a new plan. She declares that only Hercules can defeat himself, so she will drive him mad. After a choral ode extolling the virtues of the simple life, Hercules's stepfather, Amphitryon, revels how the kingdom of Hercules's wife, Megara, has been usurped by Lycus. Now the tyrant is asking for Megara's hand in marriage, thinking that Hercules has failed in his final task and died. Megara calls on Hercules to return to the light of day and takes refuge from Lycus in a temple. The tyrant is not moved and orders the temple to be burned with the suppliants inside.

Just in time, Hercules returns from below with Theseus, who, as we will learn from *Phaedra*, became trapped there while on another mission. Although exhausted from his labours, Hercules murders Lycus. At the start of act four he proceeds to make a sacrifice in gratitude to the gods. He does not heed his father's warning that he should purify himself first. As he begins the ritual, Hercules is affected by a fit of hallucinatory madness. He rushes off into the palace in order to kill the children of Lycus. Amphitryon describes how Hercules has mistaken his own children for those of his enemy. He unknowingly kills his children and then his wife, thinking that she is Juno. He then falls into a deep slumber and when he wakens has no idea what he has done. As the truth is gradually revealed, Hercules wishes to kill himself and demands the weapons that Theseus and Amphitryon are keeping from him. In the end, he decides to live, considering that living on in his grief will be his newest labour (1316–17). Asking what river will cleanse him of his blood-guilt, Theseus responds that Hercules can be restored to purity at Athens.

This is the longest of Seneca's genuine plays (1,334 lines), and although it contains key themes that we will see in Seneca's other plays, such as madness, tyranny and infanticide, two elements set it apart. First, this is the only play that ends with a note of reconciliation and hope. Although he has committed unspeakably horrible acts, Hercules can rely on his father and his friendship with Theseus to carry him through his grief. Hercules will be purified. As the prologue makes clear, Hercules's madness is sent from Juno, the only Olympian deity to appear in Seneca's plays. Yet the connection to Juno is not stressed during the onset of Hercules's madness. A comparison with Euripides's *Heracles* is informative. Iris, the messenger of the gods and Lyssa, madness personified, appear in the middle of the play to do Hera's bidding and afflict Heracles (815–74). In Seneca's play, no divine messengers appear. Rather, the onset of Hercules's madness appears to be at least in part self-inflicted. As we have noted, after killing Lycus, Hercules does not heed his father's warning that he purify himself before sacrificing to the gods. Indeed, Hercules is polluted from his time among the dead in the Underworld and with the blood of the tyrant and his attendants whom he has killed. As he begins to perform the sacrifice, Hercules utters a prayer that reveals his hubristic and megalomaniacal sense of his own heroism. He notes that his prayer will be worthy of Jupiter and of himself (926–7). At this point he is afflicted by madness.

At the same time, Hercules's madness is similar to its portrayal in Euripides's play in that Hercules is entirely blinded by it and has no knowledge of what he has done after the fit leaves him. This portrayal of madness is unique in Seneca's plays, and is closer to how it is represented in Greek plays.[33] Atreus and Medea, Seneca's other child-murderers, do call on the Furies and spirits of the Underworld for inspiration, and Medea even briefly thinks she sees them. Yet they remain fully aware of their actions, urge themselves on to their crimes and even take pleasure in the slaughter. Thus, unlike *Hercules*, a defining characteristic of many of Seneca's plays is the performance of self-willed crimes.

Troades, or *Trojan Women*, details the events in the immediate aftermath of the sack of Troy. These include the division of the women of Troy to be taken back as slaves of the victorious Greeks, and the sacrifice of Iphigenia and Astyanax. By including the deaths of both Iphigenia and Astyanax, Seneca brings together two plays of Euripides, who portrays each in his *Hecuba* and *Trojan Women* respectively. This play is unusual among Seneca's plays in that it does not focus on one individual. Rather, the play moves back and forth between the Trojan women and the Greek heroes. The play opens with Priam's aged wife, Hecuba, giving a lengthy monologue. A chorus of Trojan women soon join her. Their funeral dirge turns into a celebration of the dead. Hecuba calls on the chorus to declare that Priam is blessed, since he is removed from the sadness, pain and suffering that the women will experience (145). The chorus responds by repeating Hecuba's declaration that the dead king is blessed (156). The theme of the death, and questions about what comes after it, will be taken up again throughout the play.

The second act shifts to the Greek camp and gives a very different picture of the 'blessed' state of the dead in the Underworld. The messenger

Talthybius reports that the ghost of Achilles appeared and demanded the sacrifice of Polyxena as his bride. A lengthy debate ensues between Achilles's son, Pyrrhus, and Agamemnon. Pyrrhus is adamant that his father's demands must be met, but Agamemnon refuses. Agamemnon has learnt mercy and restraint from the ten-year-long siege. He also remembers his own act of human sacrifice, the killing of his daughter, Iphigenia, in the port of Aulis, so that the Greek fleet could gain a favouring wind to sail to Troy. The prophet Calchas is called in to divine the will of the gods. He declares that the girl must be killed, but adds that further blood is needed. The Greeks must also kill Hector's son, Astyanax. Only then will the fleet be able to return home. Thus, the murders that inaugurated the war must be redoubled in order to conclude it.

The next act moves back to the Trojans, as Andromache recounts how the shade of Hector visited her and told her to hide their son, Astyanax. She decides to hide him in Hector's tomb and engages in a lengthy battle of wits with Ulysses as he tries to discover the boy's location. The play ends with the deaths of the two youths as narrated by a messenger to the Trojans. Their deaths are portrayed in a vividly metatheatrical manner. The messenger describes how the Greeks eagerly watched as Astyanax fearlessly jumped from the last surviving tower of Troy. He then narrates how Polyxena's sacrificial wedding took place in a valley that is shaped 'in the manner of a theatre' (1125). He also notes how Polyxena's undaunted soul and disregard for death caused all to 'marvel and pity her' (1148). Thus, the internal audience within the play offers a variety of the emotional responses to the sacrifices.[34] It is worth considering that in his descriptions of the Greeks' reactions, Seneca is referencing Aristotle's (now) famous claim that tragedy elicits 'pity and fear'.[35] Yet a range of emotions and responses to the sacrifices are suggested, even perhaps a form of Stoic joy (*gaudium*). Before he begins speaking, Andromache urges the messenger to give his report by noting 'great pain enjoys [*gaudet*] dealing with all of its sorrows' (1066–7).

The *Troades* also focuses on death and the various ways that people respond to it and wonder about what happens afterwards. The first choral ode declares Priam to live a blessed life in Elysium. The second ode, however, takes a more Epicurean approach and states that death is nothing to us. It destroys the soul along with the body. The stories about the Underworld are 'empty rumours and hollow words' (405). This belief is of course contradicted by the appearance of the ghosts of Achilles and Hector, before and after this ode. One might criticise Seneca for philosophical inconsistency here, but like the descriptions of the various responses to the deaths of Polyxena and Astyanax at the play's conclusion, the play presents various visions of death. The nihilism of the second ode is only one option.

The *Phoenissae*, or *Phoenician Women*, relates what happens to Oedipus and his family after his tragic self-realisation that he has killed his father, Laius, and married his mother, Jocasta. We will consider this story fully when we discuss Seneca's *Oedipus*. After Oedipus's blinding, he left the throne of Thebes to wander with his daughter, Antigone. His two sons, Eteocles and Polynices, agreed to rule Thebes in alternating years. Eteocles ruled first, but when his year was up, he unsurprisingly refused to abdicate. Polynices married and gained an army during his year of exile and now is marching against his brother. In this play Seneca combines various aspects of the myths surrounding Oedipus's family. The opening scene of the play is reminiscent of Sophocles's final play, *Oedipus at Colonus*. In Sophocles's play, Oedipus and Antigone travel to Colonus, a deme of Athens. The play ends with Oedipus's death and the establishment of his cult in the city. Seneca omits any mention of these events. The second half, which portrays the impending war between the brothers, is also told in Acschylus's *Seven Against Thebes* and Euripides's *Phoenician Women*. In both plays Eteocles and Polynices die; Seneca's play abruptly ends before they join battle. Seneca's *Phoenissae* consists of only 664 lines and does not contain a chorus. This suggests that Seneca did not complete this work and that it may have been the last play he was working on before his death. Conversely, it has also been suggested that this play is complete and demonstrates Seneca's experiments with dramatic convention.[36]

As the play now stands, it consists of two sections of roughly equal length. In the first, Antigone tries to restrain her father from committing suicide. The majority of this part consists of lengthy speeches by the two characters. Oedipus states that the vengeance he took by blinding himself was insufficient. He must fulfil his father's curse and drive his hand into his brain

(180). Oedipus also notes the unnatural and retrograde quality of his family line; the progress of generations has not been allowed to develop normally. He orders Antigone to leave him, because he might sin against her: 'Leave your father / leave a virgin. After our mother I fear everything' (49–50). Despite the violence that defines this family, Antigone remains resolute and she stoically exhorts her father to do so as well. Oedipus notes this paradox and states that Antigone is improperly following the Roman ideal of *pietas*, or duty to one's family. Oedipus states that by helping her father, Antigone is confusing the order of the world and adding to Oedipus's punishments:

> Nature turns itself into new laws: rivers will turn back and carry their waves swiftly back to their sources; the lamp of Phoebus will bring the night, and the Evening Star will make it day; in order that something else may be added to my miseries, we also will act dutifully.
>
> (84–9)

Despite his lengthy claims that death is the only natural act he can perform, Oedipus quickly changes his mind and agrees to follow Antigone. A messenger arrives and urges Oedipus to use his new-found sense of familial duty to stop the fratricidal civil war between his two sons. Oedipus refuses to do so, however. He declares that he will act as the raging muse to the second half of the play, and orders the brothers to kill each other. In typically Senecan fashion, Oedipus conjures up even worse horrors. He orders his sons to give their weapons to their mother, so that she may join in the war. Oedipus delights in the coming war, and declares that he will hide in the woods so that he can be the spectator, or rather auditor, of the battle (350–62).

The second section shifts to the Theban palace. In this version of the myth, Jocasta is still alive (she kills herself in Seneca's and Sophocles's *Oedipus*), and does in fact rush down to the battlefield. She does not do so in order to fight, as Oedipus hoped, but rather to restrain her children. First, she speaks with Polynices. Eteocles interrupts and engages with a dialogue on kingship with either Jocasta or Polynices – the manuscript tradition is unclear and modern editors assign the lines differently.[37] Eteocles plays the role of the tyrant. Echoing the famous line from the Republican tragedy *Atreus* by Accius, 'Let them hate, provided that they fear', Eteocles notes that one should not rule who fears to be hated (654).³⁸ The play breaks off with Eteocles's ominous declaration that no price is too high to pay for power (664).

Although this play is brief, and possibly incomplete, it vividly illustrates key themes that resonate throughout Senecan tragedy. It dramatises passion versus restraint. Seneca uses Greek myths to demonstrate the inversion of the key Roman concept of duty (*pietas*). Suicide is shown as a way out of intolerable situations. There is a debate on the nature of kingship and tyranny. This play also highlights the fratricidal nature of civil war.

Seneca's *Medea* is an important link in the oft-told tale of Medea's revenge for her abandonment by her husband, Jason.³⁹ Medea was the daughter of King Aeetes of Colchis, which was located at the eastern end of the Black Sea, once considered to be the end of the world. Jason was sent there from Iolcus by his uncle, Pelias, in order to retrieve the Golden Fleece. He assembled a group of heroes for whom a magical ship was constructed, the Argo. Medea fell in love with Jason, and with the help of her magic, he was able to perform the tasks demanded by Aeetes to reclaim the fleece – typically yoking a fire-breathing bull and sowing the ground with dragon's teeth. When Aeetes still refused to grant the fleece, Medea helped Jason to steal it. Having betrayed her father, she fled with the Greeks along with her brother, Apsyrtus. In order to prevent her father from following, Medea killed and dismembered her brother and then scattered his limbs.

Medea and Jason married and had two children. They did not live happily ever after, however. Medea continued to use her magic to help Jason. When Jason returned to Iolcus, Medea deceived the aged Pelias's daughters into killing and dismembering him with the expectation that Medea's magic arts would rejuvenate him. When this expectation was not met, and the daughters learn that they have in fact been tricked into butchering their father, Medea and Jason were forced to flee again. They went to Corinth, where, in order to protect himself against the vengeance of Pelias's son, Acastus, Jason agreed to marry Creon's daughter. According to Seneca's version, Creon wished to kill Medea, but Jason convinced him to simply exile her. In the early part of her story, we can see how Medea serves as a 'helper maiden' to enable Jason to fulfil his quest. In Seneca's play she repeatedly reminds the Greeks of the services she has performed for Jason and indeed all the heroes of Greece by enabling the Argonauts to fulfil their task. Now that Medea has served her purpose, the Greeks fear her continued presence and Jason has moved on to another marriage of expediency. Medea repeatedly tries to convince the Greeks that they share the guilt in the murders she performed to help Jason. Medea also feels crushing guilt for betraying her father, murdering her brother and having Pelias killed. Thus, the past defines her revenge in a paradoxical way. She uses her past crimes as models to surpass in her revenge. The deaths of Creon, his daughter Creusa and her two children also atone for her past crimes.[40]

Medea's plan for revenge develops slowly throughout the play. In her opening monologue, however, Seneca prepares the audience for the infanticide that will conclude the play: 'Already it is born, my revenge is born. I have given birth' (25–6). Medea's status as mother is one of her defining qualities. At the end of the play, before killing her children, Medea *mater* almost wins out and prevents her from fully playing her traditional role. Indeed, this play focuses on the conflicts and paradoxes involved in what it means to 'be Medea'. In addition to her status as mother, she also sees herself as a heroic avenger and magician from the savage ends of the earth. She commands herself not to act like a woman but to take on the qualities of her homeland: 'Drive out feminine fears / and place the inhospitable Caucasus in your mind' (42–3). Ultimately, Seneca's play dramatises how Medea becomes this figure of revenge, who looks to her past crimes, surpasses them, and by doing so is able to paradoxically undo her history and return to her origins. After killing her first son, Medea declares that she has restored her family and status as a virginal princess of Colchis (982–4). Thus, Medea enacts the fantasy that revenge can undo the wrongs of the past. She imagines that the voyage of the Argonauts never took place.

Medea's obsession with herself can be seen most clearly in the number of times she refers to herself as Medea (for example 166–7). She declares to her Nurse that she will 'become' Medea (171). Then before deciding to kill her children, Medea declares, 'Now I am Medea, my character/intellect [*ingenium*] has grown through evils' (910). This line is significant for several reasons. On one level, Seneca is making a scholarly joke. The root of her name was thought to come from the Greek *medomai* or *metomai*, meaning 'I think, I have cunning intelligence' (See Pindar *Pythian* 4.27 and Euripides *Medea* 402).[41] On a metaliterary level, this line draws attention to Medea's place as coming late in the literary tradition. Her story was well known and told not only in Euripides's play, but also by Pindar in *Pythian Odes* 4 and by Apollonius, as well as several times by Ovid, in *Heroides* 12, *Metamorphoses* 7 and in his lost tragedy. Thus, Seneca is placing his play within that tradition and cleverly giving his title character awareness of her place and reputation. To cite again an oft-quoted remark that encapsulates the literary self-awareness of Seneca's character, 'This Medea has read Euripides's *Medea*.'[42] As we have noted earlier, Seneca's Medea also problematises what it means to be Medea, as various conflicting visions of herself, as mother, witch, avenger and virgin, are all referenced by her. Indeed, after Medea's declaration of selfhood, Seneca vividly demonstrates in a lengthy monologue the struggles that she undergoes to become the child-murdering avenger (916–77).

Her final perfection can only be achieved in full view of the Corinthians and, most importantly, Jason. Medea declares that the people must approve of her works otherwise her valour (*virtus*) will be hidden and lost (976–7). Here we see a combination of Senecan metatheatrics, as Medea will perform her murders before spectators, with Stoic terminology. As we noted in the previous chapter, *virtus* is the highest good for the Stoics. Paradoxically, Medea declares that the final act of her revenge will display her virtue for all to see and applaud. Thus, Medea mirrors Seneca's Stoic hero Cato, who gives a bloody performance of his *virtus* on the world stage to the delight of the gods (*On Providence* 2.8–12).

At the end, Medea is granted her opening wish to fly off in the chariot of her ancestor, the Sun. She demands that Jason look up and recognise his wife as she flies away. Jason is given the final, shocking lines of the play: 'Through the upper regions of the sky journey on high; bear witness that where you are carried there are no gods' (1026–7). These enigmatic lines can be interpreted in various ways. Medea's acts have made Jason an atheist. Or, perhaps more plausibly, the gods flee from wherever Medea is present. She has created a hole in the divine fabric of the universe.[43] It also should be noted that Seneca has carefully set up the last word of the play (gods, *deos*) to echo Medea's opening prayer to the gods of marriage (*di coniugales*). Thus, although Seneca's play shows how Medea's revenge is a greater crime than anything she committed before, there also is an element of symmetry in this play, reflected in the ring composition of the opening and closing words.

On the one hand, our reaction may be pure horror to what Medea has done. Yet as we have noted earlier, Medea declares that she is owed better treatment from Jason and the Greeks. The deeds she did in the past have cut her off from her homeland, but they were done in service to her new family and home in Greece. During their meetings with Medea, neither Jason nor Creon will admit her points. Only at the end, when his new bride and father-in-law have perished and one of his children has been killed, does Jason admit his guilt. He calls to Medea, 'strike my guilty head' (1005). The play also suggests that the blame for Medea's acts should be placed at the feet of the Argonauts, whose journey was motivated by greed and encouraged false beliefs in technological mastery over nature. The Roman tradition stresses that the Argo was the first ship. Thus, although the exploits of the Argonauts took place in the generation before the Trojan War, the sailing of the Argo represents the beginning of the decline of humanity. Seneca's play addresses the consequences of this decline and suggests how Jason's quest opened the door for the avarice that motivates people today. The second and third choral odes show how the voyage of the Argo precipitated the fall from the self-sufficiency of the Golden Age. By sailing across the sea, basic boundaries were broken for which the heroes have been punished. The chorus declares that Medea is a fitting payment for these transgressions (361–3). In fact, Seneca's chorus notes how the sailing of the Argo has brought about the present day of world empire in which 'every boundary has been removed' (369). The chorus concludes with a prophecy that eventually 'Ocean will loosen the chains of the universe ... and Tethys will reveal new worlds' (375–9). In later centuries these lines would be cited to justify exploration. Christopher Columbus's son triumphantly declared that his father fulfilled this prophecy in 1492.[44]

Phaedra tells the story of another unhappy marriage of a descendant of the Sun. Whereas *Medea* ends with the heroine flying off in her ancestral chariot, Phaedra believes her family is cursed to love that which is forbidden. She commits suicide when she realises that the false accusation that her stepson,

Hippolytus, raped her has led to his destruction. According to the mythical tradition, Phaedra's father was Minos, king of Crete. He angered the gods by refusing to sacrifice a beautiful white bull. Phaedra's mother, Pasiphaë, was a daughter of the Sun and was cursed with a desire to copulate with the bull. Venus was also angry at the Sun, and by extension his descendants, for revealing her illicit meeting with Mars to her husband, Vulcan. Luckily for Pasiphaë, the master craftsman, Daedalus, constructed a cow suit to enable her to consummate her desire. The result was the half-man, half-bull Minotaur, whom Minos hid in the labyrinth, also constructed by Daedalus. In order to appease Minos's anger at Athens, where his son, Androgeos, was killed, the Athenians were forced to send children annually to be consumed by the Minotaur. Eventually, the king's son, Theseus, volunteered to journey to Crete, where he killed the Minotaur with the help of Minos's daughter, Ariadne. On the journey back to Athens, Theseus abandoned Ariadne on Naxos. Later, he married the Amazon, Antiope, with whom he had Hippolytus. Moving from abandonment to murder, Theseus killed Antiope and later married Phaedra. When the play opens Theseus has gone off on a mission with Pirithous to steal away the queen of the Underworld, Proserpina. Phaedra is left alone in Athens wasting away with her love for Hippolytus.

Hippolytus, however, has inverted the hatred of men that typically characterises Amazons, and despises women. He has devoted himself to hunting and is a virginal follower of Diana. The play begins with his lengthy song commanding his followers to hunt. He vividly describes the natural surroundings of Athens and delights in the beauty of nature and his power over its animals. His song concludes with a prayer to Diana, whose power over the beasts of the wild he describes as encompassing the entire world. Thus, human control over the wildness of nature is signalled as a key theme of the play. For Hippolytus, nature is a world of purity, which, thanks to his devotion to the virginal goddess of the hunt, he may dominate. This vision of nature will prove to be illusory.

Phaedra's opening speech also describes the vastness of the world, but she views herself as trapped by her father's domination of the seas, her isolation from Theseus and especially the cursed passions of her mother. As Phaedra sees it, her desire to follow Hippolytus on his hunts is connected to her mother's 'crimes in the forests' (114). This view contradicts Hippolytus's ideal of sylvan purity. Phaedra's Nurse, however, does not agree with Phaedra's claim that she is cursed and dominated by the universal power of love. Speaking with strong Stoic overtones, the Nurse advises Phaedra to 'check the flames of her impious love' (165), and to 'expel the terrible crime from her chaste mind' (169). Phaedra's reply is significant. She states, 'I know what you say is true, Nurse, but madness drives me to follow the worse course. My soul goes knowingly over the edge and returns seeking sane judgement in vain' (177–80). This acknowledgement that she wishes she could act otherwise but cannot references lines spoken by Euripides's and Ovid's Medea (Eur. *Medea* 1077–80, Ovid *Met.* 7.20–1). These lines also deal with the philosophical question of *akrasia*, weakness of will, or knowing the better and doing the worse. Socrates famously declared that people do not do wrong willingly. If one knows the better course and is not hindered from following it, one will act rightly (Plato *Apo.* 25d–e and *Prot.* 358b7–c1). The Stoics adopted this position and in some ways strengthened it, by theorising that the soul was entirely rational. Thus, following a strict Socratic or Stoic argument, it seems difficult to account for the fact that, like Medea or Phaedra, a person can recognise the good but follow the bad. It might be argued that the passion of love has taken over Phaedra's soul and hence she is not acting freely. However, Phaedra is still able to approve of what the Nurse says, which suggests that her reason remains while she is in the grips of her amorous frenzy.

Here again we can see how Seneca is able to place his characters in the literary tradition. He slyly changes it by taking words spoken by the Medeas of Euripides and Ovid and places them in Phaedra's mouth. At the same time, this literary game may also be part of a philosophical debate about weakness of will. Even if we choose not to read Phaedra's lines as investigating the problem of *akrasia*, we can still appreciate how this play focuses on Phaedra's mental turmoil. Phaedra knows what is right and her feelings for Hippolytus generate a strong sense of shame within her. She is deeply concerned with her *pudor*, a virtue that was central to the Roman system of values but is difficult to translate into English. It contains ideas of honour and self-respect, which spring mainly from acting with propriety and restraint, especially in sexual matters. It can be rendered as 'shame' or 'chastity', but has much deeper connotations. Phaedra is eventually persuaded by her Nurse's demands for restraint. She states that her *pudor* has not left her soul (250) and decides to kill herself (254). Paradoxically, this Stoic decision causes the Nurse to give up her Stoic advice and help Phaedra with Hippolytus. The Nurse's love for Phaedra and Phaedra's love for Hippolytus win out over reason and propriety.

After speaking much like a Stoic while trying to restrain Phaedra's passion, the Nurse adopts a different rhetorical line when speaking with Hippolytus. She advises him to relax his austere ways, enjoy his youth, the city and the company of women (435–82). Her 'eat, drink, be merry and have sex' attitude outlines a hedonistic way of life that can be given philosophical justification only by misunderstanding of the true message of Epicureanism. As should be apparent, the Nurse radically changes her advice, from Stoicism, to an emotional appeal that Phaedra not kill herself, to encouraging hedonism in Hippolytus. These sudden changes are characteristic of Senecan drama, but perhaps are no more frequent and pronounced as here. Seneca provides brief insight into the Nurse's motivation. It is due to her subservient position, which requires that the virtue of *pudor* be denied. As she notes before approaching Hippolytus, 'Shame is a bad attendant of royal power' (430).

Hippolytus's reply continues the praise of the forest's purity with which he opened the play. He also gives a lengthy account of the decline of civilisation from the Golden Age, which mixes elements from Lucretius's account of the development of the human race in *On the Nature of the Universe* book five, and Ovid's opening account of the five ages from the *Metamorphoses*. Unlike Lucretius, who notes that civilised life developed from settled families having children, Hippolytus declares that women are the greatest evil in the world (559–64). He simply hates them, despite the fact that he does not know why (566–8). It is clear that the Nurse will get nowhere with him. Phaedra wanders on stage, faints in Hippolytus's arms, and after a lengthy speech, confesses her love. When Hippolytus prepares to kill her for this confession, Phaedra welcomes death by his sword as paradoxically fulfilling her desire and saving her chastity (*pudor* 710–13). Too disgusted or confused by Phaedra's delight, Hippolytus flees into the woods, leaving his sword behind. The Nurse accuses him of rape.

When Theseus returns from the Underworld and learns of the accusations against his son, he condemns Hippolytus to death and calls upon his father Neptune to grant his wish and destroy his son. A giant bull is sent from the sea, which so frightens Hippolytus's horses that he is unable to control them and is dragged behind his chariot to his death. When Phaedra realises that she has destroyed Hippolytus, she reveals the truth and kills herself. Theseus is left to condemn the gods for only granting prayers that ask for evil, and to reassemble his son's mangled body.

The play focuses on the helplessness of humans to understand themselves and the powers that guide the universe. It seems that human reason and control over self and nature is an illusion. As the chorus notes, nature and love, which are both creative and destructive, have power over everything. A comparison with Euripides's *Hippolytus* offers some insight as to how bleak Seneca's vision is. At the start of Euripides's play, Aphrodite makes it clear that she will punish Hippolytus for not respecting her, and that Phaedra will simply be an instrument of this punishment (47–50). Her purity will remain intact. At the end, Hippolytus and Theseus are able to reconcile with each other. Artemis appears and absolves Theseus of guilt. As she notes, humans cannot help but go wrong when the gods wish (1433–4). This is not to say that Seneca wrote his play with Euripides as his only model. He likely had access to Euripides's lost Hippolytus play, as well as a lost version by Sophocles. Ovid's telling of the story in *Heroides* 4 and the *Metamorphoses* (15.497–546) are also likely models. We should note, however, how the tenor of Seneca's play changes with the removal of the divine epiphanies that bookend Euripides's play. The workings of the universe, the gods and human psychology are presented as inscrutable in Seneca's *Phaedra*. Phaedra's love is the result of a divine curse according to her; or it springs from her own volition, according to the Nurse. Hippolytus may hate women due to reason or passion. Nature is a place of virginal purity, as Hippolytus believes, or of love, violence and death, as the chorus acknowledges early on and the play's conclusion makes clear.

Thanks to Sigmund Freud, *Oedipus* has become the story of family violence and romance par excellence. As Oedipus himself notes in Seneca's *Phoenissae*, he was cursed and condemned to death before he left the womb.

His father Laius received an oracle from Apollo that his son would kill him and marry his mother. In order to avert this fate, the infant Oedipus was taken by his shepherd, Phorbas, to be exposed on Mt. Cithaeron. A metal spike was driven through his ankles, hence one of the meanings of his name, 'swollen foot'. After performing this bloody act, Phorbas took pity on the child and gave him to a Corinthian shepherd, who in turn took the baby to the childless king and queen of Corinth, Polybus and Merope. Oedipus grew to manhood as a prince in Corinth, but when he was accused of being a bastard by one of his companions, he journeyed to Delphi in order to learn of his parentage. While on this trip he met an older man at a crossroads who, along with his attendants, violently forced Oedipus off the road. In a fit of rage, Oedipus killed the old man and all but one of his companions. Upon reaching Delphi, Oedipus learnt of his fate and, determined not to ruin his supposed family in Corinth, refused to return home. He went to Thebes, which had just lost its king and was afflicted by the Sphinx. Oedipus heroically solved the riddle and saved the city. In gratitude, the citizens awarded him kingship and marriage to the recently widowed queen, Jocasta, with whom he had two sons and two daughters. When the play opens, Thebes is afflicted by a terrible plague. Determined to find out the cause, Oedipus has sent his brother-in-law, Creon, to the oracle at Delphi.

For those who come to Seneca's play from Sophocles's, the transformation of Oedipus himself is striking. Gone is the confident hero of the Greek play. He is replaced by a fearful and guilt-ridden king. In his opening lines, Oedipus offers the same message given by several of Seneca's choruses and characters. Kingship is joyless and deceptive (6–7). This Oedipus seems to already know his story, but feels unable to escape his fate. He believes that he has safeguarded nature's laws by fleeing from Corinth (25). At the same time, he does not trust himself (27), and believes that he remains untouched by the plague because he is reserved for a special evil. Although he does not yet know the specific cause of the plague, he declares that his guilt affects the heavens (36). His fears are such that Jocasta's first words are to reproach her husband for acting unmanly and turning his back to fortune (86). Oedipus's response is significant for many reasons. Recalling his old victory over the Sphinx, he declares that his wife is wrong to accuse him of cowardice. Here we see something of the bravado of Sophocles's hero. After publicly declaring his past bravery and ability to solve the 'knotted words and the entwined traps and the terrible riddle of the winged beast', Seneca uses the post-classical technique of the aside to give us access to Oedipus's internal world. His heroism and ability to discover the truth have vanished. He wishes that instead of solving the riddle the Sphinx had killed him. He also surmises that the Sphinx is sending the plague in revenge for her death (98–109).

Oedipus's self-confidence in his past heroism again appears briefly when he encourages Creon to reveal the Delphic oracle's 'entangled' response. Playing with another meaning of his name, Oedipus declares that 'knowing riddles is given to Oedipus alone' (216).[45] Yet when Creon reveals how Laius was murdered, Oedipus fails to see the similarity to his own history. It is only when Laius's ghost unambiguously declares Oedipus to be his murderer that Oedipus starts to remember his past. He begs Jocasta to help with his confusion (773) and offer details about the time and manner of Laius's death. Her description, with the help of the two herdsmen who saved him, leads to Oedipus's final revelation.

Once Oedipus learns the truth about himself, he transforms from being fearful and guilt-ridden to accepting and even embracing his status. When the herdsman Phorbas reveals that the boy he saved was born of Oedipus's wife, Oedipus responds in typical Senecan fashion. He calls for the earth to split open and demands that the Thebans kill him. Yet he also begins to act like Seneca's most powerful characters, Medea and Atreus. Oedipus starts to think of how his evil reputation will continue with him, as he declares, 'I will wander as the crime of the ages' (875). He urges himself on to accomplish some as yet unknown action that will be worthy of his crimes (878–9). The messenger describes Oedipus as plotting 'something great' (*grande nescio quid* 925). Before deciding on self-blinding as a punishment, Oedipus commands himself to use his intellect (947). Once his punishment is accomplished, he appears on stage declaring that he has appeased his father's ghost. He delights in his blindness (999), and states that it is properly fitting for Oedipus (1003). The appearance of his mother, however, causes Oedipus to realise that he has not fully punished himself. When she kills herself in front of him, Oedipus realises that he has outdone the horrors that Apollo predicted for him and declares, 'I have surpassed my impious fate' (1046). Thus, Oedipus exhibits the Senecan aesthetic of going beyond past crimes.

One's inability to escape fate is a problem central to the myth of Oedipus. In Seneca's play, fate is particularly cruel and inscrutable. Oedipus is not confident or assured in his position as king. It is only when he realises the truth about himself that he fully uses his mental abilities (947) and takes pleasure in becoming Oedipus. After he blinds himself, a unique moment in Senecan drama occurs. A brief choral ode interrupts the action to offer a Stoic interpretation of fate: 'By fate we are driven, we must yield to fate' (980). This ode suggests that Seneca breaks dramatic convention and scripted a play with six acts, or imagines the final act as divided into two scenes. This choral ode also references the Stoic view of the power of fate. The opening lines are reminiscent of the conclusion of the Stoic Cleanthes's 'Hymn to Zeus', which Seneca translates in his letters as 'the fates lead the willing, drag the unwilling' (*Ep.* 107.11). The fact that the Stoics viewed fate as ultimately guided by divine providence, and reason remains difficult to reconcile with the malignancy of fate in *Oedipus* and in the world of Senecan tragedy. While it is hard to imagine that his ode offers the key to the play, it does encourage the audience to think about the role of fate in the world. Oedipus's ultimate submission does offer him respite from his former self who fought against his destiny. Furthermore, the Stoics did claim that if one is fated to be sick, this destiny should be embraced wholeheartedly.[46] As is always the case with Seneca's plays, Stoicism is only one avenue for interpretation. The macabre excesses of Seneca's *Oedipus* and the pleasure that the title character takes when he becomes himself can be seen along metapoetic lines, as Seneca inserts his Oedipus into the tradition and surpasses it.

Seneca's *Agamemnon* tells the story of the Greek leader's return from Troy after the ten-year war. This is a story about revenge and the bloody repayment of debts, both old and new. Before setting sail for Troy, Agamemnon was forced to sacrifice his daughter, Iphigenia, in order to appease the gods and gain a favourable wind. Agamemnon's wife, Clytemnestra, now plans to execute her husband to atone for their child's death. Yet the forces of revenge conspiring against Agamemnon go back even further. In her husband's absence, Clytemnestra has been sharing her throne with Aegisthus, Thyestes's son, who was tricked by his brother and Agamemnon's father, Atreus, into eating his own children. Thus, the crimes of the earlier generation of the house of Atreus are given prominent place in this play. It serves as the sequel to Seneca's *Thyestes*. Indeed, Thyestes's ghost opens *Agamemnon*, and describes his cannibalistic feast and the terrible manner in which he conceived his son. The Delphic oracle advised him that he could take revenge on his brother by producing a child through an incestuous union with his daughter. Aegisthus's reason for existence is to carry on the familial slaughter. Of course, Agamemnon has more recent debts to pay as well. His death is also seen as atoning for the destruction of Troy. For a Roman audience, the fall of Troy marked the start of Rome with Aeneas's flight from the city, and the destruction of Greece's heroes could be seen as well-deserved. Yet, as in the *Troades*, in *Agamemnon* the instability of kingship and royal power is stressed. Seneca undermines any nationalistic pride that could have been scripted into this story. In addition to the theme of the relentless turning of Fortune's wheel, Troy and Greece are continually equated throughout this play.

Agamemnon is unique among Seneca's plays in that act two doubles the typical reason versus passion debate. When Clytemnestra enters to begin the act, she declares that her soul is wavering in its plans (108–24). Nevertheless, like many of Seneca's characters, Clytemnestra is able to fight against her diminishing desire for revenge both by talking to herself and by resisting her Nurse's calls for restraint (125–225). Aegisthus then enters, rebuking himself for his fear and hesitation. When he sees Clytemnestra he notes that her face is pallid and trembling and that she appears stupefied (237–8). Despite her previous self-encouragement and resistance to the Nurse's advice, Clytemnestra admits that now 'married love has won and called her back' (239). Another debate ensues and this time Clytemnestra declares that she can no longer continue with her plot against Agamemnon. Only when Aegisthus states that he is ready for death or exile does Clytemnestra turn back to her old self, declaring that she must remain faithful to her crime, rather than her husband (307).

These two scenes of passion versus restraint do not appear to be fully joined, as the Nurse, but not her advice, seems to leave the stage once Aegisthus arrives. Perhaps Seneca wrote two versions of the opening, and did not properly link them or delete one scene. Yet this very repetition also demonstrates Seneca's focus on the psychology of his characters. He repeatedly offers detailed descriptions of psychological turmoil and determination, as well as sudden changes of mind. Senecan drama is typically more concerned with individual episodes than with dramatic unity. By having Clytemnestra not live up to her reputation, Seneca also plays with the literary tradition and suggests how the story could have gone another way.[47] As in the *Troades*, where we briefly see an overly credulous and easily deceived Ulysses, here we see a Clytemnestra who is briefly willing to welcome Agamemnon back and beg for his forgiveness.

Agamemnon and his Trojan captives only appear late in the play. Act four opens with the Greek captive Cassandra lamenting her sorrows with the chorus. Soon Apollo's prophetic power comes upon her and she immediately questions where she is (726). The doubling of Greece with Troy now becomes explicit as she claims that she sees 'a twofold Argos' (729). She is swept back to Troy, the groves of Mt. Ida and the judgement of Paris. Her vision then shifts to the immediate future as she foresees Agamemnon's death. As frequently happens at the end of Seneca's plays, the themes of spectatorship and of characters watching a play within a play are developed. Cassandra sees into the Underworld and calls on the dead Trojans to watch as 'the fates turn back on themselves' (758). Agamemnon now finally enters in celebration. He cannot understand Cassandra's equation of the present moment with the destruction of Troy. The final chorus praises the Argive hero Hercules and ends with the theme of the repetition of destruction. Hercules sacked Troy in the generation before Agamemnon.

At the play's conclusion, Electra appears and entrusts the young Orestes to Strophius for hiding in Phocis, an act that offers some semblance of moral order to the play, but also ensures that the cycle of revenge will continue. Orestes will eventually return to kill Aegisthus and his mother.[48] Clytemnestra and Aegisthus enter and confront Electra. Her mother condemns Electra to death, which she welcomes by offering up her neck. Aegisthus has warmed to his role as a tyrant and forces her to live because she desires to die. Cassandra is led off to her end, but she also declares herself happy, both because outliving Troy's fall has enabled her to witness Agamemnon's end, and because she will be the first to bring the news to her people below (1004–11). She is granted the last words of the play and predicts that the avenging Furies, in the form of Orestes, will come upon Clytemnestra and Aegisthus.[49]

Thyestes is Seneca's masterpiece. The play tells the story of the dynastic rivalry between Atreus and his brother in the generation before the Trojan War, as the appearance of Thyestes's ghost at the start of Seneca's *Agamemnon* makes clear. The sorrows of the House of Atreus continue with Orestes's matricide and are only 'solved' by the establishment of the court for homicide at Athens, celebrated in Aeschylus's *Eumenides*. The sorrows originate with the family's patriarch and child of Jupiter, Tantalus. There are several versions of the origins of the family's crimes, but Tantalus is typically seen as abusing his privilege of living among the gods. In one version of the myth, Tantalus wished to test the gods' divinity and so he killed his son Pelops and served him at a feast. All the gods recognised the trick except for Demeter, who was distraught at the loss of her daughter and so ate a piece of Pelops's shoulder. The other gods refused to partake in the meal, reassembled Pelops and added a piece of marble to the gap left in his shoulder. Tantalus was punished in the Underworld by being made to stand in water, which always recedes from his lips when he tries to drink and by having a fruit tree tantalisingly above his head, the boughs of which are blown away by the wind whenever he tries to pick some fruit. He is typically included along with Ixion, Sisyphus and Tityus as the most infamous criminals punished in the Underworld.

Tantalus's regenerated son, Pelops, travelled to Greece and married Hippodamia after beating her father, Oenomaus, in a chariot race. Oenomaus's horses were a gift from the gods, so the only way Pelops could win was through deceit. He bribed Myrtilus, Oenomaus's chariot driver, to attach the axles incorrectly. After his victory, Pelops killed Myrtilus by throwing him into the sea, but not before he cursed Pelops's line.[50] Pelops became ruler of the Peloponnese (Pelops's island in Greek) and had two sons, Atreus and Thyestes. The two quarrelled over the right to rule. In some versions their father cursed them for killing their half-brother, Chrysippus. Atreus ruled first, but with the help of Atreus's wife, Aerope, Thyestes deposed his brother by stealing the symbol of the family's royal power, a golden-fleeced ram. Atreus eventually seized power again and drove his brother into exile. Due to his wife's adultery, Atreus also doubts the legitimacy of his own children, Agamemnon and Menelaus (325–30). Seneca's Atreus believes that his brother is continuing to plot against him (199–204, 241). Thus, he must take action first. Although Thyestes is not portrayed as a criminal mastermind in the play, Atreus equates himself with his brother (271). He sees his own revenge as pre-emptively trumping Thyestes.

At the opening of Seneca's play, Tantalus's ghost reluctantly is driven by a Fury to fill the palace with madness (23,102). This prologue sets up many of the play's themes, particularly with respect to Thyestes. Tantalus's eventual capitulation to follow the Fury (100) anticipates Thyestes's eventual defeat at the hands of his brother. Similar to Tantalus's punishments in the Underworld, Thyestes is a victim of his own insatiable desire for royal power, specifically the comforts and pleasures that it affords. He also submits to the dramatically ironic arguments of his son, aptly named Tantalus, that he not fear his brother and return to the palace. Echoing his ancestor's opening capitulation, Thyestes says, 'I follow you, I do not lead' (489).

Atreus enters the play stating outright that he is a tyrant and rebuking himself for not living up to his role as one (176–80). After debating with him about how to properly behave as a ruler and brother, Atreus's minister quickly turns from trying to restrain Atreus to helping him plot his revenge. The second choral ode contrasts sharply with Atreus's glorification of tyranny. The chorus describes the ideal king as one who desires nothing and is free from fear, thus alluding to the orthodox Stoic belief that only the wise man is king. Yet at the end of the ode, the chorus defines its own ideal in Epicurean terms. They want to 'live secretly', remain aloof from politics and be unknown to their fellow citizens (391–403). In their final ode, the chorus worries that the cosmos is reverting to primeval chaos, suggesting that the triumph of tyranny destabilises the very fabric of the universe. Despite these apocalyptic fears, the universe is only affected by the evils within the play to a comparatively small extent. The sun travels backwards and the gods above have fled from Atreus, yet all else remains unaffected. Thyestes's demands after he learns that he has eaten his sons to be buried below Tartarus, or to be destroyed by Jove's thunderbolt, or to have the gods avenge him, remain unheeded.

Atreus is master of his political realm, as well as master of his emotions and those of his brother. He is able to stir up his soul and command it to develop his plan for revenge at the start of the play. Once he sees his brother approaching, he is able to control his anger and feign joy at Thyestes's return (497–505). Atreus is able to entrap Thyestes because he understands the true nature of his brother's desires. According to Atreus, hope is Thyestes's chief motivating desire. This uncontrollable desire will allow Atreus to ensnare his brother (289–94).

Thyestes is in fact undone by his own hopes and desires. Atreus's vision of his brother's psychology is confirmed by Thyestes's first words: 'The desired rooftops of my fatherland and the wealth of Argos ... I see' (404–7).[51] There are also admirable philosophical ideas spoken by Thyestes. He admits that he was carefree during his exile and that true pleasure is found in rural, rather than royal, settings (414–18). While he embraces good principles, they clearly are not deeply engrained in him. Not only do his opening words reveal that Atreus was right about his brother's desire for kingship, but also that, unlike his brother, Thyestes does not have firm control over his emotions. Thyestes continually wavers. He takes unwilling steps towards the palace (420). His son Tantalus continually dangles the benefits of kingship before his father. Tantalus's persuasion of his father reverses the typical Senecan passion versus restraint scene. He orders his father to conquer the foreboding and the fears he rightly feels. Eventually, all Thyestes can do is cast aside his better judgement and follow Tantalus.

In the final scene Thyestes becomes the picture of royal opulence and gluttony. He is anointed with unguent. His hopes for kingship have been filled to the point of satiety. His belch causes his brother to realise his own apotheosis. Thyestes, however, is still unable to control himself. He tries to cast the 'old Thyestes' out of his soul (937), but his body rebels. His real transformation is into a beast; after eating his children he longs to howl like a wolf (957). In contrast, by virtue of his power over himself and others,

Atreus has transformed himself in the other direction and achieved a form of divinity.[52]

While this play focuses on the insatiable hunger for crime and power that defines the house of Atreus, for many this is Seneca's most satisfying play. It is perhaps his most thematically unified, and like Medea, Atreus's final dominance is bewitchingly impressive.[53] Also like *Medea*, this play demonstrates the consequences of transgressing boundaries, be they geographical, political, or the lines that place humans betwixt and between gods and beasts. *Thyestes* is especially concerned with how empire and autocracy blur these boundaries. The choral odes in the play at times 'anachronistically' refer to the contemporary world of Rome. The second ode's definition of ideal kingship outlines the borders of the Roman Empire (367–90). The chorus describes its apolitical ideal as a life 'unknown to any Quirites' (396). 'Quirites' can be used broadly to refer to the citizens of any city, but it also is an official term for the citizens of Rome.

The political idealism that characterises the chorus at the opening of the play gives way to despair at the end. The fears that the universe is returning to primeval chaos (832) that are voiced in the final choral ode dramatically invert the political expectations that Virgil voiced decades earlier. Writing around 40 BCE, Virgil hoped that 'last age' had come and would usher in a return to the Golden Age of Saturn (*Ecl.* 4.4). Seneca's final chorus asks whether 'the last age has come to us?' (878). In contrast to Virgil's pastoral vision, Seneca's chorus states that the final age will bring about the destruction of the universe (884). Perhaps Seneca, long accustomed to the horrors of the Julio-Claudian dynasty, wished to show that the hopes that Virgil expressed for renewal had been proven false. The Golden Age of Virgil has turned into Seneca's apocalypse.

III

Reception

SENECA'S INFLUENCE HAS PEAKED AT three points in history: during his lifetime, during the Renaissance and at the present time. In this chapter we will investigate the history of Seneca's reception. In the context of this book, this undertaking can only be done as a survey, which must unfortunately remain incomplete and give a brief taste of how authors have engaged with Seneca over the past 2,000 years. If one had to summarise the general tenor of Senecan reception, it would be one of critical engagement. Seneca left behind an important legacy, both in terms of his life story and his literary production. This legacy has been typically a site for debate and contestation, rather than simple celebration of Seneca's achievement – although, as we will see, there have been those who celebrate Seneca, particularly during the late Middle Ages and Renaissance, as a leading light from antiquity. More often, the paradoxes and conflicts inherent in the study of Seneca that we have traced in the previous three chapters have been noted and critiqued by writers for centuries. This critical engagement began during Seneca's life and in the decades after his death. It has continued for over two millennia.

Tracing the history of the reception of Seneca after his death is a massive project, one that could easily fill several books. To give an example of the possibilities for detailed study, James Ker's fine book *The Deaths of Seneca*

(Oxford 2009) investigates the theme of death in the Senecan corpus and the reception of Seneca's forced suicide from the ancient world until modern times, and spans over 400 pages. Thus, in this chapter we can only give an outline of the importance of Seneca's legacy. As we trace the peaks and valleys of his popularity, we will consider how authors throughout the centuries have responded to his work.

Reception of Seneca during his life

Reference to the earliest attacks on Seneca can be found in Suetonius and Tacitus. Both Seneca's literary style and his morality come under fire. Caligula reportedly called Seneca's writing 'simple games' and 'sand without lime' (Suet. *Cal.* 53.2). Soon after Caligula's death, Claudius relegated Seneca to Corsica for alleged affairs with members of the royal household. Tacitus places another famous attack in the mouth of Suillius, who condemns Seneca as a hypocritical philosopher who simply used his position under Nero to amass his wealth. This condemnation of Seneca as the multimillionaire who preaches the value of poverty is one that has stuck with Seneca, and forces upon us the difficult question of philosophical and moral authority. Does what we know about Seneca's life compromise his philosophical message? Seneca himself may have been particularly stung by this critique. The conclusion of *On the Happy Life* provides a defence of philosophers who live lavishly.

Seneca was also a central, if not sacred, figure of the 'Neronian Literary Renaissance'. Indeed, given Seneca's long career, he is an important transitional figure that links the literature of the 'Golden Age' under Augustus to the spike in 'Silver Age' literature that occurred under Nero. The other two main authors during this period were Seneca's nephew, Lucan, and (most likely) Nero's judge of good taste (*arbiter elegantiae*), Petronius. Both engage with Seneca in various ways.

Lucan's epic poem, *Civil War*, tells the story of the war between Caesar and Pompey that culminated in Pompey's defeat at the battle of Pharsalus in 48 BCE. Lucan shares his uncle's love of violence and hyperbolic rhetoric. One key example of the latter is that both Seneca and Lucan love the trope of apostrophe. Lucan uses it to such an extent that he turns the narrator of his epic into an independent character who emotionally responds to the story he is telling.[1] Stoicism is also problematically portrayed by the narrator, who at times cannot believe that providence is guiding the world. In addition, a possible hero of Lucan's epic – if indeed there is a hero – is the Stoic Cato the Younger. Book nine centres on Cato's endurance as he marches a portion of what remains of the Senatorial army across the deserts of North Africa. This march would only end in Cato's defeat and suicide at Utica in 46 BCE. Lucan does not narrate Cato's death, as Seneca so loved to do (*On Providence* 2.8–12, *Ep.* 24.6–8). Rather, his poem likely remains unfinished and breaks off in the following book with Caesar hemmed in by Ptolemy's troops in Alexandria, curiously the same place that Caesar's *Civil War* abruptly ends. Perhaps Lucan would have concluded his poem with an account of Cato's death had he lived long enough to do so. Like Seneca, Lucan was forced to commit suicide in the aftermath of the failed Pisonian conspiracy. Yet, unlike Seneca, Lucan did not remain steadfast; in order to try and save himself, Lucan indicted his mother, perhaps thinking Nero the matricide would appreciate this lack of familial loyalty (*Ann.* 15.70).

Most scholars believe that Petronius the author of the *Satyricon* and the courtier whose death Tacitus describes as an inversion of Seneca's philosophical death in the *Annals* (16.18–20) are the same person. If so, this would demonstrate how Seneca's life, literature and death could become the basis for critical engagement and imitation.[2] The *Satyricon* is typically classified, along with Apuleius's *Metamorphoses*, sometimes called *The Golden Ass*, as the only surviving examples of the Roman novel. It is a novel in that it is fiction written in prose, but Petronius also intersperses several passages of poetry. Thus, it portrays on a large scale the prosimetrum that is characteristic of Menippean satire, the only complete surviving example of which is Seneca's *Apocolocyntosis*. The *Satyricon* has come down to us in a very fragmentary state and parodies a variety of genres, from philosophy, epic and tragedy to (possibly) the more decorous love stories that survive in the Greek novels. There are also several points in which Petronius parodies Seneca's philosophy and tragedy.[3] Indeed, the sham poet/philosopher Eumolpus, who pretends to be an old-fashioned moralist, but only does so to gain access to young boys, may be modelled on Seneca himself.

Also from the Neronian period, six satires, plus prologue, remain of the poet Persius (34–62 CE), who critiques contemporary mores and adopts a rigidly Stoic persona. Satire four focuses on the philosophical ideal of 'know thyself', and looks at the relationship between Socrates and Alcibiades. Satire five describes how Persius studied Stoicism under Lucius Annaeus Cornutus, who was a freedman from Seneca's family. According to the biography of Persius written by Suetonius, he eventually met Seneca himself, but was not impressed by his intellect (*ingenium*).

If Seneca did not leave an impression on Persius, Columella, who wrote a treatise on farming, praised Seneca as 'a man of outstanding talents and learning'. In this case, however, Columella is not discussing Seneca's literary output, but rather the output of wine produced at Seneca's vineyards at Nomentum (*Rust.* 3.3.3). Here we gain a brief contemporary glimpse of Seneca's economic activity. In fact, Seneca mentions his vineyards at Nomentum, but not for their impressive productivity. He writes that visiting them helps to restore his health (*Ep.* 104.1–6). The letter concludes with a touch of the hypocrisy that many find offensive. In the context of his wealth-producing estates, Seneca writes:

> Riches must be spurned: they are the wages of slavery. Gold and silver and whatever else weighs down successful homes must be abandoned; liberty cannot be gained for free. If you value this highly, you must value all else at little.
>
> (*EP.* 104.34)

Yet the crux of Seneca's thoughts on wealth is not that it must be rejected, but rather that one should not let the pursuit of riches run one's life and one should not be afraid of losing wealth, as the conclusion of the letter makes clear.

Octavia *and* Hercules Oetaeus

Seneca's importance for later Romans as they investigated the Julio-Claudian age and in particular the reign of Nero is abundantly clear in *Octavia*. As we have already noted, this play is our only complete example of Roman historical drama, the so-called *tragoedia praetexta*, which flourished from about 200 BCE to 100 CE. Aside from *Octavia*, only fragments of the genre remain. One manuscript branch preserves this tragedy with those universally believed to be by Seneca; the play's authenticity began to be suspect in the sixteenth century. Today, most scholars believe that it is by an unknown imitator of Seneca, who wrote the drama anywhere from a few months after Nero's death in June of 68 CE to several decades after the fact. The date and reasons for the authorship of the play remain a mystery. This play may have functioned as propaganda for one of the emperors who succeeded Nero. If so, the play is a problematic piece of condemnation. Rather than simply damning Nero, it brings the emperor vividly onto the stage. Thus, it demonstrates the horror and attraction that Romans felt for the Julio-Claudian period. As the conclusion of Suetonius's biography of Nero shows, the death of the last of the Julio-Claudians inspired both relief, as the citizens accordingly donned freedmen's caps, but also regret. Suetonius relates that Nero's tomb was decorated with flowers, statues of the emperor were erected, and copies of his edicts were read as if he were still alive and would soon return to avenge himself. Suetonius also notes that when he was a young man a pretender came from the east claiming to be Nero reborn (*Nero* 57).

It is within this context of fascination with the bygone age of Nero that we can understand *Octavia*. It narrates events from the first part of 62 CE, when Nero was safely free from his mother (murdered in 59 CE) and his original praetorian prefect and fellow guide along with Seneca, Sextus Afranius Burrus (died under mysterious circumstances in 62 CE, Tacitus, *Ann.* 14.51). According to Tacitus, the death of Burrus 'broke Seneca's power' (*Ann.* 14.52), and presumably prompted Seneca to ask to resign his position (14.53). Free from these constraints, Nero sought to rid himself of his arranged marriage to Claudius's daughter, his stepsister Octavia, and marry his new love, the noblewoman Poppaea Sabina. Tacitus preserves the lengthy machinations Nero must go through before eventually divorcing, exiling and murdering Octavia. The playwright, who may have been one of Tacitus's sources for these events, compresses the action into three days. Thus, unlike Senecan drama, the action of the play is not confined to one day. The play does not have a five-act structure and the action is considerably more decorous. We do not witness Octavia's murder. The play ends as she is led off to her ship to sail to the island of her exile, Pandataria. The main chorus in this play is particularly active in supporting Octavia, but their rebellious actions are quashed by Nero's troops.

Although this play is set in the Rome of recent history, the mythological horrors of the Greek world are ever present. The play's final words, spoken by the chorus, trump Seneca's aesthetic of excess by stating that the violence of Roman history outdoes that of Greek myth: 'Aulis is more gentle than our city, as is the barbarian land of the Tauri. There the gods above are appeased with the slaughter of strangers. Rome feels joy in the blood of citizens' (978–82). The powers of the Underworld are also vividly present. The play's central scene consists of the appearance of Agrippina's ghost on the morning of Nero's wedding. Her prophecy of Nero's eventual fall and death is the prime example that this play had to be written after Nero's death and thus Seneca's. Agrippina's speech concludes, 'There will come a day and a time when he will pay for his crimes with his guilty soul and pay his enemies with his throat, deserted, cast down and lacking everything' (629–31). These details are eerily close to Suetonius's account of Nero's death, most notably that Nero in fact stabbed himself in the neck. If Seneca actually did write this play, he was prophetically inspired or guessed remarkably accurately about the circumstances of Nero's death.

The play expands upon Senecan drama in that it multiplies the reason versus passion scenes. First Octavia and her Nurse debate which course of action they should follow, then Seneca and Nero, and finally Poppaea and her Nurse. In the opening debate, Octavia is advised to submit to Nero by her Nurse. Unlike Seneca's passionate female characters, such as Medea and Clytemnestra, Octavia ultimately cannot act on her hatred for Nero. In comparison to Seneca's active heroines, Octavia is a martyr. She is not able to confront Nero and speak to the power that oppresses and ultimately destroys her.

After the first choral ode, Seneca enters. His monologue begins by asking why Fortune has lifted him up to so high a position only to cast him down (377–80). Then in language that contains strong echoes of his praise of exile in his *Consolation to Helvia*, Seneca ruefully remembers how he enjoyed studying nature while away in Corsica (381–90). As Rolando Ferri notes in his commentary on the play, the portrayal of Seneca is positive, but not hagiographical.[4] In other words, *Octavia* critically engages with and reshapes Seneca, both his life and what he wrote. His praise of exile as giving him uninterrupted time for study does have its basis in Seneca's own statements to his mother. Yet his opening questioning of Fortune's reasons for bringing him home from exile provide a commentary on Seneca's other, considerably less positive views of exile contained in his *Consolation to Polybius*. Readers of both of Seneca's consolations might recognise that his published works provide an ambiguous evaluation of his exile. From the standpoint of history, this play ironically comments on Seneca's hypocrisy and ambition. Perhaps he should have remained content in his place, as he claims to have been in the *Consolation to Helvia*.

The bulk of Seneca's monologue is a prophecy that the universe is approaching its final day and will collapse into chaos. This apocalyptic vision can be connected with the final chorus in *Thyestes* as well as the Stoic theory of the *ekpyrosis*, or periodic destruction and renewal of the universe by fire. Seneca's philosophy, in particular *Natural Questions*, also discusses past and future world destructions, either by fire or by water. Seneca then discusses how the world will be reborn in a better state, as when it was young and Saturn, not Jupiter, ruled the cosmos (*Oct.* 391–406).

At the conclusion of Seneca's monologue, the playwright swerves back to Neronian Rome and back to Senecan tragedy. Returning to his opening apocalyptic prophecy, Seneca claims that the current age is the logical result of the accumulation of past crimes. Nero comes to be the personification of the universe's degradation. Here we can see something of the implied propaganda in this play. If the age of Nero represented the culmination of the Iron Age, the present must be the happy age that Seneca 'prophesied' would come after his destruction. Thus, the end of the Julio-Claudian line and the civil wars that ensued are portrayed as a cosmic and universally cleansing cataclysm, which ushered in a new and happy era. There is a similar apocalyptic fear in the final chorus of Seneca's *Thyestes* (*Thy.* 875–8). In *Thyestes*, however, there is no renewal after destruction. Here we can see another key difference between *Octavia* and Senecan drama: the theme of hope. There is an element of dramatic irony to all of Nero's cruelties. The audience knows that Nero cannot continue with impunity. This fact is suggested by the active role the chorus takes against him and by Seneca's monologue. It is also made clear by Agrippina's ghost.

The links between Greek myth and Julio-Claudian history, which are mostly latent in Seneca's plays, are turned into an important theme in *Octavia*. As we have seen, the play concludes by one-upping Seneca's master trope and states that Rome is crueller than Greek tragedy. In addition, the *Octavia* poet is one of our earliest readers, if not the earliest, to suggest how the world of Senecan tragedy and the world of imperial Rome can map on to one another. This connection is clearly seen in the reason versus passion debate between Seneca and Nero. Seneca plays the role of the Minister and Nero plays the role of Atreus from *Thyestes*. The comparison does not neatly line up, however. While Nero may be a tyrant like Atreus who invites the people's fear and is bent on destroying a member of his own family, unlike the Minister in *Thyestes*, Seneca never acquiesces to help the tyrant he serves.

Of the play's 982 lines, 192 (nearly 20 per cent) are taken up by the debate between Seneca and Nero (lines 440–582). The two characters employ stichomythia, or the rapid exchange of lines, occasionally even half-lines, and lengthy speeches, to debate how an autocrat should wield his power, the true character of Augustus and the nature of love. The debate concerning the limits of autocratic power is structured around key themes of Seneca's *On Mercy*. For example, Seneca calls on Nero to think of how the gods would judge his deeds (448, see *On Mercy* 1.7.1–2). Referring to the divinisation of his father Claudius, Nero responds with one of the greatest lines in Latin literature: 'I would foolishly fear the gods, because I myself create them' (449). We can see that *Octavia* does not just take passages from Seneca and plug them in. By giving Nero the ability to counter Seneca's claims, the dialogue of the play undoes the carefully scripted words that Seneca constructs for Nero in *On Mercy*. As Tacitus's Nero points out, his rhetorical abilities, specifically the ability to provide counter-arguments *ex tempore*, were the priceless gift that Seneca gave to him (*Ann.* 14.55). Now here, as in Nero's reply to Seneca's request for retirement in Tacitus, Seneca's gift of eloquence is used against him.

Nero's characterisation as a rhetorically adept tyrant can be linked to Seneca's Atreus. And like Atreus, Nero's lust for violence verges on self-destruction. Both direct their anger against their families and both make grandiose statements that show they do not fear their own destruction. As he plots his revenge against his brother, Atreus says, 'Let this famous house of Pelops fall even on me, so long as it also falls on my brother' (*Thy.* 190–1). Nero concludes the opening debate with a brief speech outlining why he must kill his relatives. His last words are reminiscent of Atreus's paradoxically Stoic disregard for personal safety, but in the context of *Octavia*, they also look proleptically to Nero's eventual fate, 'Let everything that stands high fall!' (471).

The final movement of the dialogue concerns Nero's love for Poppaea, and Seneca's countercharge that Nero must remain faithful to his wife, Octavia. Here the debate becomes reminiscent of that between the Nurse and Phaedra at the opening of Seneca's *Phaedra*. Nero declares that he cannot help whom he loves. He declares that love is the 'tyrant of heaven' and the most powerful of the gods (see *Pha.* 184–94). Sounding like Phaedra's Nurse, Seneca responds that love has been falsely divinised by humans' foolishness. Love is not an external god that carries a bow, arrow and a torch. Rather, love is a product of human psychology, 'a great force of the mind and a seductive heat of the soul' (561). Unlike *Phaedra*, however, the debate in *Octavia* does not come to any resolution. Seneca does not agree to help Nero with his plans and is simply dismissed by the emperor (588–90). Seneca may not win, but at least he does not submit.

If we accept the earliest possible date for *Octavia*, that is during the brief reign of Galba immediately following Nero's death (June 68–15 January 69 CE), then this play represents one of the earliest surviving post-mortem receptions of Seneca. The unknown author was a close and careful reader of Seneca, and it is noteworthy how he intertwines an investigation of Seneca's life, philosophy and tragedy. The *Octavia* playwright turns Seneca into a prophet of the apocalypse that will be brought on by Nero, and by extension makes him serve posthumously as a political propagandist for the next regime. Nero in turn becomes not simply a bad emperor, but a world-destroyer, and we may possibly see the beginnings of the beast of the apocalypse that he will become in the Christian tradition.[5]

The other major classical reception of Senecan drama is *Hercules Oetaeus*. There are some who believe this play is in fact by Seneca, but the majority of scholars date this play to the late first or early second century.[6] It may possibly be as late as 200 CE. It is the longest play to survive from antiquity (1,996 lines), and likely represents the end of the classical dramatic tradition. It tells the story of Hercules's death as the result of a poisoned cloak given to him unwittingly by his wife, Deianira. At the opening of the play, she is jealous of Hercules's return with the young Iole after the sack of her father's city, and she remembers that the centaur Nessus had given her a 'love potion' made from his blood after Hercules killed him. She smears it on a cloak for Hercules. Rather than causing him to fall in love with her again, Nessus's poison destroys Hercules. He builds a massive pyre on which to immolate himself. The play ends with Hercules's apotheosis, which is confirmed by his voice from on high comforting his sorrowing mother, Alcmene. This story is also recounted in Sophocles's play *The Women of Trachis* (*Thraciniae*), but the author does not provide a simple translation of the Greek text. Perhaps the most notable difference is that at the end of Sophocles's play Hercules's divinisation is not assured. Hercules's final words command his son Hyllus to marry Iole (1221–9) and then he orders his son to lift him on the pyre (1252–6). The most immediate source for this play's portrayal of Hercules's death and apotheosis is Ovid's *Metamorphoses* (9.152–272). Ovid's version stresses Hercules's patient endurance of the flames (9.240–1), and repeatedly notes that only Hercules's mortal body will be affected by the fire. The part of him that was given by Jupiter is eternal (9.250–3, 262–70).

Some have taken this play to reflect the Stoic belief that the apotheosis of Hercules represents the rewards for the wise man after a life of suffering and endurance.[7] Given the points that Ovid makes, however, the apotheosis of Hercules in this play does not necessarily reflect Stoic theory. Nevertheless, at the play's end, there is a continual focus on Hercules's *virtus* (manly courage). Hercules appears from heaven to rebuke his mother for lamenting his death. He notes, 'my *virtus* has made a path for me to the stars and to the gods themselves' (1942–3), and '*virtus* leads to the stars, fear to death' (1971). Like *Octavia*, but unlike the eight plays securely attributed to Seneca, *Hercules Oetaeus* ends with a choral ode. Whereas the chorus of

Octavia laments how the savagery of Roman history outdoes that of Greek myth, the chorus of *Hercules Oetaeus* concludes with a prayer to Hercules to protect the earth and gives 'Stoic' advice on how, like the hero of the play, to avoid passing to the shades below:

> Never is renowned *virtus* carried to the shades of Styx. Live bravely, and the cruel fates will not convey you over the river Lethe, but when your final day will complete your last hours, glory will open up a path to the gods above.
>
> (1983–8)

Virtus is central to Stoicism; it is the only good in life, and, along with the exclusive exercise of reason and the banishment of the passions, it is one of the defining characteristics of the wise man. In this play, *virtus* need not have a specific Stoic connotation, however, as valour and courage were the defining ideals of Roman manhood in general.

It is true that in some contexts, Hercules could be seen as a Stoic exemplar. At the same time, the deeply ambiguous nature of Hercules's character must be remembered. On the one hand, Hercules is seen as a civilising force. For example, his twelve labours helped to rid the world of tyrants and wild beasts. Yet there also is a deep undertone of savagery at the core of Hercules, which is clearly seen in his madness and murder of his wife and children. The literary tradition also speaks to Hercules's ambiguity. In the Greek tradition, he appears in epic (Apollonius's *Argonautica*), tragedy (appearing in plays by Aeschylus, Sophocles and Euripides), comedy (Aristophanes's *The Frogs*) and as a party-loving oaf in Euripides's satyr play, *Alcestis*.

Seneca also investigates the varied nature of Hercules's character. As we have seen, *Hercules Furens* stresses the hero's megalomania and dramatically links his claim to have pacified the world with the onset of his family-destroying madness. In the *Apocolocyntosis*, Hercules appears as a comic hero, who unsuccessfully lobbies for another mortal to be admitted to Olympus. Seneca's dialogue *On the Constancy of the Wiseman* admits the Stoics have claimed Hercules as an example of the Stoic ideal, but Seneca claims that the Roman Cato is a better model. In language that echoes Lucretius's dismissal of the benefits provided to the human race by mythological heroes, Seneca denigrates Hercules's accomplishments:[8]

> As for Cato, I urge you not to be concerned: for the wise man can neither suffer injury nor insult. The immortal gods have given us in Cato a better example of the wise man than Ulysses and Hercules were for earlier ages. For we Stoics have proclaimed them to be wise men, unconquered by labours and despisers of pleasures and victors over all fears. Cato did not fight with wild beasts, which huntsmen and farmers also pursue; he did not pursue monsters with fire and sword, nor did he happen to live in an age when it was possible to believe that the heavens rested on one man's shoulders.
>
> (*CONST.* 2.1–2)

With the complexity of Seneca's engagement with Hercules in mind, from his tragic madness, to his comic role as Claudius's champion, to his being surpassed by Cato, we should be wary of thinking that the author of *Hercules Oetaeus* is basing his hero directly on his portrayal in Seneca. A better knowledge of Seneca's own writings and of the ambiguities of the Hercules figure in general enables us to question the easy answers that this play seems to give about *virtus* and how endurance leads divinisation. It is worth noting that both of the dramatic receptions of Senecan drama focus on martyr-like characters. Seneca's own death may also be an important model for *Octavia* and *Hercules Oetaeus*.

Classical Rhetoric and Philosophy

While poets and historians turned to Seneca in the years following his death, his influence began to decline quickly, particularly in the fields of rhetoric and philosophy. Seneca was the most famous rhetorician in his own day, but with the passage of time and change in tastes and political regimes, his style fell out of favour – at least according to some. In his *Education of the Orator*, the rhetorician Quintilian (*c.*35–*c.*100 CE), also a Spaniard who rose to fame in Rome through his rhetorical abilities, reserves his judgement of Seneca for the conclusion of book ten's lengthy discussion of Greek and Latin literature. Quintilian states that he has delayed his treatment of Seneca because in the past people have believed that he condemned Seneca and was his enemy. Quintilian states that such claims are false (10.1.125). This popular view seems to have come about somewhat earlier in Quintilian's teaching career, when Seneca was almost the only author read by his students. Rather than categorically forbidding the reading of Seneca, Quintilian took pains to make sure that his students did not prefer him to better authors (10.1.126). Quintilian's concluding summation of Seneca is worth quoting at length:

> In philosophy he was not diligent enough, but he was an exceptional persecutor of vices. There are many excellent *sententiae* in his works, and much that should be read for the sake of morals, but his style is mostly corrupt and extremely dangerous because it abounds in pleasing vices.
>
> As I said, there are many things to approve of in him and many things to admire, provided that one take the care to be selective. If only he had done this himself! For his nature was worthy of the better things that it wished for; but he achieved what he wanted.
>
> (*INST.* 10.1.129; 131)

The paradox of Quintilian's condemnations of Seneca's pointed style, in favour of the more ample periodic style of Cicero, is that in many ways Quintilian's own rhetorical style appears influenced by Seneca. The fact that he still feels it necessary to condemn Seneca's style several years after his death suggests that Seneca still remained a popular model, despite the protests of Quintilian and others.[9]

Aulus Gellius (*c.* 130–80 CE) bears witness to the fact that Seneca's style remained a topic of debate (*NA* 12.2). According to Gellius some 'judge that Seneca is a writer of little value, whose works are not worth the trouble of taking up'. Others, however, admit that his style is inelegant, but that 'he is not lacking learning and knowledge of the subjects that he discusses and that in castigating the vices of people he has a severity and seriousness that is not without charm' (12.2.1). Gellius himself will not pass judgement upon

Seneca's overall talents or writings. Instead, he discusses Seneca's criticism of three lines from Ennius's *Annals* (306 Warmington) and condemnation of Cicero for praising them (*Brut.* 58), which he states comes from the now lost 22nd book of the *Moral Epistles*. Only the first 20 books have survived. According to Gellius, Seneca also criticised Virgil for imitating Ennius in his epic. He states that Virgil did so in order that people who were fans of the archaic poet would favour his new composition (12.2.10). Despite his opening statement that he will not judge Seneca, Gellius condemns him as an 'inept and foolish human being' (12.2.11). He concludes that Seneca has made some worthy statements, such as, 'What difference does it make how much you have? There is much more that you do not have'. Yet Gellius's final summation is that the good things that Seneca says are overshadowed by the bad, and for this reason he is all the more dangerous for students to read (12.2.13–14).

Similarly, Marcus Cornelius Fronto (*c.* 100–76 CE), who was the emperor Marcus Aurelius's teacher of rhetoric, advises the emperor to stay away from a hybrid style that weds the rustic simplicity of Cato (literally, pine nuts, *pineis nucibus*) with the 'soft and feverish little plums of Seneca' (Loeb vol. 2: 102–3). He later criticises the repetitious nature of the opening of Lucan's *Civil War*, claiming this corrupt style signalled he was like his uncle (Loeb vol. 2: 104–5). While Seneca's literary style would be analysed and attacked, his philosophy seems to have been completely ignored by the two important Stoics who came after him. Epictetus and Marcus Aurelius show little, if any, evidence of being acquainted with Seneca's works. Writing philosophy in Latin, a project started by Lucretius and Cicero at the end of the Republic and then continued by Seneca, was largely rejected during the classical period. Epictetus's philosophy, as transcribed by his student Arrian, is in Greek, as is the *Meditations* of Marcus Aurelius.

Early Christian Writers

Seneca would return to favour, but only to a limited degree, in the writings of Christian authors in the Latin west. The first direct reference to Seneca by a Christian author comes in Tertullian's (*c.*160–240 CE) *On the Soul*, where a quote is introduced, 'As even Seneca, who is often ours, says ...' (20.1). The designation of Seneca as 'often ours' suggests that Tertullian may have seen in Seneca ideas that come close to 'our' Christian faith, but also that he does not fully harmonise with it, hence the qualifying 'often' (*saepe*).

The *Divine Institutes* of Lactantius (*c.*240–320 CE) contain the most quotations of Seneca during the early Christian period and the most favourable assessments of him. Lactantius cites Seneca 22 times. At one point, he calls him 'the smartest of all the Stoics' (2.8.23). He also declares, 'If you want to learn about everything, take up Seneca's books. He was a most accurate describer of the public's conduct and vices and a most fierce attacker of them' (5.9.19, cf. 5.22.11).[10] But again, Lactantius can only go so far in his praise; Seneca still would have needed to reject the Stoics Zeno and Sotion to obtain true wisdom (6.24.14).

Jerome (*c.*348–420 CE) relied 'heavily on Seneca's lost *De matrimonio* for his discussion of virginity in *Adversus Iovinian* 1.41–9'.[11] Like Tertullian, he also refers to Seneca as 'ours' (*noster*). Here the significance of this designation seems clearer than Tertullian's. It seems unlikely that Jerome is claiming Seneca for the Christian cause. Before mentioning Seneca, Jerome named Greek philosophers, such as Aristotle, and so by referring to Seneca as 'ours', Jerome may simply mean that he wrote in Latin.

Jerome's notice for Seneca in *De viris illustribus* is worth quoting in full:

> Lucius Annaeus Seneca of Corduba, a student of Sotion the Stoic and the uncle of the poet Lucan, lived a life characterised by the greatest self-control. I would not have placed him in my catalogue of holy men, if I were not encouraged to do so by those letters from Paul to Seneca or from Seneca to Paul, which are read by a great many people. In these letters, written when he was Nero's teacher and the most powerful man of his time, he says that he wishes to hold the same place among his own people that Paul holds among the Christians. This Seneca was killed by Nero two years before Peter and Paul were crowned with martyrdom.
>
> (12)

The ambiguity that Jerome feels about including Seneca in this work is significant. He notes that Seneca indeed led a morally upright life, but this fact alone does not mean he should be included in Jerome's catalogue of holy men. Jerome is also fascinated by the connections that Seneca shares with Peter and Paul. All three were killed by Nero within a few years of each other. Yet Jerome's main reason for including Seneca is the fact that Seneca and Paul exchanged a series of letters. Jerome provides us with the first surviving reference to this correspondence. This work was shown to be a forgery in the fifteenth century, although today there is at least one scholar who believes that these letters represent a genuine correspondence.[12] The exchange consists of 14 short letters in Latin. The author seems unconcerned, or unaware, that Paul's canonical letters are written in Greek. Many of the letters have a positive tone. Seneca is presenting Paul's ideas (and perhaps his letters) to Nero, who initially receives them favourably. Nero remarks that Paul's writing abilities and education do not measure up to the sublime topics he discusses (*Ep.* 7). In order to help Paul with his Latin, Seneca serves as his teacher. Paul refers to Seneca as 'the teacher of so great a princeps and indeed a teacher of everyone' (*Ep.* 2). Seneca sends Paul a work on how to improve his writing (*Ep.* 9). The only real threat to Paul is Nero's wife, Poppaea, who according to tradition was favourable to the Jews and might not encourage the new religion (*Ep.* 5).

The later letters curiously add dates and the names of the consuls at their conclusion, so we can luckily assign 'dates' to them. Letters 10 and 12–14 are imagined to have been written in 58 CE. The oddly placed letter nine is dated to 28 March 64 and refers to the Great Fire in Rome, which Tacitus states started in July of that year. This letter leaves behind the fantasy world of the other letters. Not only does it refer to an actual historical event, but it also shows that Nero was no friend to the Christians. The dating of the letters may serve several purposes. It gives the letters an air of authenticity. By having so many set in 58, perhaps the author imagined what could have been during the early good years of Nero's reign.[13] The author completely ignores the tradition that Seneca was responsible for turning Nero into a tyrant, and instead portrays him as a sympathetic teacher who will make Paul more acceptably Roman, and hopefully spread

Christianity himself, as the final letter, which contains the only reference to Jesus Christ, demonstrates.[14]

Underlying the fiction of these letters is not simply that Seneca's philosophy can at times be harmonised with Christianity, but also, as Jerome shows us, the fact that Seneca lived at the same time as Jesus and the Apostles. He was present in Rome for the Great Fire and had to have witnessed Nero's persecutions. This synchronicity, in addition to any intellectual connections, contributes to the idea that Seneca *could have* at least known something of Christianity. Indeed, Seneca's brother knew Paul as governor of Achaea, according to Acts of the Apostles 18:12–17. Seneca, like Peter, Paul and the Christians after the Great Fire, was a victim of Nero. This desire to set Seneca as a witness to the early Church has not died out, as seen from his albeit minor role in Henryk Sienkiewicz's 1895 novel, *Quo Vadis?*, famously brought to the silver screen by MGM in 1951.

Augustine (354–430 CE) also mentions the letters between Seneca and Paul (*Ep.* 153.14). In *The City of God*, he states that Seneca lived during the time of the Apostles (*De civ. D.* 6.10). In this work, Augustine's magnum opus, Augustine quotes extensively from Seneca's lost *De superstitione*. He praises the freedom with which Seneca condemns Roman state religion, but also criticises Seneca's hypocrisy for still taking part in the rituals. Augustine claims that Seneca states, 'The wise man will observe all of these rites as if ordered by the laws, but not as if pleasing to the gods' (*De civ. D.* 6.10). Augustine condemns Seneca's acceptance of the importance of keeping up appearances for the good of the state:

> But that man, whom the philosophers have made a free man, so to speak, nevertheless, because he was a famous senator of the Roman people, worshipped what he renounced, did what he argued against, and revered that which he faulted.
>
> (*DE CIV.* D. 6.10)

In the following chapter, Augustine cites Seneca to criticise the Jews, especially the observance of the Sabbath, which, according to Augustine, Seneca claimed forced the Jews to waste a major portion of their life, by spending every seventh day in idleness. Possibly echoing Horace on how Greek culture has influenced that of their Roman conquerors, Seneca states that the customs of Jews, the 'most wicked race', have been received throughout the world and paradoxically, 'the conquered have given laws to the victors' (*De civ. D.* 6.11). In his final quote on the topic, Augustine cites Seneca as claiming, 'The Jews, however, know the reasons for their rites; the greater part of humanity is ignorant of why they do what they do' (*De civ. D.* 6.11). In his extant works, Seneca does criticise the practice of lighting lamps on the Sabbath, 'since the gods do not lack light, nor are humans delighted by soot' (*Ep.* 95.47). As for the Christians, Augustine is right in noting that Seneca does not mention them (*De civ. D.* 6.11), at least as far as we can tell from what has survived of his work.

Seneca in the Late Middle Ages and Early Renaissance

After the sixth century, Seneca is mentioned sporadically.[15] He would come to be read with increasing frequency starting in the twelfth-century renaissance. Perhaps one of the most important and familiar Christian authors to praise Seneca is Peter Abelard (1072–1142). Interestingly, some of this praise comes in the context of Abelard's reading of 'Seneca's' correspondence with 'Paul'. Abelard refers to Seneca as 'The greatest follower of poverty and self-control, and the best teacher of morals among all the philosophers.' Elsewhere, he notes, 'Seneca is as famous for his eloquence as for his morals.'[16] Today, Abelard is perhaps most famously known for his ill-fated love affair with his student, Héloïse. Her uncle had Abelard castrated for his affair. Several letters between Abelard and Héloïse survive, and Seneca is quoted by both parties. Many of the citations of Seneca come from Héloïse, thus offering us possibly the earliest evidence of a woman reading Seneca. For example, in her first letter, she quotes a lengthy passage from the opening of *Moral Epistles* 40, and notes with approval Seneca's statement to Lucilius that letters are a way to make absent friends present. She hopes that Abelard will follow this advice and continue to write to her.[17]

Abelard and Héloïse's engagement with Seneca is part of the renewed interest in his works and life that began during the renaissance of classical learning that took place in western Europe during the twelfth century. From this point until the 1600s, Seneca's reputation would only grow as his texts and biography served as inspiration for scholars and artists. During these centuries we can note the development of two, often interconnected paths for Seneca's reception. First, he serves as a moral authority from pagan antiquity. For example, John of Salisbury (1110–80) worked with Seneca in his *Policraticus* and *Metalogicon*. In the latter work, he defends Seneca's reputation, saying: 'With all due respect to Quintilian, there is no, or at least hardly any, other moralist among the pagans, whose words and opinions can be more conveniently alleged in all sorts of discussions' (1.22).[18] Dante calls him 'Seneca morale' and places him among the 'great spirits' of the pagans in Limbo (*Inferno* 4.141). Second, this focus on Seneca's moral authority leads to an increased interest in his biography, which often focuses on his death scene and portrays him as a martyr who, like the Christians, suffered under Nero's cruelty. For example, Jacobus of Voraigne's collection of saints' lives, the *Legenda aurea* (*c.*1260), includes Seneca's death, as well as those of his two brothers and nephew, in his account of Peter the Apostle (Chapter 84). He even ascribes prophetic significance to Seneca's name, stating that it alludes to his final act of self-killing, even if he was forced to do so (*se necans... se necavit* 84.3).[19]

The bibliographical tradition would be immeasurably bolstered by Boccaccio's rediscovery of the later books of Tacitus's *Annals* in 1370 at Monte Cassino. In his *Commentary on Dante*, Boccaccio gives a lengthy account of Seneca to explicate Dante's brief reference to 'Seneca morale' in Limbo (4.1.435–64). He recounts Seneca's death scene from Tacitus and suggests that Dante misplaced Seneca. Boccaccio understands Tacitus's account of Seneca's dying in a bath as a reference to Christian baptism and Seneca's alleged invocation of 'Jove the Liberator' as a cryptic reference to Jesus Christ (4.1.462–4). Thus, Boccaccio hopes that Seneca was saved.[20] This belief in Seneca's possible conversion is stated explicitly in several biographies written in Italy during the fourteenth century.[21]

Yet Seneca's life and works were not universally praised. In the letter to Seneca from his *Letters on Familiar Matters* (*Rerum familiarum libri*

24.5), Petrarch begins by apologetically noting that he will speak so frankly with Seneca. His criticisms do come from close engagement with Seneca's works. Despite the fact that Seneca is 'to be revered' and, on the authority of Plutarch, is an 'incomparable teacher of morals', Petrarch will devote this letter to showing 'the error' of Seneca's life (24.5.5). He criticises Seneca for his relationship with Nero. Why did such a wise man knowingly seek out such dangers? He also condemns Seneca for flattery and hypocrisy. One example focuses on the praise that Seneca piles upon Nero in *On Mercy* and *Consolation to Polybius*, only to condemn Nero in *Octavia*. Here we can see Petrarch's confusion about what Seneca wrote. He does not realise that the praise in *Consolation to Polybius* is directed at Claudius, rather than Nero (although it is a good example of Seneca's hypocrisy, when we compare this consolation to the treatment of Claudius in the *Apocolocyntosis*). Secondly, Petrarch believes Seneca wrote *Octavia*, but he also casts doubt on the play's authorship, noting that Corduba was home to two Senecas (24.5.17).

Yet even if Petrarch can eventually excuse Seneca of condemning his pupil in the *Octavia*, he also bases his critique on historical sources. He focuses on Suetonius's claim that Seneca kept Nero from studying the old orators (24.5.13 = Suet. *Nero* 52). Because of this fact, Petrarch concludes, 'the root of your miseries grew from your frivolity, or rather, vanity' (24.5.13). Petrarch shows that he has read *On Mercy*, because he condemns Seneca for stating that Nero was greater than Augustus (24.5.24) and condemns Seneca for encouraging Nero's love of playing the lyre and chariot racing. Yet he stops short of blaming Seneca for the full extent of Nero's tyranny. He does not blame Seneca for Nero's persecution of the Christians. He bases this acquittal on Seneca's correspondence with St Paul as 'proof' that Seneca thought Nero's later acts were 'greatly evil' (24.5.25). Petrarch concludes his letter wishing that Seneca had stayed close with Paul:

> If only you had remained more constant and you had not torn yourself away from him at the end, so that with that preacher of the truth you would have died for the truth itself and for the promise of your eternal reward and for the name of the One who promises it.
>
> (24.5.26)

Thus, as James Ker points out, for Petrarch, Seneca died either too late or too early. Either Seneca should have followed his philosophical instincts and lived out his life as an exile in Corsica, or he should have lived long enough to accept the Christian faith.[22] While this letter demonstrates some of the standard critiques that have dogged Seneca, namely, hypocrisy, inconstancy and vanity, it also reveals some of the main questions that would surround his life during this period. Was Seneca a Christian? How many Senecas were there, and who wrote what? We can see both of these questions at work in Petrarch's letter. In fact, he ends with a note of doubt, dating his letter 'the first day of August, in the 1348th year from the birth of Him, about whom I remain uncertain whether you knew anything' (24.5.26).

We can see a critical assessment of Seneca's life, death and relationship to Nero in Chaucer's *The Canterbury Tales*. Seneca is one of Chaucer's most frequently quoted 'authorities'.[23] Yet in *The Canterbury Tales*, he is not simply quoted to lend authority. Often the references to Seneca do not fit well into their context and can reveal how Chaucer's characters simply look to old names to buttress their claims, but do not live up to the morality Seneca advises.[24] Chaucer includes a brief biography of Seneca as part of 'The Monk's Tale', *De casibus virorum illustrium* (B2 3653–740). The Monk begins with Satan and Adam and eventually comes to Nero. He cites 'Suetonius' as his source, but the version ultimately goes back to *The Romance of the Rose* (1275). Chaucer portrays the relationship between Seneca and Nero in a manner that differs from his sources.[25] The section on Nero consists of 11 stanzas; the first four tell of Nero's crimes, the middle three of Seneca, and the final four tell of Nero's fall at the hands of Fortune. The tale praises Seneca as a 'maister' who was at the time 'the flower of morality', but adds the qualification 'but if books lye' (3685–8). The Monk notes that Seneca did steer Nero away from tyranny and vice, but also states that he only taught Nero 'letturure and curteisye' (3686). Seneca's instruction made Nero 'so konnyng and so sowple' (3690). Seneca may be 'wise' and 'moral', according to the Monk, but he does not state that he made Nero so. We can see a critique of Seneca's teaching of Nero. Perhaps his ultimate goal was to bend Nero to his will by rendering him not virtuous, but rather 'supple'.[26] Indeed, according to the Monk, Nero kills Seneca because as a youth he was continually made to rise in his teacher's presence (3701–4). We can perhaps glean a faint trace of Suetonius's claims that Seneca used Nero and his position to glorify himself and his abilities, and a more distant echo of Dio's statement that Seneca actually taught Nero how to be a tyrant.

Despite the questions about the relationship between Seneca and Nero in the ancient and medieval sources, *On Mercy* served as a model for late medieval and Renaissance theories of kingship. Eventually, the favour that it had enjoyed for centuries came under attack in Machiavelli's *The Prince*. As Peter Stacey has suggested, in this treatise Machiavelli attempts to destroy Seneca's portrait of a ruler guided by the ideal of universal reason. For Machiavelli, the prince and politics are guided by self-interest, violence and deception.[27] Yet even this portrait of the prince has a Senecan parallel, not in his portrait of the ideal king, but in that of the tyrant in *On Mercy* and his plays.

This renewed engagement with Seneca also saw the writing of commentaries on his work, most notably his tragedies. The work of the English Dominican Nicholas Trevet in explicating Seneca's tragedies circulated widely. The rediscovery of the oldest surviving manuscript of Seneca's plays, now known as the *Etruscus* (E), in northern Italy, led to intensified study of Seneca's life and drama among a group of 'protohumanistic' scholars in Padova. The text was found by Lovato dei Lovati (1240/41–1309), who produced a biography and commentary. His student, Albertino Mussato, did so as well and even went so far as to call Seneca 'a silent supporter of the Christians'(1.1).[28] He mainly draws his evidence for this claim from the letters between Seneca and Paul. He praises Seneca's wisdom and learning and attributes a 'theological quality' to his plays (4). Yet Mussato's love for Seneca went even deeper; his reading of the plays inspired him to revive the tradition of Latin drama, which had died out some 1,200 years earlier with *Hercules Oetaeus*, the work of another admirer of Seneca. We will spend several pages recounting how Seneca helped to shape the development of drama in Latin and modern languages over the next 300 years. We can only offer a very general sketch of this process that began with Mussato. After considering neo-Latin dramas in Italy, we will move to considering Seneca in English tragedy.

Rebirth of Tragedy in Latin

As we noted, the Senecan *Hercules Oetaeus* represents the end of classical drama. We have sporadic evidence that Senecan drama was read throughout the Middle Ages, but it is not until the early 1300s that we see a creative reworking of his plays into new dramas that combine classical, Christian and contemporary themes. One of the major fruits of this intensified study of Senecan drama is the Latin drama *Ecerinis*, written by Albertino Mussato in 1314.

Mussato's play is not a mythological drama. Like *Octavia*, it uses Senecan themes to portray recent historical events. The play recounts the tyranny of Ezzelino III da Romano (1194–1259), who fought in northern Italy for the emperor Frederick II. As Gary Grund notes in his edition and translation of the play, the events of the previous century serve as a commentary on the contemporary threat posed to Padova by Cangrande della Scala of Verona.[29] Like *Octavia*, the chorus is made up of patriotic citizens; but unlike the Roman play, the tyrant is punished at the end. This play had such an effect on the people of Padua that Mussato

> was crowned with the poetic laurel on December 3, 1315 ... and a statute was passed that the play should be recited every Christmas season to strengthen the patriotism of the citizenry. The readings took place in Mussato's presence in the town hall of Padua.[30]

The play itself is an impressive and surrealistic amalgamation of thirteenth-century Italian history, Christianity, Senecan tragedy – *Thyestes* in particular – and *Octavia*. It is particularly interesting to note how the latent Republicanism in *Octavia* is accentuated centuries later to support the independence of Padua. As we have seen, Seneca was no champion of restoring the Republic, but his plays, his life and particularly his representation in *Octavia*, which during this period was believed to be by Seneca himself, provided not only a powerful way of representing the outrages of tyranny, but also suggested how to stand against it. Like Seneca's Atreus, Ezzelino is proud to be a tyrant and glories in his evil lineage. According to his mother,

Ezzelino's father is Satan himself, who raped her to produce the tyrant and his brother. The impetus driving this play, and Ezzelino himself, is the Senecan ideal of outdoing past horrors, creating something greater and more terrible than anything previously known. By making Ezzelino proud of his Satanic origins, Mussato can have him surpass his pagan Roman predecessors. As Ezzelino declares after learning his parentage from his mother:

> What more do you want, brother? Do you feel shame, madman, to have so great a father? Do you deny our divine origin? We are born from the gods. In the past, Romulus and Remus were not elevated by Mars with so great a family line. This god is greater and has the widest kingdom. He is the king of vengeance, at whose command mighty princes, kings and leaders suffer punishment.
>
> (75–81)

A Neronian context is invoked throughout the play. The chorus declares that Ezzelino's tyranny surpasses that of Nero (246). Ezzelino sees himself as the scourge of God, noting that all the murders committed by Nero 'of happy memory' (393) happened through God's will (395–7). This declaration comes at the conclusion of a brief Senecan reason versus passion debate between Ezzelino and a Friar.

In this play, however, the tyrants are punished. The final act is one long scene dominated by a messenger speech relating joyfully and in vivid detail the deaths of Ezzelino, his brother and his brother's family. The horrors of infanticide that so dominate Seneca's plays now turn into a cause for celebration as the tyrant's line has been extirpated. The play ends with a piece of moralising, as the chorus voices sentiments that only get buried by the violence that surrounds them in Seneca's plays. In the last lines of Mussato's play, the happy citizens declare, 'This stable order does not cease: virtue seeks the allurements above, crime seeks out the shadows below. You have been warned. Learn the unchanging law while you can' (625–9).

Let us turn to another neo-Latin drama to see how Seneca fares in a classical, mythological context. Gregorio Correr (1409–64) came from a Venetian family with deep ties to the papacy. He too was called to the Church, and from 1448 was the abbot at San Zenone in Verona. Yet in his youth he focused on literature, composing *Procne* with an appended discussion of Latin metre at some point between 1426 and 1431. With this play, Correr fills an important 'gap' in the Senecan dramatic corpus. As we have seen, the story of Procne, Philomela and Tereus, famous from Ovid's *Metamorphoses*, lurks behind Seneca's plays, *Thyestes* in particular (Procne and Philomela also serve as a model for Octavia in her play). Thus, Correr presents this essential Senecan intertext in dramatic form, and although the tale is from Ovid, Correr makes it clear in the opening prose *argumentum* that Seneca's *Thyestes* serves as his underlying model (6). As Seneca's play opens with the ghost of Tantalus, so Correr's play opens with the ghost of the Thracian Diomedes, who used to serve his guests to his man-eating horses until he himself was fed to them by Hercules. Like Seneca's Tantalus, Diomedes is compelled to return to his house and ensure that a greater crime happens (34–49). At the end of his speech, the Furies whip his face and summon him back to Hades (64–7; see *Thy.* 96–7). Correr also paradoxically leaves out Ovid's story of metamorphoses, where the three are transformed into birds at the end, and concludes his play in Senecan fashion. There is no resolution and Tereus's and Procne's final words echo those of Atreus and Thyestes:

> Tereus: The Furies will pursue you.
> Procne: Itys alone will pursue his father.
>
> (1060)

Seneca's *Thyestes* concludes:

> Thyestes: The avenging gods [i.e. the Furies] will be present. My prayers hand you over to them for punishment.
> Atreus: I hand you over to your sons for punishment.
>
> (1110–12)

Medea also looms large in this play and serves as a model for Procne to surpass (700–1). Once Tereus recognises his son (993–4; see also *Thy.* 1005–6, *Medea* 1021), Procne combines ideas from *Thyestes* and *Medea*. She declares that she has achieved the pinnacle of her desires (1022, see *Thy.* 911–13, 1096–7). Paradoxically, through this murder, Philomela's virginity has been restored, as has the fidelity of Procne's marriage (1023–4; see *Medea* 982–4 and *Thy.* 1098–9). Tereus also recognises Procne as having surpassed the crimes of Medea (1042–7). This play's vivid amalgamation of Senecan and Ovidian excess was popular in its own day and even won the admiration of the future Pope Pius II. Aeneas Sylvius, who, eight years before his elevation to the pontificate in 1458, published a treatise on the education of children (*De liberorum educatione*), notes that Seneca is to be read with profit, 'but we have no Latin tragedian besides Seneca, except for Gregorio Correr of Venice, who, when I was a youth, turned the story of Tereus, which comes from Ovid, into a tragedy.'[31]

Seneca and English Drama

During the sixteenth century Senecan tragedy reached the peak of its influence and esteem. Several critics declared that Senecan tragedy represented the ultimate achievement in the genre, surpassing even the Greeks (G. Giraldi Cinthio, *Discorsi* 1543, Bartolomaeo Ricci, *De Imitatione* 1545 and J. C. Scaliger, *Poetices* 1561).[32] His plays were translated into modern languages and served as models for the writers in the vernacular throughout western Europe.[33] For example, in France, the plays of Étienne Jodelle (1532–73), Robert Garnier (1544–90), Pierre Corneille (1606–84) and Jean Racine (1639–99) developed and critiqued Senecan drama. Tristan l'Hermite (*c.*1601–55) staged his *La mort de Sénèque* in 1644. With Racine's *Phèdre* (1677), we can start to see Seneca eclipsed by Euripides as the preferred classical model; but nevertheless, Seneca remains a key, if suppressed intertext.[34] In England, Elizabethan drama is typically said to begin with Thomas Sackville's and Thomas Norton's *Gorboduc* (1561), a play based upon the crisis that arose when the legendary English king divided his realm between his sons, Ferrex and Porrex. In the past, *Gorboduc* has been dubbed 'pure Seneca'.[35] This play's mingling of native English tradition and contemporary political concerns (for example, the problems of royal succession under a 'virgin queen') with Senecan elements will set the tone for the more well-known English plays of the late sixteenth and early seventeenth centuries. During this period in England, some authors, such as the Countess of Pembroke and her circle, also engaged with Seneca as filtered through French works and adhered to more stately and decorous neoclassical ideals. But their works seem not to have been part of the wider theatrical world in London.[36] Indeed it was largely the public theatres and professional playwrights, such as Thomas Kyd and William Shakespeare, who combined Senecan tragedy and philosophy with native English, Biblical and Continental traditions to provide the some of the richest and most complex engagements with and transformations of Seneca.[37]

Seneca's *Trojan Women* (*Troas*) was performed in Latin at Trinity College, Cambridge in 1551–2 and again in 1560–1.[38] During this period, Thomas Heywood translated *Trojan Women*, *Thyestes* and *Hercules Furens* in 1559, 1560 and 1561 respectively. In the preface to his translation of *Thyestes*, Heywood provides a lengthy poetic account of how he was encouraged to continue after producing his translation of *Trojan Women*. He states that Seneca appeared to him in a dream wanting to meet his translator (39–50). He encourages him to continue his works:

> 'If thou', quoth he, 'be whom I seek, if glory aught thee move
> Of mine to come in after age, if Senec's name thou love
> Alive to keep, I thee beseech again to take thy pen,
> In metre of thy mother tongue to give sight of men
> My other works, whereby thou shalt deserve of them and me
> No little thanks, when they themselves my Tragedies shall see
> In English verse that never yet could Latin understand.'
>
> (50–7)[39]

Seneca's wish was heeded.

Translations of the other plays followed quickly in the 1560s. Only the *Phoenissae* remained untranslated until 1581. A complete collection of his ten tragedies, that is, including *Octavia* and *Hercules Oetaeus*, were published together in 1581. While these translations certainly enhanced the dissemination of Seneca in England, schoolboys would have read his works in Latin from an early age. Yet 'schoolboys' is too limiting a term. Queen Elizabeth I is credited with translating (rather freely) part of the second choral ode from *Hercules Oetaeus* (600–99) around 1589. Around 1567, she translated *Moral Epistles* 107.[40] In several of the famous early English dramatic receptions of Seneca, by Christopher Marlowe, Thomas Kyd and Shakespeare's *Titus Andronicus*, we find Senecan characters providing an important model, for example the avenger in Kyd's *The Spanish Tragedy* and Shakespeare's *Titus Andronicus*, as well as the megalomaniacal overreacher, as in Marlowe's *Tamburlaine*. We also see Senecan tragedy and philosophy quoted in the original Latin. The characters often gloss these quotations to enable them to be fully understood by the audience. Yet Seneca is not quoted in the original simply to give the play an air of classicism or to show the learning of the author. Kyd's *The Spanish Tragedy*, for example, engages with both the Latin and the conflicting attitudes of Seneca's plays in an extremely complex manner. Seneca is set against himself as both a counsellor of Stoic endurance and of violent revenge. These contrasting ideals come out most clearly when Hieronimo gives a long speech in which he debates whether to avenge his son.

According to the stage direction, Hieronimo enters 'with a book in his hand' and apparently begins to read from it:

> *Vindicta mihi!*
> Ay, heaven will be revenged of every ill,
> Nor will they suffer murder unrepaid.
> Then stay, Hieronimo, attend their will,
> For mortal men may not appoint their time.
>
> (3.13.1–5)

Initially, it would seem that Hieronimo is reading from the Bible for advice and comfort after his son's murder. He may quote part of the Latin translation of Paul's letter to the Romans, 'vengeance is mine, I will repay, says the Lord' (Rom. 12:19; see Duet. 32.36). This sudden appearance of Christianity is startling. Although the play ostensibly refers to struggles between Spain and Portugal in the mid-1550s, other than this apparent quoting from the New Testament, references to Christianity are entirely absent. In fact, the world of the play is more classical than Christian. This is immediately apparent in the opening scene in which the ghost of Andrea appears and describes his time in a thoroughly classical Underworld complete with Charon, the three judges, Pluto and Proserpina. After his description, he is joined by Revenge to watch the play unfold. Readers of Seneca will be reminded of the opening of *Thyestes*, but Kyd develops the latent potential in Seneca's prologue, and has his ghost and Fury watch the entire play and serve as its chorus.

The question of what book Hieronimo has in his hand becomes even more complicated after we hear his next Latin quote and gloss:

Per scelus semper tutum est sceleribus iter.
Strike, and strike home where wrong is offered thee,
For evils unto ills conductors be,
And death's the worst of resolution.

(3.13.5–8)

This Latin quote is an adaptation of Seneca's *Agamemnon* 115: *per scelera semper sceleribus tutum est iter*, 'through crimes the way is always safe for crimes'. This quote encourages Hieronimo to take revenge and also realise that Lorenzo, the murderer of his son, will likely attempt to cover up his crime by murdering him. We can see a key conflict set out between the Christian refusal of revenge and the Senecan ideal that crime justifies further crime and is a logical means of self-preservation. If we originally thought that the book in Hieronimo's hand was the Bible, now it appears to be Seneca. How can we reconcile the two quotes with the stage direction that Hieronimo enters with one book in his hand? Perhaps we are to imagine that he is reading from a commonplace book of Latin quotations. Yet a further Senecan layer can be added to the opening quotation *vindicta mihi*. Although judging from his gloss on the Latin, Hieronimo appears to have the Biblical quotation in mind, it is noteworthy that he does not mention the Bible, God, Paul or Christ. He only notes that 'heaven will be revenged' and calls on himself to 'attend their will' (3.13.2–4). This ambiguity ('heaven', 'their will') suggests that rather than the Biblical passage, Hieronimo may be thinking of a more generalised ideal of heavenly or cosmic justice that need not be based on Christian ideas. Furthermore, the phrase *vindicta mihi* can be brought back to Seneca as well, or at least to a Senecan context, which suggests, as one commentator on the play points out, that Hieronimo may only be holding in his hand Seneca's plays.[41] In *Octavia*, which was during this period generally believed to have been by Seneca, Nero speaks in a manner that is reminiscent of the more famous Pauline quote. After putting down the riots that ensued in support of Octavia, Nero's prefect says, 'I report that the rage of the people has been suppressed by the slaughter of a few who were still recklessly resisting.' To which Nero angrily responds, 'And is this enough? In this way do you, a soldier, listen to your leader? You restrain them? Is this the vengeance I am owed?' (*haec vindicta debetur mihi*, *Oct.* 846–9). This is not to imply that the author of *Octavia* was ironically quoting from Paul's letter to the Romans, but rather to show that in the early modern context, when we can be sure that authors like Kyd had read Paul and Seneca, lines from Senecan drama can take on new meanings and have resonances that were not likely available to the original audience.

Hieronimo continues on. After using Seneca's *Agamemnon* to urge himself to strike in vengeance, he then sways himself towards a more Stoic resolve. Here again he uses Seneca as a means of justification:

> For he that think with patience to contend
> To quiet life, his life shall easily end.
> *Fata si miseros juvant, habes salutem;*
> *Fata si vitam negant, habes sepulchrum:*
> If destiny thy miseries do ease,
> Then hast thou health, and happy shalt thou be.
> If destiny deny thee life, Hieronimo,
> Yet shalt thou be assured a tomb;
> If neither, yet this comfort be,
> Heaven covereth him that hath no burial.
>
> (3.13.10–19)

The Latin is taken from Seneca's *Troades* 510–12, where Andromache is convincing Astyanax to hide in Hector's tomb. Taken out of context in Hieronimo's interpretation, these lines encourage him to lead a Stoic life of quiet, to follow destiny, be happy if he lives, content if he dies and not have any fear about what happens to his body when he leaves it. Thus, Hieronimo reveals one of the contradictions of the Senecan corpus. The tragedies, especially when brief passages are quoted out of context, may be seen to glorify and justify revenge and, along with his philosophy, to encourage a life of Stoic endurance, patience and submission to fate. Given this apparent victory of Stoicism, Hieronimo's next line comes as a surprise: 'And now to conclude, I will revenge his death!' (3.13.20). The abrupt nature of this conclusion is startling, but not without precedent in Senecan tragedy, where, for example, in *Agamemnon*, Clytemnestra suddenly gives up her desire for revenge (239–43) after Aegisthus enters and then unexpectedly regains her nerve (306–9). Yet after he makes this decision, once again like Senecan characters, Hieronimo commands himself to control his passions and follow through with his plans (3.13.39–44, with a quote from Seneca's *Oedipus* 515 at line 35; see also 4.4.21–30).

A key point that separates this play from Seneca is the public world that Kyd's characters inhabit. This is not so much the result of the play being set in the recent past as it is that the avenger is not as autonomous and self-creating as Seneca's characters. Hieronimo must perform his social tasks as the king's knight marshal. The conflict between his public life and his private need for revenge causes those around him to think him mad (4.4.119–20). In a somewhat similar vein, Shakespeare's Titus and Hamlet also appear to be mad as they plot their revenge. Yet Kyd's portrayal of Hieronimo's public duties and private hell are presented in a Senecan manner. We can clearly see the two worlds collide at the end of 3.13. Immediately after the solitary Hieronimo reads Seneca and commands himself to avenge his son, the social world enters. Several petitioners have come to his house in order to ask Hieronimo to 'plead their cases to the King' (3.13.48). One of the citizens makes clear the high reputation for justice that Hieronimo holds, 'There's not any advocate in Spain / That can prevail, or will take half the pain / That he will, in pursuit of equity' (3.13.52–4). In an aside, Hieronimo orders himself to play his public role:

> Now must I bear a face of gravity,
> For thus I used, before my marshalship,
> To plead in cases as corregidor. –
> Come on, sirs, what's the matter?
>
> (3.13.56–9)

His role playing works until he sees an old man who has come to petition for justice after the murder of his son (3.13.78–9). Hearing the old man's suit causes Hieronimo to enter into a state of overwhelming sorrow. In a long speech he talks of his own murdered son and declares that justice does not exist in this world. With language that recalls Seneca's characters echoing Virgil's angry Juno, Hieronimo declares that he will look to the Underworld for aid: 'Though on earth justice will not be found, / I'll down to hell, and in this passion, / knock at the dismal gates of Pluto's court' (3.13.108–10; cf. Virgil *Aen.* 7.312, *Acheronta movebo*). To their great consternation, he tears up the man's petitions. Then, reminiscent of Seneca's Medea, Hieronimo hallucinates that the old man is his dead son's unavenged spirit (3.13.133–51) and that he is a Fury (3.13.153–8). Nevertheless, Hieronimo still tries to use public and lawful means to avenge his son, but is thwarted from seeing the king by Lorenzo (3.14.77–8). In the end, the public world dissolves into the illusion of the play-within-a-play in which Hieronimo is able to kill his son's murderers, but not without his wife and his son's beloved Bel-imperia killing themselves as well.

A similarly complex engagement with Seneca's prose and poetry occurs in John Marston's *Antonio's Revenge*. This play likely dates from the winter of 1600–1, and is the tragic sequel to Marston's love-comedy *Antonio and Mellida* (1599). The earlier play narrates how after Piero Sforza, the duke of Venice, defeated the fleet of Andrugio, duke of Genoa, the two were reconciled and planned to marry their children, Mellida and Antonio respectively, to unite their lands. *Antonio's Revenge* opens with Piero's bloody plans to break up the marriage. He murders Andrugio, kills the son of Pandulfo Feliche and sets the corpse in his daughter's room in order to condemn her for being unchaste. He eventually plans to exonerate his daughter, marry Andrugio's recent widow, Maria, and murder her son, Antonio. The ghost of Andrugio appears to both Antonio and Maria telling them of Piero's crimes and urges his son to avenge his death. Antonio feigns madness, enlists the help of Pandulfo Feliche and others, murders Piero's son, Julio, and serves him up as 'sweetmeats' to Piero, whose tongue has been cut out. Then all three stab the duke to death. The parallels with *The Spanish Tragedy* are clear throughout, as are those to Shakespeare's *Hamlet*, which was likely written at the same time as Marston's play. It remains a matter of debate whether Marston simply copied Shakespeare's idea, or if the two playwrights decided to compose a play on a similar theme for their respective playhouses, with Marston writing a something of a parody of revenge tragedy to be acted by the boys of Paul's Playhouse.

Antonio's Revenge, despite its interest for students of Seneca and revenge plays, has its own tragic performance history. As noted earlier, it likely was contemporaneous with *Hamlet* and presents roughly the same story in Italy rather than Denmark. As such, it has been completely overshadowed by Shakespeare's play. Soon after it was performed, Marston was mercilessly ridiculed as the figure of 'Crispinus' in Ben Jonson's *The Poetaster*. It seems that the play was never performed again, save for one performance in 1967.[42]

Marston's play juxtaposes the two sides of the Senecan corpus and shows how Stoic *apatheia* gives way to emotion and revenge. Seneca is quoted copiously throughout, both in Latin and English translation. *Thyestes* is the main tragic intertext, but passages and themes from *Octavia*, *Medea* and *Agamemnon* are also present. The main philosophical texts are *On Providence* and the (possibly Senecan) *De remediis fortuitorum*, which follows the English translation by Robert Whittington.[43] At the start, Pandulfo is a Stoic. When he learns of his son's death, he laughs (1.5.26), and later gives a long speech explaining the reason for his laughter. He concludes by referencing Seneca's *On Providence* 6.6: 'This heart in valour even Jove out-goes; / Jove is without, but this 'bove sense of woes; / and such a one, eternity' (1.5.99–101). In this same revelation scene, when Antonio learns of his father's death, which he thinks is from natural causes, he brings in the world of Senecan tragedy by stating that nature should shake and the earth should crack under him for his misery (1.5.32–3).

Act 2.3 begins with Antonio entering with a book, which we soon learn contains quotes from Seneca. He tells his friends not to worry about his sorrow; he is trying to cure himself: 'I am taking physic; here's philosophy' (2.3.42). After they leave he reads aloud in Latin a passage slightly adapted from *On Providence* 6.6, which commands endurance of pain and notes that this ability allows humans to surpass god. Thus, here we have the full Latin quotation that Pandulfo alluded to in the previous act. But this 'physic' proves to be no help for Antonio. Antonio declares that he wrote it down in happier times and now finds these words to have no value (2.3.49–56). Indeed, this play reveals that Seneca's promises of surpassing god by conquering the emotions render one less than human.

Antonio is turned into a Senecan avenger by his father's ghost, who reveals the truth of his death and concludes quoting a line from *Thyestes* in Latin, *scelera non ulcisceris, nisi vincis* ('you do not avenge crimes, unless you surpass them' 3.1.51 = *Thy.* 195–6). Antonio transforms himself into Atreus by quoting a pastiche of lines spoken by the ghost of Tantalus at the opening of *Thyestes* (3.2.15–22 = *Thy.* 13–15, 75–9, 80–1). It is noteworthy that after the appearance of his father's ghost, Antonio adopts words from Seneca's ancestral ghost, but Marston has made important changes. When Seneca's Tantalus appears at the start of *Thyestes*, he does not wish for the horrors of the play to take place and only reluctantly infects his house after the Fury drives him to do so (86–105). In fact, the lines that Antonio quotes urging himself on to revenge are spoken by Tantalus, asking for more punishments to be heaped upon him rather than continue his familial crimes. Thus, it may seem that Marston has carelessly taken lines from Seneca and used them in the wrong context. Seneca's Tantalus does not wish the cycle of blood to continue. Yet Marston seems to correct this opening scene of the reluctant Tantalus. Not only does he take lines that reject revenge and turn them into lines that encourage it, he also adds his own Latin to the Senecan text: '*Antonii vocem excipe / Properantis ad vos: Ulciscar*' ('hear the voice of Antonio / as he hurries to you: I shall be avenged' 3.2.21–2). In both texts, the 'you' refers both to the judges of the Underworld and those punished within it. Marston has changed *Tantali* to *Antonii* and added the final declaration of revenge. Seneca's text was a model, but also one that could be cut up and emended. Antonio's name is inscribed into *Thyestes*, as Marston does away with the fear and hesitation of Tantalus that opens Seneca's play.

Pandulfo, too, rejects Seneca's philosophy and joins with Antonio. When he sees his dead son's 'trunk' he first continues with his Stoic laughter. Overcome with grief, he realises that human emotion must win out: 'Man will break out, despite philosophy'. He continues with a metatheatrical reference to the child actors who are performing this play:

> Why, all this while I ha' but played a part,
> Like some boy that acts a tragedy,
> Speaks burly words and raves out passion;
> But when he think upon his infant weakness,
> He drops his eye. I spake more than a god,
> Yet I am less than a man.
>
> (4.5.46–52)

For Pandulfo, Stoicism is childish acting, which allows one to think he can surpass god (as Seneca promises in *On Providence* 6.6), but in reality denies one's essential humanity.

Indeed, revenge not only guides the world of this play, but also the world above. Echoing Medea and Atreus, Antonio declares, 'O, my soul's enthroned / in the triumphant chariot of revenge' (3.5.18–19). Inverting the ideals of endurance quoted from Seneca's *On Providence*, at the start of the final act the Ghost states, 'Now down looks providence / T'attend the last act of my son's revenge' (5.1.10–11). After giving up his Stoicism, Pandulfo states that heaven supports their revenge (5.3.15). There is also a political element that justifies the play's revenge. Although Piero and his son are killed to settle personal vendettas, by the end of the play it is clear that the people wish to overthrow the tyrant and are near revolt (5.1.20, 5.3.20). After the Thyestean feast of revenge, the final scene contributes to the play's political dimension. The Senators of Venice congratulate Antonio and his followers, declaring them to be 'blest' (5.6.10). The Senators hope that the tyrannicides' 'honours live / religiously held sacred, even for ever and ever' (5.6.10–11), and thank them for their Herculean efforts in ridding the state of pollution (5.6.12–13). In fact, the Senators offer as a reward the 'chiefest fortunes of the Venice state' (5.6.24). Antonio and Pandulfo reject any reward; for them revenge is more personal than political. They make it clear that they will spend the rest of their lives in voluntary atonement for their murders (5.6.28–36). We can see how this play cycles through and builds upon several themes from Seneca. The Stoic world of *apatheia* is rejected for the tragic world of revenge. Although this world seems to be justified, the excesses of Senecan revenge do not have the final word. Private revenge is justified politically, but still must be further tamed by penitence 'enclosed / in holy verge of some religious order' (5.6.34–5).[44]

Although Seneca is only one of many factors that shape Shakespeare's plays, his drama and philosophy are crucial ingredients.[45] Indeed, Shakespeare portrayed events from Roman history in *Titus Andronicus*, *Julius Caesar*, *Antony and Cleopatra*, *Coriolanus* and *Cymbeline*. The famous passage from *Hamlet* is often cited as evidence for Shakespeare's admiration of Seneca. When the troupe of actors arrives at the Danish court, Polonius declares:

> The best actors in the world, either for tragedy, comedy, history, pastoral, pastoral-comical, historical-pastoral, scene individable or poem unlimited. Seneca cannot be too heavy, nor Plautus too light for the law of writ and the liberty. These are the only men.
>
> (*HAMLET* 2.2.333–7)

The context of this praise of Seneca must also be taken into account. The speaker is of course Polonius, not Shakespeare himself. Polonius is a comic character, not particularly aware of what is going on around him and prone to bombastic and sententious statements. His hyperbole and citation of the different genres and hybrid genres that the players are able to perform also suggests that we should be wary of seeing in the passage simply unadulterated praise of Seneca and Plautus.

Like his contemporaries Kyd and Marston, Shakespeare dutifully quotes Senecan tag lines, though rarely in Latin and never as explicitly as Hieronimo's reading of quotes. The line from *Agamemnon* that a criminal's safety can only come from committing more crimes (*per scelera semper sceleribus tutum est iter* 115) is referenced by Shakespeare twice in *Macbeth* (1606):

> Things bad begun make strong themselves by ill.
>
> (3.2.55)
>
> I am in blood
> stepp'd in so far that, should I wade no more,
> returning were as tedious as go o'er.
>
> (3.4.135–7)

In *Richard III* (1597), King Richard urges himself on similarly:

> Murder her brothers and then marry her –
> Uncertain way of gain! But I am in
> So far in blood that sin will pluck on sin
>
> (4.2.62–4)

In his comedy *The Malcontent* (1604), John Marston quotes the Latin to show how the idea has become commonplace in English:

> MENDOZA: Then she's but dead; 'tis resolute she dies.
> Black deed only through black deed safely flies.
> MALEVOLE: Pooh! *Per scelera semper sceleribus tutum est iter.*
> MENDOZA: What! Art a scholar? Art a politician?
> Sure thou art an arrant knave.
>
> (5.4.13–16)

Shakespeare also makes use of Seneca's prose works. For example, Macbeth's famous metatheatrical lines of despair at the end of his play allude to a passage from Seneca's *Moral Epistles*:[46]

> Life's but a walking shadow; a poor player,
> That struts and frets his hour upon the stage,
> And then is heard no more; it is a tale
> Told by an idiot, full of sound and fury,
> Signifying nothing.
>
> (*MACBETH* 5.5.24–8)

Seneca

Seneca writes:

> The laughter of those, who are called happy, is false; but their sadness is heavy and a festering sore. In fact, their sadness is all the heavier because they cannot openly show that they are sad, but rather in the midst of their sorrows that eat away that their very hearts, it is necessary for them to act happy. I rather frequently make use of this example, for nothing else is better at expressing this mime of human life, which assigns parts to us, which we play poorly.
>
> (EP. 80.6–7)

Indeed, it is in *Macbeth* that we can trace one of Shakespeare's most sustained and creative uses of Seneca, in particular his *Medea*. As Robert Miola has shown, in *Macbeth* Shakespeare separates the character of Medea into multiple players.[47] Medea the murderous infanticide becomes Lady Macbeth and Medea the witch is portrayed by the Three Weird Sisters. At the start of the play, Lady Macbeth claims that she would murder her child rather than break her oath (1.7.54–9). She also echoes Seneca's Medea's command to herself to 'drive off feminine fears' (42). Before plotting the murder of King Duncan with Macbeth, Lady Macbeth calls on the spirits, 'unsex me here, / and fill me from crown to the toe top-full / of direst cruelty!' (1.5.39–41). The overall movement of Seneca's play is inverted as well. Medea grows in strength throughout her play and the murder of her children leads to her climactic quasi-apotheosis. Macbeth, Lady Macbeth and the Witches start off as powerful and confident, but they lose their power by the end. In fact, it is the murder of King Duncan, Macbeth's kinsman, at the start of the play, which causes the fall of Macbeth and Lady Macbeth. Murder does not allow the two to soar to the heights of heaven as it does for Medea.

Shakespeare makes further radical departures from Seneca. As Macbeth laments that after killing King Duncan, his hands will never be clean (2.2.59–62), words likely based on Senecan models (see *Pha.* 715–8 and *Herc.* 1323–9), he and his wife hear a knocking on the castle gate. In the next scene, we are taken to the source of that knocking and treated to the comical scene of the drunken Porter pretending that he is at Hell's gate receiving damned souls (2.3.1–20). Thus, we see the union of tragedy and comedy, which is almost entirely absent from Seneca's plays – although Atreus's self-proclaimed apotheosis once he hears his brother belch provides an important exception. Furthermore, despite the humour in this scene, the Porter's pretending that Macbeth's castle is Hell is not simply a joke. Macbeth and Lady Macbeth are now damned. As Macbeth states, he has given up his 'eternal jewel' by killing Duncan (3.1.65–71). Under Macbeth's reign, Scotland has become a hellish tyranny, as Rosse makes clear (4.3.164–73; see also 3.4.32–8). Yet like Medea, who declares that 'her talents have grown through evils' (910), at the end, Macbeth has 'supp'd full with horrors' and has learnt 'almost' to live without fear (5.5.8–15). With this qualification, we see Macbeth still is not able to be granted the paradoxical Stoic triumph that Seneca grants his most powerful characters, Medea and Atreus.

Indeed, Stoic ideas of self-perfection and creation come under scrutiny in Shakespeare. Macbeth foolishly thinks that by killing all who threaten him he can become perfect (3.4.20–1). We can also compare the villain Iago's parody of Biblical parable and Stoic self-creation at the opening of *Othello*. Once Roderigo realises that his love for Desdemona will not be returned, he declares that suicide is the only answer, as he cannot control his love: 'I will incontinently drown myself' (1.3.306). After Iago asks why he has foolishly chosen this end, Roderigo notes, 'It is silliness to live when to live is a torment; and then have we a prescription to die, when death is our physician' (309–11). We may note echoes of Seneca's thoughts on death as the ultimate remedy for an intolerable life, as well as Phaedra's resolve to end her life rather than act on her love for Hippolytus. Iago's response to Roderigo's claim that it is not in his 'virtue to amend' his love for Desdemona uses Stoic ideas of the power of the will and reason set within a Christian context, which would have been familiar from Jesus's parable of the sower (Matt. 13) and Paul's declaration that one reaps what one sows (Gal. 6.7). Iago notes:

> Virtue? A fig! 'tis in ourselves that we are thus, or thus. Our bodies are gardens, to which our wills are gardeners ... But we have reason to cool our raging motions, our carnal stings, our unbitted lusts; whereof I take this, that you call love, to be a sect or scion.
>
> (1.3.320–2; 330–3)

When Roderigo still is not convinced of his own powers over himself, Iago sums up Stoic theory on the passions, reminiscent of passages from both *On Anger* and Phaedra's Nurse: 'It is merely a lust of the blood and a permission of the will' (1.3.335–6).

While Shakespeare problematises the Senecan ideal of perfection as presented in both his philosophy and tragedy, during this period there also develops a minor, but important, tradition of the 'anti-revenge' play, as seen in *The Atheist's Tragedy* and *The Revenge of Bussy D'Ambois*.[48] As with the other plays we have considered, especially *The Spanish Tragedy* and *Antonio's Revenge*, ideals from Seneca's two bodies of work are set against each other, but in the two 'anti-revenge' plays, while the demands for vengeance are still acted upon, violence is downplayed and the petty need for revenge is set against the ultimate cosmic order. To conclude our investigation of Seneca on the English Renaissance stage we will consider George Chapman's *The Revenge of Bussy D'Ambois* (1610 or 1611) because it looks closely at Stoic philosophy and even declares its hero to be a follower of Seneca. The play tells of events that occurred in France during the reign of Henry III (1551–89). Chapman dedicates his play to Thomas, the earl of Arundel, who was Catholic. Chapman may have hoped that the portrayal of events in this Catholic country and their recent bloody struggles with Protestantism (the St Bartholomew Day massacre is mentioned) would have impressed his dedicatee. In his opening letter, Chapman fears that his 'scenical presentation' might 'meet with some maligners' (Maus 1995: 176). Indeed, the avenging hero in this play, Clermont, the brother of the murdered Bussy D'Ambois, is more of a philosopher than an Atreus. Echoing Seneca, Clermont agrees with the trope that all the world is a stage (1.1.330). But he then offers a long speech clarifying that stages are only to be respected if we follow what 'the good Greek moralist says of them' and proceeds to quote ideas that may come from Epictetus on the subject (1.1.334–40).[49] According to Clermont, plays are only worthy if they teach us detachment and allow us, like Democritus, to laugh at all of the events that occur (1.1.340–72). Clermont's admiring patron, the Guise, notes that this was a 'virtuous digression' but then encourages him to avenge his brother (1.1.373–7). Clermont coolly responds that he has written a formal challenge and asks one of his servants to bear it.

Throughout the play, Clermont patiently waits and frequently offers his own take on the order of the universe that combines Christianity with Stoicism:

> Good and bad hold never
> Anything in common: you can never find
> Things' outward care, but you neglect your mind.
> God hath the whole world perfect made and free,
> His parts to th' use of th' All; men then that [be]
> Parts of that All must, as the general sway
> Of that importeth, willingly obey
> In everything without their power to change.
> He that, unpleased to hold his place, will range
> Can in no other be contained that's fit,
> And so resisting th' All, is crushed with it.
>
> (3.4.54–65; see also 4.1.131–4)

When King Henry asks the Guise what makes 'this Clermont such a rare one' (4.4.12), the Guise gives a long speech praising Clermont's imperviousness to Fortune and his ability to put aside his anger, despite the wrongs done to him. He concludes:

> In short, this Senecal man is found in him:
> He may with heaven's immortal powers compare,
> To whom the day and fortune equal are.
> Come fair or foul, whatever change can fall,
> Fixed in himself, he still is one to all.
>
> (4.4.42–6)

All of this philosophising, however, has led to such an interminable delay in the action that finally, at the start of act five, the world of Senecan tragedy intrudes. The last act opens with the ghost of Clermont's brother appearing and demanding revenge. His opening words are reminiscent of Seneca's ghosts. Yet the world of Senecan vengeance is given a more decorous twist.

The ghost speaks to his brother and urges him on by noting that getting revenge will suit the Christian idea of justice (5.1.78–99). Clermont confines his vengeance to Montsurry, his brother's killer, who dies forgiving his killer and his wife and urges them to spend the rest of their life in penitence (5.5.111–12). Clermont declares these final words to be 'Noble and Christian' (5.5.113). Yet when Clermont learns that the Guise has been killed, he realises that he cannot live without him and decides to kill himself. Having succumbed briefly to the violence and petty demands of this world, Clermont declares that he can no longer live 'ready every hour / to feed thieves, beasts, and be a slave of power' (5.5.191–2). In this play, Senecan violence is Christianised, but suicide is still seen as a noble way to leave the prison of the body.

Seneca in Seventeenth-Century Art and Opera

During this period there was a particular interest in discovering the 'true image' of Seneca. Yet we can also see how this zeal to discover what Seneca looked like led to two famous misidentifications. Peter Paul Rubens's painting, *The Death of Seneca* (c.1614–15 now in Munich, Alte Pinakothek), is based on a black marble statue of a muscular older man, with bent knees, who is slightly crouching at the waist. His right arm is bent; his left arm at his side, but not relaxed. The hands on both arms are large and expressive. His face is turned upwards, perhaps in a look of quiet endurance. At the time, this statue was identified as the dying Seneca. Today it is declared to be a second-century Roman copy of a Hellenistic original, which does not depict Seneca, but rather a fisherman.

A second image of Seneca, of which many copies have been found, is a bust which depicts a bearded man with lines on his cheeks and forehead and a full head of hair. This bust was identified as Seneca in 1598. Rubens himself purchased a copy in 1608, and it can be seen in his painting *The Four Philosophers* (1611, now in Florence, Galleria Palatina, Palazzo Pitti). Today, it remains unknown whom this bust portrays; an idealising portrait of the archaic Greek poet Hesiod is one accepted possibility.[50]

In 1813 a double herm bust of Seneca (his name is inscribed) and Socrates was discovered on the Caelian Hill in Rome. This image exploded the idealisations of Seneca as a heroic-looking, bearded and muscular figure. This 'true image' of Seneca depicts a bald, clean-shaven man, with a full and perhaps overfed-looking face. Although the statue dates from the early third century, scholars have suggested that the bust of Seneca is based on a public honorific statue of Seneca, which was erected during his lifetime.[51] In this statue we see a much more comfortable and aristocratic Seneca, perhaps stressing his political influence, as his face looks strikingly like that of a bust of Cicero.

During the sixteenth century, Seneca appeared on the stage in a new genre. He is a central character in Claudio Monteverdi's opera *L'incoronazione di Poppea*, which was first performed at the Teatro Giovanni e Paolo in Venice 1643. As scholars have pointed out, this is likely to have been the first opera based on a historical event.[52] It starts a long line of operas and other dramatic works that focus on Nero and in which Seneca plays a role.[53] *Octavia* is its main source, but the librettist Giovanni Francesco Busenello made several important changes. *Poppea* is an opera in three acts with a prologue between Fortuna, Amore and Virtù, in which the three debate their superiority. Since the play concludes, unlike *Octavia*, with the wedding of Nerone and Poppea, it seems that Amore wins. Yet this triumph of love is not without its ambiguities, both from the standpoint of history and from the fact Fortuna cannot be held in check for long. Busenello also plays with history by including Seneca's death, which of course came three years after Nero's divorce and wedding.

The portrayal of Seneca is ambiguous. The role is written for a bass, which limits the range of his expressiveness and can make him sound ridiculously pompous. Even before we hear Seneca sing, he is ridiculed by two of Nero's soldiers, who call him a 'cunning fox' and a greedy old man who has built his fortune on the graves of others (1.1).[54] Unlike the Roman play, in this opera Seneca tries to console Ottavia by encouraging Stoic constancy. She and her page (Valetto) find Seneca's advice to be ineffectual, 'useless remedies for the unhappy' (1.4). The opera follows *Octavia,* by having Nerone and Seneca meet and debate Nero's plans and the nature of kingship. Nero finally grows tired of the discussion and dismisses Seneca with a degree of scorn not found in the play, calling him 'an impertinent teacher, and an insolent philosopher'. Yet unlike *Octavia*, Seneca is given the last word, 'The worse argument wins when power clashes with reason' (1.9). Nevertheless, insult and unheeded advice highlight Seneca's lot in Rome. In the next scene, immediately before he passes Seneca's death sentence, Nero calls him 'a decrepit and crazy man' (1.10).

Even in his death scene, Seneca is unable to convince those around him of his beliefs. While Seneca gladly greets the announcement of the capital sentence passed by Nerone as the final test of his philosophy, the group of Famigliari around him respond differently. They beg Seneca not to die and reject Stoicism and Seneca's celebration of death as they sing about how they prefer the joys of this world (2.3).

In this opera Seneca is a central, if ambiguous, character. His death occurs near the midpoint of the play, and as one scholar argues, it 'dissects the drama and sets its moral opening against its immoral conclusion'.[55] Even after his death he remains on the mind of Nerone (2.6) and Poppea (2.12).[56] Despite his baritone pomposity and inability to connect with the characters in the opera, some scholars have declared that Seneca is the hero of the work – although this remains a matter of considerable debate.[57] While Seneca is not favoured by mortals, he is favoured by the gods. Pallade (1.8) comes to Seneca and informs him that his end is close at hand. At the start of the second act, Mercurio announces to Seneca that he will die on this day (2.1). In language that is reminiscent of the final chorus of *Hercules Oetaeus*, Mercurio declares that virtue deifies mortals and so the virtuous Seneca will be allowed to ascend to the heavens. In fact, Busenello wrote a scene that was not included in the opera in which Seneca ascends to heaven heralded by a chorus of virtues.[58] Virtue may be the route to heaven, but this opera suggests that very few, if any, would wish to follow Seneca. The life of a Stoic is a life set apart; Seneca may be loved by the gods, but he cannot connect with humans.

The sixteenth and early seventeenth centuries represent the high point of Seneca's influence. His influence may have even been greater than it was during his lifetime and certainly lasted longer than it did in the years after his death. Yet this was not a period of simple adulation, as we have seen. The old criticisms of Seneca's style by Quintilian and Aulus Gellius were frequently brought up, as were the accusations of hypocrisy, which, according to Tacitus, began during Seneca's lifetime. Seneca was a starting point for critical engagement with a variety of topics, such as the relationship between tragedy and philosophy, the viability of living a Stoic life, the dangers of tyranny and especially the perils of living close to autocratic power.

Decline and Rebirth of Seneca

The nineteenth century was not kind to Seneca. His life and work, when they were even discussed at all, came under withering attack. We can single out August Wilhelm von Schlegel's judgement of his plays as representative of the feeling that would prevail well into the twentieth century. He declares:

> But whatever period may have given birth to the tragedies of Seneca, they are beyond description bombastic and frigid, unnatural both in character and action, revolting from their violation of propriety, and so destitute of theatrical effect, that I believe they were never meant to leave the rhetorical schools for the stage.[59]

Lord Macaulay gives a humorous twist to the criticism of Seneca's style first voiced by Caligula:

> I read through the works of both the Senecas, father and son. There is a great deal in the *Controversiae* both of curious information, and of judicious criticism. As to the son, I cannot bear him. His style affects me in something the same way with that of Gibbon. But Lucius Seneca's affectation is even more rank than Gibbon's. His works are made up of mottoes. There is hardly a sentence which might not be quoted; but to read him straightforward is like dining on nothing but anchovy sauce.[60]

He also points out the futility of Seneca's philosophy:

> For our own part, if we are forced to make a choice between the first shoemaker and the author of the three books *On Anger*, we pronounce

for the shoemakers. It may be worse to be angry than to be wet. But shoes have kept millions from being wet; and we doubt whether Seneca ever kept anybody from being angry.[61]

It would not be until the 1920s that Seneca's fortunes would begin to change for the better: 1927 saw the republication of Thomas Newton's *Seneca: His Tenne Tragedies* of 1581, which contained an introduction by T. S. Eliot. In this introduction, Eliot provides a re-evaluation of Seneca as a dramatist and reminds readers of his importance for the development of early modern drama throughout western Europe.[62] Eliot takes on what he believes to be the three major misunderstandings of the relationship between Seneca and later drama. He states that Seneca is not in fact responsible for the bloody horrors that are spilt across the Renaissance stage, but rather that Seneca's plays are considerably more decorous than they are given credit (Eliot 1932: 64–8). Secondly, Eliot notes that Senecan rhetoric had as much to do with the progress of English verse drama 'as with its faults and delays' (Eliot 1932: 75). Finally, Eliot argues that Seneca was one of the major influences on the 'thought' of Elizabethan drama. He even goes so far as to claim that Seneca was the philosopher lying behind Shakespeare's poetry in the same way that Aquinas lies behind Dante (Eliot 1932: 80–1). This is not to say that Eliot 'forgives' Seneca for the sins of which he is often accused. Eliot does not think that Seneca's plays were intended to be performed, but he does make the intriguing suggestion that they are a distant forerunner of 'modern "broadcasted drama"' (Eliot 1932: 55). He also notes that Seneca's plays suffer in comparison to classical Greek drama, specifically because his characters lack life and credibility. As he notes in his oft-quoted summation:

> In the plays of Seneca, the drama is all in the word, and the word has no further reality behind it. His characters all seem to speak with the same voice, and at the top of it; they recite in turn.
>
> (ELIOT 1932: 54)

Yet Eliot is also careful to place this love of declamatory rhetoric in its cultural context, by noting that it is a product of the age and specifically

Roman tastes, rather than simply evidence that Seneca is an inferior poet (Eliot 1932: 56). We can see here the seeds for the re-evaluation of Seneca that would gradually bloom later in the century. As Eliot argues, Seneca must be treated on his own terms, not simply in comparison to the Greeks. Understanding the history of Seneca's reception during the sixteenth and seventeenth centuries can not only help us to understand 'better' authors such as Shakespeare, but also allows us to reconsider Seneca's place in the history of drama and philosophy.

It is of course difficult, if not impossible, to explain why literary and intellectual tastes change. Can they be related to larger cultural contexts and social forces, as Seneca himself argues in *Moral Epistles* 114? Speaking generally, we may note that after centuries of being seen as the dominant cultural paradigm, the Romans lost precedence to the Greeks during the nineteenth century. In addition, the positive links between empire and progress as well as ideals of good taste and decorum during the nineteenth century also spoke against Seneca. World War I and the ensuing decadence of the 1920s, as well as the rise of new forms of autocracy, may have contributed to a new appreciation of Seneca.

Yet this new appreciation only caught on slowly, and it was not until the last decades of the twentieth century that the new renaissance of Seneca truly began. The main impetus for today's scholarly interest in Seneca may be traced to France, namely, the focus of Pierre Hadot and Michel Foucault on Hellenistic and Roman philosophy.[63] As we have seen, Foucault argued that during the first centuries CE a new model of the self emerged that focused on its care and cultivation. Foucault only considered philosophical texts to articulate his points. As scholars have demonstrated, by limiting himself to philosophy, which typically prescribes norms for the ideal way to act, Foucault misses the full complexity of ancient thought about the self. This point is especially apparent in the case of Seneca, who wrote philosophy, tragedy and satire. Thus, Seneca's philosophy only represents one side of how he pictured the universe and how individuals should relate to themselves and others. Senecan tragedy represents a serious challenge to the ideal of Stoicism, a fact that Foucault does not consider. Nevertheless, Foucault took Seneca seriously as a philosopher and saw him as a thinker central to understanding our modern views about ourselves, our emotions and our place in the universe. Classicists soon began to show interest in Roman thought and literature and to critique Foucault's points about the ancient world.

Martha Nussbaum's *The Therapy of Desire: Theory and Practice in Hellenistic Ethics* (Princeton 1994) vividly demonstrates the importance and relevance of the ancient schools of thought that have existed in the shadows of Plato and Aristotle. As she notes, Stoicism, Epicureanism and Scepticism

> all conceived of philosophy as a way of addressing the most painful problems of human life ... They practiced philosophy not as a detached intellectual technique dedicated to the display of cleverness but as an immersed and worldly art of grappling with human misery.[64]

The final chapters of this important book focus on Seneca, specifically on how anger and the emotions relate to our humanity (Chapter 11) and how Seneca's *Medea* sets up a 'countercosmos' to the Stoic ideal (Chapter 12). In both chapters Nussbaum demonstrates how Seneca brings out the unresolved tensions that lie at the core of living a Stoic life. According to her, these tensions are muted in *On Anger*, but come out particularly when Seneca tells two stories of fathers' dispassionate and flattering reactions to their children being murdered by tyrants (3.14–15). Interestingly, it is Seneca who gets angry, and calls on the gods to curse Praexaspes for his slavish flattery (3.14.3). Seneca soon composes himself and explains what Praexaspes should have done, but as Nussbaum suggests, here

> we find Seneca wrestling with the tensions in his own position ... He can't really say that these parents were right to detach themselves that much, to give way to the demand for flattery as if it didn't really matter.[65]

Her analysis of *Medea* takes this point further:

> What we have discovered, then, is that there are two selves, two pictures of selfhood in the world; two pictures, even, of morality; and that we

must choose between them. The choice is not simple, but tragic. If we go for *eros* and *audacia*, we get crime and murderous anger; if we go for purity, we get flatness and the death of heroic virtue.[66]

Some scholars have questioned the close relationship that Nussbaum sets up between Senecan tragedy and philosophy. Yet her analyses of both bodies of Seneca's work and their possible connections are crucial for understanding the complexity and richness of Seneca and of contemporary Seneca studies.[67]

While the major shift in scholarly interest in Seneca would not begin in earnest until the last years of the twentieth century, the revival of Seneca as a dramatist began much earlier. Despite Schlegel's criticisms of Seneca's plays as not being true dramas – a criticism that has been repeated in scholarly circles ever since – in recent times poets and dramatists have again looked to Seneca for inspiration. This trend began slowly, with Percy Shelley's *The Cenci*.[68] Written in 1819, this play has also been considered 'unstageable'. It tells the story of a Roman aristocratic family domineered by their father, Count Francesco Cenci, who tyrannically wishes to destroy his children, until they have him murdered. The plot was discovered and on 11 September 1599 Cenci's wife, daughter and oldest son were publicly executed on the Ponte Sant'Angelo. Shelley takes this piece of history and weaves a combination of Senecan tragedy refracted through Renaissance drama. *Macbeth* is a key intertext. As in Seneca's plays, here nature turns back on itself, as Cenci's son Bernardo notes: 'He has cast Nature off, which was his shield, / and Nature casts him off, who is her shame' (3.1, p. 47). At the start of the play, Cenci celebrates the sudden death of two of his sons in Spain with a feast. In a moment reminiscent of Atreus, he wishes that the wine he drinks were mixed with his children's blood (1.3, p. 15). He ruins his daughter, Beatrice, by raping her, an act that leads her and her family to plot the Count's murder. The origins of this plot recall Seneca (and Ovid). Beatrice never says explicitly what has been done to her, but as she collects herself and begins to plan her revenge, she channels Ovid's Procne and Medea, as well as Seneca's Medea and Atreus: 'Aye, something must be done; what yet I know not ... something which shall make / the thing that I have suffered but a shadow / In the dread lightning which avenges it' (3.1, p. 38).

After the murder is discovered, Beatrice takes on a Stoic attitude. She remains indifferent to the tortures to which she has been repeatedly subjected. She does have a brief moment where she declares that the universe is not guided by a beneficent god, but rather by the malevolence that was her father (5.4, p. 100). In the end, however, Beatrice dies cheering on her condemned family members by enjoining them, 'So mayest thou die as I do; fear and pain / Being subdued. Farewell! Farewell! Farewell!' (5.4, p. 104). Beatrice's revenge against her father destroys herself and her family. But her final Stoic constancy turns the Christian martyr drama on its head. After the death of her father, the Pope from whom Cenci has repeatedly bought indulgences for his crimes comes to be the authority figure. He condemns the family because he worries that, if he is merciful, there will be more parricides in Rome (a reference to Seneca's critique of Claudius in *On Mercy* 1.23?). Although Beatrice's body has been tortured and she now will be beheaded, she refuses to submit to the Pope. She remains a law unto herself. Despite the violence that has been done to her and the violence she has committed in retaliation against her father, Beatrice declares her purity: 'I lived ever holy and unstained' (5.4, p. 104). *The Cenci* begins as a Senecan revenge drama and ends with the avenger turning into a Stoic martyr, thus harmonising Seneca's two bodies of work in one play. It is likely that Shelley engaged in a close reading of Seneca before writing *The Cenci*. Although she does not note the specific texts, Mary Shelley wrote in her journal for 10 May 1815, 'Shelley reads Seneca every day and all day.'[69]

The violence of the malevolent universe of Seneca's plays, as filtered through Elizabethan, Jacobean and later drama, has shaped the contemporary aesthetic in drama and film. This fascination with Seneca can be demonstrated by the increased performances of his plays in recent years, in both Latin and in translation. It can also be seen in the creative reworkings of Senecan drama. *Phaedra's Love* by the British playwright Sarah Kane (1971–99) stands out as a particularly notable example. Traces of Racine's and Euripides's versions can be found as well. For example, as in Euripides, in Kane's version Phaedra hangs herself. This play premiered on 15 May 1996 at the Gate Theatre in London. In this brief work, Kane transforms Hippolytus into the bored noble that her Nurse accuses Phaedra of being in Seneca's play. Unlike the mythical version in which Hippolytus is a virginal follower of Diana, here he continually engages in sex, but without any pleasure. The set opens with Hippolytus sitting in a dark room, eating a hamburger, watching an increasingly violent Hollywood film and masturbating without emotion into a sock. Phaedra and a doctor look on. She is concerned about her stepson's health, but is continually assured by the doctor that nothing is wrong with him. Kane's Hippolytus shows the darker side of Stoic *apatheia*. Despite the protests of her daughter Strophe, a character invented by Kane, Phaedra confesses her love to Hippolytus, and after over two millennia there is sexual contact between the two. Phaedra performs fellatio. Hippolytus is unimpressed; the only concern he shows for his stepmother is to tell her to see a doctor as he has gonorrhoea (Kane 2001: 84).

Kane magnifies the incestuous theme of self-consuming families that characterises Senecan drama, as we soon learn that Hippolytus is having sex with Strophe, as is Theseus, who did so on the night of his wedding to Phaedra. The play ends with a pummelling combination of sex and violence, which makes the traditional dismemberment of Hippolytus look tame. Instigated by the disguised Theseus, Hippolytus is torn apart by a mob, members of which have come from as far as 'Newcastle' to watch the execution. Hippolytus's genitals are cut off, thrown onto a grill and then thrown to some children, after which his entrails are cut out and grilled. During this cannibalistic violence, Theseus unknowingly rapes and kills Strophe, who is also in disguise but speaking in favour of Hippolytus to the crowd. When Theseus realises what he has done, he kills himself. The three bodies are left on stage as vultures circle overhead. Hippolytus is given the last words and expresses his satisfaction. As he looks at the birds, he says, 'If there could have been more moments / like this' (Kane 2001: 103). Kane has come to be seen as one of the most important contemporary dramatists, and *Phaedra's Love* is testament to the creative possibilities and continuing influence of Senecan tragedy.

To take an even more recent example, Charles Mee's *Night (Thyestes 2.0)* includes translations from Seneca's *Thyestes*, mostly the opening scene, and places them within a contemporary dinner party. Mee encourages further reworking by any and all interested parties. The text of the play, along with several other plays by him, including ones based on Aeschylus and Euripides, is available on his website.[70] Mee wants others to take his texts and transform them into their own works, as he has done to Seneca and others.

Seneca's legacy is not simply confined to the stage, but also influences modern films. Gian Biagio Conte has suggested that Peter Greenaway's *The Cook, The Thief, His Wife & Her Lover* (1989) taps into Seneca's aesthetic, and demonstrates the violence and suffering that tyranny causes.[71] One might also note how the aesthetics of violence create a link between Seneca and Quentin Tarantino's *Reservoir Dogs* (1992) and *Pulp Fiction* (1994). Indeed, Tarantino's later two-film cycle, *Kill Bill* (Vol. 1, 2003, Vol. 2, 2004) is *Medea* in reverse, as the avenging mother has to save her child from her murderous father. The opening of Volume 2 is reminiscent of the domineering self-reflexivity of Seneca's Medea. The main character, The Bride, played by Uma Thurman, looks directly into the camera, tells the audience of her past crimes and congratulates herself for how the critics have praised her acts of revenge in the first film. Unlike Medea, who wishes Jason to live, The Bride is clear from the outset that she will 'kill Bill', the father of her child who attempted to execute her on her wedding day. In the end, she is reunited with her daughter.[72]

Charles Mee's open-ended invitation to rework Seneca provides a fitting way for us to draw this chapter and book to a close. As Mee demonstrates, concluding a chapter on the reception of Seneca is an impossible task, as this process continues in both the scholarly and creative worlds. Seneca's legacy shapes us and will continue to be shaped by us. The contemporary revival of interest in Seneca speaks to the fears and aspirations of the late twentieth and early twenty-first centuries, particularly in Europe and North America.[73] For some, Seneca provides an example for how (not?) to try to live a moral life in what appears to be an irredeemably corrupt and corrupting society. Seneca can offer examples for the modern cult of self-help, and also speaks to our desires to help others live a better life. Seneca provides a source of morality that is free from the Christian God, but, as recognised for centuries, Seneca's moral teachings have parallels with the New Testament. Yet Seneca's hope for the betterment of the self and of humanity is also coupled with despair for and delight in depicting a world overrun by horrific violence and political and emotional tyranny.

Seneca's concerns with the evils of empire speak to our worries about the cost and consequences of globalisation. At the same time, Seneca's own indulgence in the benefits of empire also reveals something of our own paradoxical ability to decry the excesses of the modern world while simultaneously and tacitly accepting them. On an even more disturbing note, Seneca also speaks to contemporary fears about the fate of the human race, the planet and even the cosmos. The chorus's question in *Thyestes* about whether we are living in the 'final age' (*ultima aetas* 878) is echoed today. Indeed, the trajectory has been sped up, as the title of Sir Martin Rees's warning, *Our Final Hour*, reveals.[74] Seneca could not have dreamt of the technological advances of the last century that shape much of our contemporary anxieties about the possibility of humanity's imminent end. Yet if Seneca's life and works teach us anything, it is about the difficulties of living a good life in a world that seems racing towards its own self-inflicted destruction.

NOTES

INTRODUCTION

1 Ker 2009: 197–8.
2 This is the famous passage concerning 'the number of the beast, for it is the number of a person. Its number is six hundred sixty-six'. Hebrew, like Latin and Greek, used letters for numbers. The Hebrew letter equivalent of 666 is *Neron Caesar*. There is a variant reading of 616, which also works for Nero, if the final 'n' is omitted. See *New Oxford Annotated Bible* (NSRV) 1991, and Usher 2013.
3 The Greek historian Cassius Dio, who as we shall see is generally hostile towards Seneca, famously refers to him as a 'tyrant teacher' (*tyrannodidaskalos*).
4 Syme 1958: 552; Griffin 1992: 1.
5 Barthes 1977: 148.
6 Griffin 1992: 177.
7 Star 2016.
8 Griffin 1992: 31.
9 Trillitzsch 1971: 357.
10 Stewart 1953: 82.
11 Scholiast to Juv. 5.109.
12 Nauta 1987.
13 On the fire and Nero's blaming of the 'Chrestiani', see Tacitus *Annals* 15.44.
14 Macaulay 1880: 106.
15 Edwards 1993: 173–206.
16 Rosivach 1995.
17 See also Griffin 1992: 442.
18 Ker 2009: 269–71.

1. SENECA'S PHILOSOPHY

1 Sedley 2003: 17.
2 Ibid.: 20–4.
3 See *On the Nature of the Universe* 3.1023.
4 Brunschwig and Sedley 2003: 173. See also *On Anger* 2.31.6–8, and *On the Private Life* 4.
5 Inwood 1985: 28–30; for the key Stoic texts on the soul, see Long and Sedley 1987: section 53.
6 Long and Sedley 1987: section 58.
7 Graver 2007: 53–60, and Long and Sedley 1987: section 65.
8 Inwood 1985: 5.
9 Griffin 1992: 177.
10 Foucault 1986.
11 Ibid.: 43, 46.
12 Griffin 1992: 398.
13 See the helpful list in Harris 2001: 127–8.
14 There is, however, a large lacuna in the early sections of the text.
15 Seneca responds to Achilles's claim that revenge is sweet. See *On Anger* 2.32.1.
16 Graver 1999 argues that Seneca's discussion is not innovative. Sorabji 2000: 66–92 posits that it is.
17 Already noted in *On Anger*, see 2.2.2.
18 Roller 2001: 97–108, and Star 2012: 23–30.
19 Newman 1989: 1482.
20 Griffin 1992: 256–87, 515.
21 Stacey 2007.
22 It does remain unclear whether this work was in fact one of Varro's Menippeans. See Conte 1994: 215.
23 Nauta 1987.
24 Star 2012: 152–60.
25 See discussion in Braund 2009: 16–17.
26 Stacey 2007: 45.
27 MacMullen 1986: 521.
28 Concept of *gratia*, Roller 2001: 129–212; Seneca and Roman elite, Griffin 2003a, 2003b and most fully, 2013. See also Inwood 1995a.
29 For questions surrounding the date of this work, as well as the political life of Paulinus, see Griffin 1992: 398.
30 This is the first book, according to many of the manuscripts. Today, most scholars believe that the original order of the books was 3, 4a, 4b, 5, 6, 7, 1 and 2. See Hine 2010: 1–2, and Williams 2012: 13–14.
31 Williams 2012.
32 Hine 2006: 42, Star 2012: 34–5.
33 *On Providence* is also addressed to Lucilius. The dating of this work is uncertain. See Griffin 1992: 396, 400–1.
34 Ker 2009: 153.
35 *Vindico* can also mean to avenge, a central theme of Seneca's tragedies, as we will see in the following chapter.

II. SENECA'S TRAGEDIES

1. Nisbet 1987: 250.
2. Bishop 1985.
3. Fitch 1982. See now Marshall 2014.
4. E.g. *Apocol.* 7.2.2 and *Herc.* 1296; see the full comments of Eden 1984: 94–5.
5. Davis 2003: 15–16, 69–74.
6. Tarrant 1978: 229.
7. Eliot 1932: 64–5.
8. Trinacty 2014.
9. On how the first choral ode of *Hercules* incorporates elements from Euripides's fragmentary play, *Phaethon*, and the Augustan poets, see Star forthcoming.
10. Schiesaro 2003.
11. We have no way of knowing how Ovid's tragedy *Medea* portrayed Medea's infanticide.
12. Most 1992.
13. On metatheatre in Senecan drama, see Boyle 1997, Schiesaro 2003, Erasmo 2004 and Littlewood 2004.
14. Staley 2010.
15. Bartsch 1994.
16. Beacham 1991: 171–4.
17. Tarrant 1995: 220 n. 22.
18. Ibid.: 222.
19. Ibid.: 221.
20. Fitch 2000, and Fitch 2004: 14.
21. Eliot 1932: 54.
22. Herington 1966: 444–5.
23. Fitch 1987: 311. See also 314.
24. Eden 1984: 4–5
25. Fitch 1987: 312–14
26. Mader 2003.
27. On the Romans' hatred of the word 'king' (*rex*), see Cic. *Rep.* 2.47–9, Livy 2.19.4 and Tac. *Ann.* 3.56.2.
28. For an overview, see Ker 2009: 125–9, Star 2015 and Star 2016.
29. Star 2012: 50–2.
30. See Hijmans 1966, and Traina 1974.
31. Nussbaum 1993: 146–9.
32. Schiesaro 1997, 2003: 244–51.
33. Padel 1992, 1995, and Gill 1997: 218–28.
34. Littlewood 2004: 16.
35. Staley 2010.
36. Tarrant 1978: 229
37. Fitch 2002 assigns the final lines to Eteocles and Polynices. Zwierlein 1986 gives them to Eteocles and Jocasta.
38. On the history of quotations of this line by Seneca and others, see Star 2015: 256–9.
39. The commentary by Boyle 2014 is helpful for tracing the long history of Medea's reception.
40. Gill 1997, Winter 2014: 103–11.
41. Fitch 2002: 339.

42 von Wilamowitz-Moellendorff 1919: 162; see also Schiesaro 2003: 18.
43 Nussbaum 1994: 463–4.
44 Clay 1992.
45 *Oedipus* was taken to mean 'swollen foot' (*oideo + pous*). It could also mean 'he who knows feet', based on the Greek verb to know, *oida*. The riddle of the Sphinx asked, 'what walks on four feet at dawn, two feet at noon, and three feet in the evening?'
46 Epictetus *Diss.* 2.6.9, quoting Chrysippus.
47 Her reference to the 'treacherous wife' (*coniunx perfida* 117) in her list of criminal women may obliquely refer to herself. See Tarrant 1976: 196.
48 Fitch 2004: 122, Shelton 1983: 183 n.61.
49 See Tarrant's explication of *furor* 1976: 361.
50 Parts of the family's early history are related in the opening choral ode 136–75.
51 Davis 2003: 46.
52 See especially line 714, where the messenger says that Atreus performs a sacrifice to himself (*mactet sibi*), and Atreus's own declarations, 'I walk equal to the stars ... I send away the gods above' (885, 888) and 'I am the highest of the gods in heaven and the king of kings!' (911–12).
53 Cicero (*On Duties* 1.97) notes and Seneca (*On Mercy* 2.2.2–3) laments the approval that Accius's Atreus meets with.

III. RECEPTION

1   Bartsch 1997: 93–100.
2   Star 2012 provides a full explication of the relationship between Seneca and Petronius.
3   Sullivan 1968b: 193–213.
4   Ferri 2003: 70–5.
5   Usher 2013.
6   Nisbet 1987: 250.
7   Marti 1945, Larson 1991.
8   See *On the Nature of the Universe* 5.22–54.
9   Conte 1994: 515, Dominik 1997: 52.
10 Ross 1974: 127, 156 n.51.
11 Ross 1974: 129.
12 Berry 1999.
13 Stivala 2009: 70.
14 Ibid.: 73–81.
15 Ross 1974: 131–5.
16 Latin quoted ibid.: 135.
17 Radice 1974: 110.
18 Translation by McGarry 1982: 62.
19 Graesse 1969.
20 Ker 2009: 201–2.
21 Ibid.: 200.
22 Ibid.: 315–17.
23 He is mentioned over 33 times in *The Canterbury Tales*: 'The total number of references to Seneca in the *Tales* is greater than the number to any other philosopher except Solomon.' Wilson 1993: 135.

24 Wilson 1993: 136–40.
25 Ibid.: 138.
26 Ibid.
27 Stacey 2007.
28 Latin text from Megas 1967.
29 Grund 2011: xx.
30 Ibid.: xxi.
31 Ibid.: xxviii–xxix.
32 See the judgements of Senecan drama assembled in Boyle 1983: 1–3.
33 Braden 1985: 115–52; see also Jacquot 1964 and Dodson-Robinson 2016.
34 Levitan 1989.
35 Cauthen 1970: xvi.
36 Braden 1985: 171. There was also a tradition of Nero Latin dramas, such as Matthew Gwinn's *Nero*, a hypertext of which has been edited by D. Sutton, available at http://www.philological.bham.ac.uk/Nero/. Accessed 21 June 2016. See also Binns 1974.
37 Cunliffe 1925 [1893], Kastner and Charlton 1921, Charlton 1946 [1921], Lucas 1969 [1922], Braden 1985, Miola 1992, Winston 2009.
38 There may have been a performance of *Hippolytus* at Westminster in 1546; see Ker and Winston 2012: 4 n.12. *Phaedra* was performed at the Palace de Cardinal St George in France in 1474, and *Hippolytus* in 1485 in Rome. For a full list of performances of Seneca's plays, see The Archive for the Performance of Greek and Roman Drama (APGRD) http://www.apgrd.ox.ac.uk/.
39 The text is taken from Ker and Winston 2012: 141.
40 For the text of both translations, see Mueller and Scodel 2009. It is generally accepted that the translation by *Hercules Oetaeus*, although not in her hand, is by the Queen. See Mueller and Scodel 2009: 439–46.
41 Bevington 1996: 94.
42 Gair 1978: 39, 46 n104.
43 On the disputed authorship of *De remediis fortuitorum*, see Newman 1988.
44 See 2.2.50–69, where Pandulfo and Piero debate how to rule, with lines taken from *Thyestes*'s debate between the Minister and Atreus and *Octavia*'s debate between Seneca and Nero. Piero sends Pandulfo away, saying, 'Hence doting Stoic' (2.2.70).
45 Miola 1992.
46 Staley 2010.
47 Miola 2004: vii–x.
48 Maus 1995: ix.
49 Ibid.: 381.
50 Several other representations of Seneca, particularly his death scene, were painted throughout the seventeenth and eighteenth centuries; see Ker 2009: 212, 217–18, 226–36, 303–12.
51 Zanker 2000: 54–8, Ker 2009: 182.
52 Boyle 2008: lxxxvi, Manuwald 2013: 4.
53 See list compiled by Manuwald 2013: 386.
54 Text taken from Curtis 1989.
55 Rosand 2009: 122.
56 Ibid.
57 Ibid.: 121–3, 136.
58 Ibid.: 134.

59 Von Schlegel 1883: 211.
60 Macaulay 1976: 178; a letter from Calcutta, dated 30 May 1836.
61 Macaulay 1880: 106.
62 For another important early twentieth century re-evaluation of Senecan tragedy, see Regenbogen 1961: 429–62 (originally published in 1930).
63 Hadot 1995, Foucault 1986 and Foucault 2005.
64 Nussbaum 1994: 3.
65 Ibid.: 434.
66 Ibid.: 470.
67 Hine 2000: 29 and Boyle 2014: civ–cv.
68 See Slaney 2015.
69 Quoted in Curran 1970: 246 n187.
70 http://www.charlesmee.org/night-thyestes.shtml. Accessed 24 September 2015.
71 Conte 1994: 424.
72 Seneca is also alive and well in the world of young adult fiction, as seen in the character from *The Hunger Games* books and films, Seneca Crane, a merciful follower of the president, who ultimately is forced to kill himself for his clemency.
73 To move from our primary focus on Seneca in the English-speaking world, Seneca has been a central figure in German literature since 1945, see Ziolkowski 2004 and Ker 2009: 238–44.
74 This is the title of the American edition. Interestingly, the apocalyptic urgency was toned down in the UK, where the book is published as *Our Final Century*.

Select Translations, Commentaries and Collections of Essays

THE COMPLETE WORKS OF SENECA, in Latin and English, can be found in the Loeb Classical Library (in ten volumes, Harvard University Press, 1928–74). The original translations of the tragedies have been replaced by John Fitch (2002 and 2004).

The University of Chicago Press is publishing in translations *The Complete Works of Lucius Annaeus Seneca* (2010–). As of November 2015, all of his prose works are available. The tragedies are forthcoming.

Selections from Seneca's works are also available in the Penguin Classics and Oxford World's Classics series:

Seneca. 1969. *Letters from a Stoic*. R. Campbell, trans. London.
Seneca. 1997. *Dialogues and Letters*. C. D. N. Costa, trans. London.
Seneca. 2009. *Dialogues and Essays*. J. Davie, trans. Oxford.
Seneca. 2010. *Selected Letters*. E. Fantham, trans. Oxford.
Seneca. 2010. *Six Tragedies*. E. Wilson, trans. Oxford.

Select Translations, Commentaries and Collections of Essays

For those looking to read Seneca in the original, there are commentaries on all of the plays.

J. Fitch, ed. 1987. *Seneca's Hercules Furens*. Ithaca, NY.
E. Fantham. 1982. *Seneca's Troades*. Princeton, NJ.
A. J. Boyle. 1994. *Seneca's Troades*. Leeds.
M. Frank. 1994. *Seneca's Phoenissae*. Leiden.
C. D. N. Costa. 1973. *Seneca. Medea*. Oxford.
H. Hine. 2000. *Seneca. Medea*. Warminster.
A. J. Boyle. 2014. *Seneca. Medea*. Oxford.
M. Coffey and R. Mayer. 1990. *Seneca. Phaedra*. Cambridge.
A. J. Boyle. 2011. *Seneca. Oedipus*. Oxford.
R. J. Tarrant. 1976. *Seneca. Agamemnon*. Oxford.
R. J. Tarrant. 1985. *Seneca. Thyestes*. Atlanta, GA.
R. Ferri. 2003. *Octavia. A Play Attributed to Seneca*. Cambridge.
A. J. Boyle. 2008. *Octavia, Attributed to Seneca*. Oxford.

See also:

P. T. Eden. 1984. *Seneca: Apocolocyntosis*. Cambridge.
G. D. Williams. 2003. *Seneca: De otio, De brevitate vitae*. Cambridge.
M. D. Usher. 2006. *A Student's Seneca. Ten Letters and Selections from De providentia and De vita beata*. Norman, OK.
S. Braund. 2009. *Seneca, De Clementia. Edited with Text, Translation, and Commentary*. Oxford.
B. Inwood. 2010. *Seneca: Selected Philosophical Letters*. Oxford.
J. Ker. 2012. *A Seneca Reader: Selections from Prose and Tragedy*. Mundelein, IL.

In addition, there are two books that focus on individual plays:

R. Mayer. 2002. *Seneca: Phaedra*. London.
P. J. Davis. 2003. *Seneca: Thyestes*. London.

Select Translations, Commentaries and Collections of Essays

Detailed considerations of recent trends in Senecan scholarship can be found in three companions to Seneca:

G. Damschen and A. Heil, eds 2014. *Brill's Companion to Seneca*. Leiden.
S. Bartsch and A. Schiesaro, eds 2015. *The Cambridge Companion to Seneca*. Cambridge.
E. Dodson-Robinson, ed. 2016. *Brill's Companion to the Reception of Senecan Tragedy*. Leiden.

For a collection of influential essays, see J. Fitch, ed. 2008. *Seneca*. Oxford Readings in Classical Studies. Oxford.

The standard scholarly work on Seneca's life is Miriam Griffin, *Seneca: A Philosopher in Politics* (Oxford 1976, 1992). Recently, a biography of Seneca that focuses also on his political life but is for a more general audience was published by James Romm: *Dying Every Day: Seneca at the Court of Nero* (New York 2014). Emily Wilson's biography provides a full account of Seneca's life and focuses on his philosophy: *The Greatest Empire: A Life of Seneca* (Oxford 2014). See also P. Veyne. 2003. *Seneca: The Life of a Stoic*. D. Sullivan, trans. New York.

Bibliography

Barlow, C. W., ed. 1938. *Epistulae Senecae ad Paulum et Pauli ad Senecam* <*QuaeVocatur*>. Papers and Monographs of the American Academy in Rome.
Barthes, R. 1977. *Image – Music – Text*. S. Heath, trans. New York.
Bartsch, S. 1994. *Actors in the Audience: Theatricality and Doublespeak from Nero to Hadrian*. Cambridge, MA.
——— 1997. *Ideology in Cold Blood*. Cambridge, MA.
——— 2006. *The Mirror of the Self: Sexuality, Self-Knowledge, and the Gaze in the Early Roman Empire*. Chicago, IL.
——— 2007. 'Wait a moment, *Phantasia*: Ekphrastic interference in Seneca and Epictetus'. *Classical Philology* 102: 83–95.
Bartsch, S. and D. Wray, eds 2009. *Seneca and the Self*. Cambridge.
Beacham, R. C. 1991. *The Roman Theater and its Audience*. Cambridge, MA.
Berry, P. 1999. *The Correspondence Between Paul and Seneca, A. D. 61–65*. Lewiston, NY.
Bevington, D., ed. 1996. *The Spanish Tragedy: Thomas Kyd*. Manchester.
Binns, J. W. 1974. 'Seneca and neo-Latin tragedy in England', in Costa, ed., 205–34.
Bishop, J. 1985. *Seneca's Daggered Stylus: Political Code in the Tragedies*. Meisenheim.
Boyle, A. J., ed. 1983. *Seneca Tragicus*. Berwick.
——— ed. 1994. *Seneca's Troades*. Leeds.
——— 1997. *Tragic Seneca: An Essay in the Theatrical Tradition*. New York.
——— ed. 2008. *Octavia, Attributed to Seneca*. Oxford.
——— ed. 2014. *Seneca: Medea*. Oxford.
Braden, G. 1970. 'The rhetoric and psychology of power'. *Arion* 9: 5–41.
——— 1985. *Renaissance Tragedy and the Senecan Tradition: Anger's Privilege*. New Haven, CT.
Braund, Susanna. 2009. *Seneca, De Clementia. Edited with Text, Translation, and Commentary*. Oxford.

Braund, S. and C. Gill, eds 1997. *The Passions in Roman Thought and Literature*. Cambridge.
Brunschwig, J. and D. Sedley. 2003. 'Hellenistic philosophy', in D. Sedley, ed. 151–83.
Brunschwig, J. and M. C. Nussbaum, eds 1993. *Passions and Perceptions: Studies in Hellenistic Philosophy of Mind: Proceedings of the Fifth Symposium Hellenisticum*. Cambridge.
Cauthen, I. B. 1970. *Thomas Sackville and Thomas Norton. Gorboduc, or Ferrex and Porrex*. Lincoln, NE.
Charlton, H. B. 1946 [1921]. *The Senecan Tradition in Renaissance Tragedy*. Folcroft, PA.
Clay, D. 1992. 'Columbus' Senecan prophecy'. *American Journal of Philology*. 113: 617–20.
Coffey, M. and R. Mayer, eds 1990. *Seneca, Phaedra*. Cambridge.
Conte, G. B. 1994. *Latin Literature: A History*. J. Solodow, trans. Baltimore, MA.
Cooper, J. and J. F. Procopé, eds 1995. *Seneca: Moral and Political Essays*. Cambridge.
Costa, C. D. N., ed. 1973. *Seneca: Medea*. Oxford.
—— ed. 1974. *Seneca*. London.
Cunliffe, J. W. 1925 [1893]. *The Influence of Seneca on Elizabethan Tragedy*. New York.
Curran, S. 1970. *Shelley's Cenci: Scorpions Ringed with Fire*. Princeton, NJ.
Curtis, A., ed. 1989. *Claudio Monteverdi: L'Incoronazione di Poppea*. London.
Davis, P. J. 2003. *Seneca: Thyestes*. London.
De Vivo, A. and E. Lo Cascio, eds 2003. *Seneca uomo politico e l'età di Claudio e Nerone*. Bari.
Dingel, J. 1974. *Seneca und die Dichtung*. Heidelberg.
Dodson-Robinson, E., ed. 2016. *Brill's Companion to the Reception of Senecan Tragedy*. Leiden.
Dominik, W. J. 1997. 'Style is the man: Seneca, Tacitus and Quintilian's canon', in *Roman Eloquence: Rhetoric in Society in Literature*. W. J. Dominik, ed. New York: 50–70.
Eden, P. T. 1984. *Seneca: Apocolocyntosis*. Cambridge.
Edwards, C. 1993. *The Politics of Immorality in Ancient Rome*. Cambridge.
—— 1997. 'Self-scrutiny and self-transformation in Seneca's *Letters*'. *Greece and Rome* 44: 23–37.
—— 1999. 'The suffering body: philosophy and pain in Seneca's *Letters*', in *Constructions of the Classical Body*. J. Porter, ed. Ann Arbor, MI. 252–68.
—— 2000. *Suetonius: Lives of the Caesars*. Oxford.
—— 2005. 'Archetypally Roman? Representing Seneca's ageing body', in *Roman Bodies: Antiquity to the Eighteenth Century*. A. Hopkins and M. Wyke, eds, London. 13–22.
—— 2007. *Death in Ancient Rome*. New Haven, CT.
—— 2009. 'Free yourself! Slavery, freedom and the self in Seneca's *Letters*', in Bartsch and Wray, eds, 139–59.
Eliot, T. S. 1932. *Selected Essays*. New York.

Elsner, J. and J. Masters, eds 1994. *Reflections of Nero: Culture, History and Representation*. Chapel Hill, NC.
Erasmo, M. 2004. *Roman Tragedy: Theatre to Theatricality*. Austin, TX.
Ferri, R. 1998. 'Octavia's heroines: Tacitus *Annales* 14.63–4 and the *Praetexta Octavia*'. *Harvard Studies in Classical Philology*. 98: 339–56.
—— ed. 2003. *Octavia*. Cambridge.
Fitch, J. G. 1982. 'Sense-pauses and relative dating in Seneca, Sophocles and Shakespeare'. *American Journal of Philology*. 102: 289–307.
—— ed. 1987. *Seneca's Hercules Furens*. Ithaca, NY.
—— 2000. 'Playing Seneca?' in Harrison, ed. 2000. 1–12.
—— 2002. *Seneca VIII: Tragedies*. Cambridge, MA.
—— 2004. *Seneca XI: Tragedies II*. Cambridge, MA.
Foucault, M. 1984. *The Foucault Reader*. Paul Rainbow, ed. New York.
—— 1985. *The Use of Pleasure: The History of Sexuality, Volume 2*. Robert Hurley, trans. New York.
—— 1986. *The Care of the Self: The History of Sexuality, Volume 3*. Robert Hurley, trans. New York.
—— 2005. *The Hermeneutics of the Subject: Lectures at the College de France 1981–1982*. G. Burchell, trans. New York.
Fyfe, H. 1983. 'An analysis of Seneca's *Medea*', in Boyle, ed. Berwick. 77–93.
Gair, W. R., ed. 1978. *John Marston, Antonio's Revenge*. Manchester.
Gill, C. 1987. 'Two monologues of self-division: Euripides, *Medea* 1021–80 and Seneca, *Medea* 893–977'. In Whitby, Hardie and Whitby, eds, 24–37.
—— 1996. *Personality in Greek Epic, Tragedy and Philosophy: The Self in Dialogue*. Oxford.
—— 1997. 'Passion as madness in Roman poetry', in Braund and Gill, eds, Cambridge: 213–41.
—— 2006. *The Structured Self in Hellenistic and Roman Thought*. Oxford.
Goldhill. S. 1995. *Foucault's Virginity: Ancient Erotic Fiction and the History of Sexuality*. Cambridge.
Graesse, T., ed. 1969 [1890]. *Jacobi a Voragine. Legenda aurea. Vulgo historia Lombardica dicta*. Osnabrück.
Graver, M. 1998. 'The manhandling of Maecenas: Senecan abstractions of masculinity'. *American Journal of Philology* 119: 607–32.
—— 1999. 'Philo of Alexandria and the origins of the Stoic *Propatheiai*'. *Phronesis* 44: 300–25.
—— 2002. *Cicero and the Emotions: Tusculan Disputations 3 and 4*. Chicago, IL.
—— 2007. *Stoicism and Emotion*. Chicago, IL.
Griffin, M. T. 1984. *Nero: The End of a Dynasty*. London.
—— 1986. 'Philosophy, Cato and Roman suicide I & II'. *Greece and Rome* 33: 64–77, 192–202.

—— 1992. *Seneca: A Philosopher in Politics*. Oxford.
—— 2003a. '*De Beneficiis* and Roman society'. *Journal of Roman Studies* 93: 92–113.
—— 2003b. 'Seneca as a sociologist: *De Beneficiis*', in De Vivo and E. Lo Cascio, eds, 89–121.
—— 2013. *Seneca on Society: A Guide to De Beneficiis*. Oxford.
Grund, G. 2011. *Humanist Tragedies*. Cambridge, MA.
Hadot. P. 1995. *Philosophy as a Way of Life: Spiritual Exercises From Socrates to Foucault*. M. Chase, trans. Oxford.
Harris, W. V. 2001. *Restraining Rage: The Ideology of Anger Control in Classical Antiquity*. Cambridge, MA.
Harrison, G. W. M., ed. 2000. *Seneca in Performance*. London.
—— ed. 2015. *Brill's Companion to Roman Tragedy*. Leiden and Boston, MA.
Henderson, J. 2004. *Morals and Villas in Seneca's Letters: Places to Dwell*. Cambridge.
—— 2006. 'The Journey of a lifetime', in Williams and Volk, eds, 124–46.
Heil, A. and G. Damschen, eds 2014. *Brill's Companion to Seneca: Philosopher and Dramatist*. Leiden and Boston, MA.
Herington, C. J. 1966. 'Senecan tragedy'. *Arion* 5: 422–7.
Hijmans, B. L. 1966. 'Drama in Seneca's Stoicism'. *Transactions and Proceedings of the American Philological Association*. 97: 237–51.
—— 1976. *Inlaboratus et Facilis: Aspects of Structure in Some Letters of Seneca*. Leiden.
Hine, H. M. 1995. 'Seneca, Stoicism and the problem of moral evil', in *Ethics and Rhetoric: Classical Essays for Donald Russell on His Seventy-Fifth Birthday*. D. Innes, H. Hine and C. Pelling, eds. Oxford. 93–106.
—— 2006. 'Rome, the cosmos, and the emperor in Seneca's *Natural Questions*'. *Journal of Roman Studies* 96: 42–72.
—— 2010. *Seneca: Natural Questions*. Chicago, IL.
Inwood, B. 1985. *Ethics and Human Action in Early Stoicism*. Oxford.
—— 1993. 'Seneca and psychological dualism', in Brunschwig and Nussbaum, eds, 150–83.
—— 1995a. 'Politics and paradox in Seneca's *De Beneficiis*', in *Justice and Generosity: Studies in Hellenistic Social and Political Philosophy*. A. Laks and M. Schofield, eds. Cambridge. 241–65.
—— 1995b. 'Seneca in his philosophical milieu'. *Harvard Studies in Classical Philology* 97: 63–76.
—— 2000. 'The will in Seneca the Younger'. *Classical Philology* 95: 44–60.
—— ed. 2002. *The Cambridge Companion to the Stoics*. Cambridge.
—— 2007a. 'The importance of form in Seneca's philosophical letters' in *Ancient Letters: Classical and Late Antique Epistolography*. R. Morello and A. Morrison, eds. Oxford. 133–48.
—— 2007b. *Seneca: Selected Philosophical Letters*. Oxford.
—— 2009. 'Seneca and self-assertion', in Bartsch and Wray, eds, 39–64.

Jacquot, J., ed. 1964. *Les Tragédies de Sénèque et le théatre de la renaissance.* Paris.
Johnson, W. R. 1988. 'Medea nunc sum: The close of Seneca's version', in *Language and the Tragic Hero: Essays on Greek Tragedy in Honor of Gordon M. Kirkwood.* P. Pucci, ed. Atlanta, GA: 85–95.
Kane, S. 2001. *Complete Plays.* London.
Kastner, L. E. and H. B. Charlton, eds 1921. *The Poetical Works of Sir William Alexander, Earl of Stirling.* Manchester.
Ker, J. 2006. 'Seneca, man of many genres', in Williams and Volk, eds, 19–41.
——— 2009a. *The Deaths of Seneca.* Oxford.
——— 2009b. 'Seneca on self-examination: re-reading *On Anger* 3.36', in Bartsch and Wray, eds, Cambridge. 160–87.
Ker, J. and J. Winston, eds 2012. *Elizabethan Seneca: Three Tragedies.* London.
Kohn, Thomas. 2013. *The Dramaturgy of Senecan Tragedy.* Ann Arbor, MI.
Larson, V. T. 1991. 'The *Hercules Oetaeus* and the picture of the *Sapiens* in Senecan prose'. *Phoenix.* 45: 39–49.
Lavery, G. B. 1980. 'Metaphors of war and travel in Seneca's prose works'. *Greece and Rome* 27: 147–57.
Leach, E. W. 1989. 'The implied reader and the political argument in Seneca's *Apocolocyntosis* and *De Clementia*'. *Arethusa* 22: 197–230.
Levick, B. 2003. 'Seneca and money', in De Vivo, and Lo Cascio, eds, 211–28.
Levitan, W. 1989. 'Seneca in Racine'. *Yale French Studies.* 76: 185–210.
Littlewood, C. 2004. *Self-Representation and Illusion in Senecan Tragedy.* Oxford.
Long, A. A. 1986. *Hellenistic Philosophy: Stoics, Epicureans, Sceptics.* Berkeley, CA.
——— 1991. 'Representation of the self in Stoicism', in *Companions to Ancient Thought 2: Psychology.* S. Everson, ed. Cambridge. 102–20.
——— 2001. *Stoic Studies.* Berkeley, CA.
——— 2006. *From Epicurus to Epictetus: Studies in Hellenistic and Roman Philosophy.* Oxford.
Long, A. A. and D. Sedley, eds 1987. *The Hellenistic Philosophers.* 2 vols, Cambridge.
Lucas, F. L. 1969 [1922]. *Seneca and Elizabethan Tragedy.* New York.
Macaulay, T. 1880. *The Miscellaneous Works of Lord Macaulay, Volume IV.* Lady Trevelyan, ed. New York.
——— 1976. *The Letters of Thomas Babington Macaulay, Volume 3: Jan. 1834–Aug. 1841.* T. Pinney, ed. Cambridge.
MacMullen, R. 1986. 'Personal power in the Roman empire'. *American Journal of Philology* 107: 512–24.
Mader, G. 1998. '*Quod nolunt velint:* Deference and doublespeak at Seneca, *Thyestes* 334–335'. *Classical Journal* 94: 31–47.
——— 2003. 'Thyestes' Belch: Seneca, *Thy.* 911–12'. *Classical Quarterly.* 53: 634–6.
Manuwald, G. 2013. *Nero in Opera: Librettos as Transformations of Ancient Sources.* Berlin and Boston, MA.

Marshall, C. W. 2014. 'The works of Seneca the Younger and their dates', in Heil and Damschen, eds, 33–44.
Marti, B. 1945. 'Seneca's tragedies: A new interpretation'. *Transactions and Proceedings of the American Philological Association* 76: 216–45.
Maus, K., ed. 1995. *Four Revenge Tragedies*. Oxford.
McGarry, D. 1982, trans. *The Metalogicon of John of Salisbury*. Westport, CT.
Megas, A. 1967. *The Pre-humanistic Circle of Padua (Lovato Lovati – Albertino Mussato) and the Tragedies of Seneca*. Thessaloniki.
Meltzer, G. 1988. 'Dark wit and black humor in Seneca's *Thyestes*'. *Transactions of the American Philological Association*. 118: 309–30.
Miola, R. 1992. *Shakespeare and Classical Tragedy*. Oxford.
—— ed. 2004. *Macbeth: A Norton Critical Edition*. New York.
Montiglio, S. 2006. 'Should an aspiring wise man travel? A dilemma in Seneca's thought'. *American Journal of Philology*. 127: 553–87.
Morford, M. 1973. 'The Neronian Literary Revolution'. *Classical Journal*. 68: 210–15.
—— 1991. *Stoics and Neo Stoics*. Princeton, NJ.
Most, G. W. 1992. '*disiecti membra poetae:* The rhetoric of dismemberment in Neronian poetry', in *Innovations of Antiquity*. R. Hexter and D. Selden, eds, London. 91–419.
Motto, A. L. 2001. *Further Essays on Seneca*. Frankfurt am Main.
Motto, A. L. and J. Clark. 1988. *Senecan Tragedy*. Amsterdam.
—— 1993. *Essays on Seneca*. Frankfurt am Main.
—— 1997. 'Seneca's visionary drama'. *Listy filologické* 70: 34–41.
Mueller, J. and J. Scodel, eds 2009. *Elizabeth I: Translations 1544–1589*. Chicago.
Nauta, R. R. 1987. 'Seneca's *Apocolocyntosis* as Saturnalian literature'. *Mnemosyne* 40: 69–96.
Newman, R. J. 1988. 'Rediscovering the *De remediis fortuitorum*'. *American Journal of Philology*. 101: 92–107.
—— 1989. '*Cotidie Meditare*. Theory and practice of the *Meditatio* in imperial Stoicism'. *ANRW* 36.3: 1473–517.
Newton, T., ed. 1581 [1966]. *Seneca: His Tenne Tragedies*. Bloomington, IN.
Nisbet, R. 1987. 'The oak and the axe: symbolism in Seneca, *Hercules Oetaeus* 1618ff', in Whitby, Hardie and Whitby, eds, 243–52.
Nussbaum, M. 1993. 'Poetry and the passions: two Stoic views', in Brunschwig and Nussbaum, eds, 97–149.
—— 1994. *The Therapy of Desire: Theory and Practice in Hellenistic Ethics*. Princeton, NJ.
O'Gorman, E. 2000. *Irony and Misreading in the Annals of Tacitus*. Cambridge.
—— 2005. 'Citation and authority in Seneca's *Apocolocyntosis*', in *The Cambridge Companion to Roman Satire*. K. Freudenberg, ed. Cambridge. 95–108.
Osgood, J. 2007. 'The *Vox* and *Verba* of an emperor: Claudius, Seneca and *Le Prince Ideal*'. *Classical Journal* 102.4: 329–53.

Padel, R. 1992. *In and Out of Mind: Greek Images of the Tragic Self*. Princeton, NJ.
—— 1995. *Whom Gods Destroy: Elements of Greek and Tragic Madness*. Princeton, NJ.
Padoan, G., ed. 1994. *Giovanni Boccaccio: Esposizioni sopra la Comedia di Dante*. Milan.
Radice, B. 1974. *The Letters of Abelard and Heloise*. London.
Rees, M. 2003. *Our Final Hour: A Scientist's Warning: How terror, error, and environmental disaster threaten humankind's future in this century – on earth and beyond*. New York.
Regenbogen, O. 1961. *Kleine Schriften*. Munich.
Relihan, J. C. 1993. *Ancient Menippean Satire*. Baltimore, MA.
Reydams-Schils, G. 2005. *The Roman Stoics: Self, Responsibility, and Affection*. Chicago, IL.
Richardson-Hay, C. 2009. 'Dinner at Seneca's table: the philosophy of food'. *Greece and Rome*. 56: 71–96.
Rist, J. M. 1989. 'Seneca and Stoic orthodoxy'. *ANRW* 2.36.3: 1993–2012.
Roller, M. B. 2001. *Constructing Autocracy: Aristocrats and Emperors in Julio-Claudian Rome*. Princeton, NJ.
Rosand, E. 1985. 'Seneca and the interpretation of "L'coronazione di Poppaea"'. *Journal of the American Musicological Society*. 38: 34–71.
—— 2009. 'Il retorno a Seneca'. *Cambridge Opera Journal*. 21: 119–37.
Rosenmeyer, T. 1989. *Senecan Drama and Stoic Cosmology*. Berkeley, CA.
Rosivach, V. J. 1995. 'Seneca on Fear of Poverty in the *Epistulae Morales*'. *Antiquité Classique*. 64: 91–8.
Ross, G. M. 1974. 'Seneca's philosophical influence', in Costa, ed. 116–65.
Rossi, V. ed. 1942. *Francesco Petrarca. Le familiari. Volume quarto*. Florence.
Rudich, V. 1993. *Political Dissidence Under Nero: The Price of Dissimulation*. New York.
—— 1997. *Dissidence and Literature under Nero: The Price of Rhetoricization*. New York.
Sambursky, S. 1987. *Physics of the Stoics*. Princeton, NJ.
Schiesaro, A. 1994. 'Seneca's *Thyestes* and the morality of tragic *Furor*', in Elsner and Masters, eds, 196–210.
—— 1997. 'Passion, reason and knowledge in Seneca's tragedies', in Braund and Gill, eds, Cambridge: 89–111.
—— 2003. *The Passions in Play*: Thyestes *and the Dynamics of Senecan Tragedy*. Cambridge.
Schofield, M. 1991. *The Stoic Idea of the City*. Cambridge.
Sedley, D. 2002. 'The school, from Zeno to Arius Didymus', in Inwood, ed. 7–32.
—— ed. 2003. *The Cambridge Companion to Greek and Roman Philosophy*. Cambridge.
Segal, C. 1982. '*Nomen Sacrum*: Medea and other names in Senecan tragedy'. *Maia* 34: 241–6.
—— 1984. 'Senecan baroque: the death of Hippolytus in Seneca, Ovid, and Euripides'. *Transactions of the American Philological Association*. 114: 311–25.
—— 1986. *Language and Desire in Seneca's Phaedra*. Princeton, NJ.

BIBLIOGRAPHY

Schlegel, A. W. von. 1883. *Lectures on Dramatic Art and Literature*. J. Black, trans. London.

Shelley, P. B. 1991. *The Cenci (1819)*. Oxford.

Shelton, J. 1983. 'Revenge or resignation: Seneca's *Agamemnon*', in Boyle, ed., 159–83.

Sherman, N. 2005. *Stoic Warriors: The Ancient Philosophy Behind the Military Mind*. Oxford.

Sienkiewicz, H. 1905. *Quo Vadis? A Tale of the Time of Nero*. S. Binion and S. Malevsky, trans. New York.

Slaney, H. 2015. 'Schlegel, Shelley and the "death" of Seneca', in Harrison, ed., 311–29.

Sorabji, R. 2000. *Emotion and Peace of Mind: From Stoic Agitation to Christian Temptation*. Oxford.

Stacey, P. 2007. *Roman Monarchy and the Renaissance Prince*. Cambridge.

Staley, G. 2010. *Seneca and the Idea of Tragedy*. Oxford.

Star, C. 2006. 'Commanding *constantia* in Senecan tragedy'. *Transactions of the American Philological Association*. 136: 207–44.

——— 2012. *The Empire of the Self: Self-Command and Political Speech in Seneca and Petronius*. Baltimore, MD.

——— 2015. 'Roman tragedy and philosophy', in Harrison, ed. 238–59.

——— 2016. 'Seneca *Tragicus* and philosophy', in Dodson-Robinson, ed. 34–56.

——— forthcoming. 'Euripides and Senecan drama', in *A Companion to Euripides*. L. McClure, ed. Malden, MA.

Stewart, Z. 1953. 'Sejanus, Gaetulicus, and Seneca'. *American Journal of Philology* 74: 70–85.

Stivala, J. 2009. *The Christian Afterlife of Seneca the Younger: The First Four Hundred Years*. Diss. Australian National University.

Striker, G. 1991. 'Following nature: a study in Stoic ethics'. *Oxford Studies in Ancient Philosophy* 9: 1–73.

Sullivan, J. P. 1968a. 'Petronius, Seneca, and Lucan: a Neronian literary feud?' *Transactions of the American Philological Association* 99: 453–67.

——— 1968b. *The Satyricon of Petronius: A Literary Study*. Bloomington, IN and London.

——— 1985. *Literature and Politics in the Age of Nero*. Ithaca, NY.

Syme, R. 1958. *Tacitus*. Oxford.

Tarrant, R. J. ed. 1976. *Seneca: Agamemnon*. Cambridge.

——— 1978. 'Senecan drama and its antecedents'. *Harvard Studies in Classical Philology* 82: 213–63.

——— 1985. *Seneca's Thyestes*. Atlanta, GA.

——— 1995. 'Greek and Roman in Seneca's tragedies'. *Harvard Studies in Classical Philology* 97: 215–30.

Too, Y. L. 1994. 'Educating Nero: a reading of Seneca's *Moral Epistles*', in Elsner and Masters, eds, 211–24.

Traina, Alfonso. 1974. *Lo stile 'drammatico' del filosofo Seneca*. Bologna.

Trillitzsch, Winfried. 1971. *Seneca im literarischen Urteil der Antike.* 2 vols. Amsterdam.
Trinacty, C. 2014. *Senecan Tragedy and the Reception of Augustan Poetry.* Oxford.
Usher, M. D. 2013. '*Teste galba cum Sibylla*: Oracles, Octavia, and the East'. *Classical Philology* 108: 21–40.
Whitby, M., P. Hardie and M. Whitby, eds 1987. *Homo Viator: Classical Studies for John Bramble.* Bristol.
Wilamowitz-Moellendorff, U. von. 1919. *Griechische Tragödien vol. 3.* Berlin.
Wilcox, A. 2008. 'Nature's monster: Caligula as *exemplum* in Seneca's *Dialogues*', in *KAKOS: Badness and Anti-Value in Classical Antiquity.* I. Sluiter and R. Rosen, eds, Leiden. 451–76.
—— 2012. *The Gift of Correspondence in Classical Rome: Friendship in Cicero's Ad Familiares and Seneca's Moral Epistles.* Madison, WI.
Williams, G. D. 2012. *The Cosmic Viewpoint: A Reading of Seneca's Natural Questions.* Oxford.
Williams, G. D. and K. Volk., eds 2006. *Seeing Seneca Whole: Perspectives on Philosophy, Poetry and Politics.* Leiden.
Wilson, G. 1993. '"Among othere wordes wyse": the medieval Seneca and the *Canterbury Tales*'. *The Chaucer Review* 28: 135–45.
Wilson, M. 1987. 'Seneca's letters to Lucilius: a revaluation', in *The Imperial Muse: Ramus Essays on Roman Literature of the Empire: to Juvenal Through Ovid.* A. J. Boyle, ed. Berwick. 102–21.
—— 1997. 'The subjugation of grief in Seneca's "Epistles"', in Braund and Gill, eds, Cambridge. 48–67.
Winston, J. 2009. 'English Seneca: Heywood to *Hamlet*', in *The Oxford Handbook of Tudor Literature.* M. Pincombe and C. Shrank, eds, Oxford. 472–87.
Winter, K. 2014. *Artificia mali: Das Böse als Kunstwerk in Senecas Rachetragödien.* Heidelberg.
Zanker, P. 2000. 'I ritratti di Seneca', in *Seneca e il suo tempo.* P. Parroni, ed. Rome. 47–58.
Ziolkowski, T. 2004. 'Seneca: a new German icon?' *International Journal of the Classical Tradition.* 11: 47–77.
Zwierlein, O. 1986. *Senecae Tragoediae.* Oxford.

INDEX

Abelard, Peter 134–5
Aeschylus 71–2, 97, 112, 127, 168
Agrippina 10, 12, 14–17, 20, 44, 46, 84–5, 112, 114
Alexander the Great 26, 38
Antonio's Revenge 148–52, 156
apatheia 28, 30, 149, 152, 167
Apollinaris, Sidonius 2
Aristotle 4, 26–7, 29, 35, 37, 54, 78, 90, 93, 96, 131, 164
ataraxia 27–8
Augustine 133–4
Augustus 1–2, 44–7, 53, 72, 118, 124, 136
Aurelius, Marcus 130

Barthes, Roland 4
Boccaccio 135
Boudicca 18
Brecht, Bertolt 92
Britannicus 12, 15, 46
Burrus 14–17, 20, 121

Caesar, Julius 1, 9, 13, 23, 38, 118
Caligula 1–3, 10–13, 17, 34–5, 38, 44, 51, 80, 87, 118, 161

Cato the Younger 7, 9, 23–4, 27, 54, 92, 101, 119, 127–8
Catullus 54
Chaucer, Geoffrey 137
Chrysippus 26, 35, 50, 55, 113
Cicero 26, 34, 53–4, 60, 129, 130, 159
civil war 1, 7, 9, 46, 98–9, 118–19, 123
Claudius 1, 5, 11–14, 17–18, 43–6, 48, 70, 87–8, 118, 121, 124, 128
Cleanthes 29, 61, 90, 109
Columella 120
Correr, Gregorio 140–2
cosmopolitanism 53, 55
Countess of Pembroke 143

Dante 135, 162
Dio, Cassius 3–4, 10, 17–19, 42, 138

earthquakes 57, 59
Egypt 5, 9–10, 57
ekpyrosis 29, 123
Eliot, T. S. 162–3
Elizabeth I 144
empire 1–2, 19, 23, 45, 49, 58, 80, 89, 102, 115, 163, 169

191

Index

Epictetus 6, 130, 156
Epicureanism 26, 28, 61–2, 105, 164
Epicurus 25, 27–8, 54, 61
Etruscus (early manuscript of Seneca's plays) 138
eupatheiai ('good emotions') 30–1
Euripides 71–3, 75, 79, 82, 90–1, 94–5, 97, 101, 104, 106, 127, 142, 166, 168
exile
  in *Agamemnon* 110
  in *Medea* 86, 99
  in *Octavia* 122–3
  in *Phoenissae* 97
  Publius Suillius's 19
  Seneca's 2, 11–12, 18–19, 34–5, 43–4, 46, 57, 137
  in *Thyestes* 88, 99, 113–14

fortune 32, 34, 107, 110, 122–3, 137, 157
Foucault, Michel 32–3, 163–4
Freud, Sigmund 106
Fronto, Marcus Cornelius 130
Furies 74–5, 77, 95, 112–13, 141, 145, 148, 150

Galba (Roman Emperor) 125
Gallio (Seneca's brother) 8, 13
Gellius, Aulus 61, 129, 130, 160
ghosts 77, 96–7, 108, 110, 112–13, 122, 124, 141, 145, 149, 150–1, 157–8
Golden Age 2, 45, 102, 105, 115, 118
Gorboduc 142
Graces, Three 49–50
Great Fire at Rome (64 CE) 21, 132–3
Griffin, Miriam 6, 31

Hadot, Pierre 163
Hercules Oetaeus 3, 5, 70, 126–8, 138–9, 143–4, 160
Heywood, Thomas 143
horme (impulse) 31

L'incoronazione di Poppea 159–60
infanticide 68, 75, 94, 100, 140, 154

Jerome 131–3
Juno 36, 73–5, 93–4, 148
Jupiter 24, 29, 73–4, 79, 95, 112, 114, 123, 126, 135, 149

Kane, Sarah 166–7
Ker, James 24, 117, 137

Lactantius 131
Livy 36, 89
Lucan 7–9, 58, 91, 118–19, 130–1
Lucilius Iunior 20, 58–66, 78, 134
Lucretius 28, 105, 127, 130

Macaulay, Thomas Babbington, Lord 19, 161
madness 36, 38, 54, 74–5, 86, 94–5, 104, 113, 127–8, 149
Marlowe, Christopher 144
Marx, Karl 42
Mee, Charles 167–8
metatheatre 69, 73, 78, 96, 151, 153
Mussato, Albertino 138–40

nature 11, 24, 29, 52, 55–7, 59–60, 62, 65, 73, 98, 102–3, 106–7, 123, 149, 165
Nero 1–5, 8–9, 11, 19, 55, 60, 62, 84, 89, 118–19, 131–3, 135, 140
  actor emperor 80
  in *Apocolocyntosis* and *On Mercy* 42–9, 88, 91

in *The Canterbury Tales* 137–8
in *L'incoronazione di Poppea* 159–60
looks for Source of the Nile 58–9
in *Octavia* 120–5, 146
orders Seneca's death 21–3
in Petrarch 136
refuses Seneca's request to return gifts 20–1, 51, 56
suspected model for Atreus in *Thyestes* 69, 70–1
taught and advised by Seneca 12–17
Newton, Thomas 162
Nile 9, 57–8
Nussbaum, Martha 92, 164–5

Octavia (play) 3, 5, 70, 84–5, 120–8, 136, 139, 141, 143, 146, 149, 159, 160
Octavia (wife of Nero) 12, 121–2, 125
oikeiôsis (appropriation) 28, 52
otium (leisure) 52, 54, 56, 63
Ovid 2, 11, 63, 68, 72, 74–5, 91, 101, 104–6, 126, 141–2, 165

Paul, St 5, 8, 131–4, 136, 138, 144–6, 155
Paulina 3, 22–3
passions 24, 28, 30–2, 35, 37–9, 63, 68, 85, 90–2, 103, 127, 147, 156
Persius 120
Petrarch 136–7
Petronius 7, 24, 91, 118–19
phantasia (impression) 31
pietas (duty) 37, 98–9
Plato 4, 6, 24, 26–7, 29, 42, 49, 54, 62, 90, 104, 164
Pompeii 59, 79, 81
Pompey the Great 9, 38, 80, 118

poverty 6, 19, 62, 65–6, 118, 134
preludes to emotion 39, 93
Procne 68, 141–2, 165
pudor (shame) 104–5

Quintilian 16, 81, 128–9, 135, 160

Racine, Jean 142, 166
reason
 and drama 3–4, 57, 85–6, 104–6, 109–10, 122, 124, 140, 155, 160
 in rulers 138
 in soul 30–1, 36–9
 in Stoic life 6, 24, 52–4, 64, 109, 127
recognition 33, 78–9, 90
Republic, Roman 1–2, 9, 19, 26, 48, 54, 79, 89, 130
revenge
 'anti-revenge plays' 156
 in *Antonio's Revenge* 147–52
 of Atreus 67–9, 91, 113–14, 125
 in *The Cenci* 165–6
 of Clytemnestra 108–11
 of Juno 75
 in *Kill Bill* 168
 of Medea 75, 83, 91, 99–102
 and reason 37, 39, 91–2
 in *The Revenge of Bussy D'Ambois* 156–8
 in *The Spanish Tragedy* 144–5, 147
 of the Sphinx 108
Revenge of Bussy D'Ambois, The 156–8
rhetoric 2, 11–12, 16, 19, 47, 69, 91, 105, 118, 124–5, 128–30, 161–2
Rubens, Peter Paul 158

Schlegel, August Wilhelm von 161, 165
Sejanus 10

Index

Seneca
  Agamemnon 70–1, 81, 86, 109–12, 145–7, 149, 152
  Apocolocyntosis 2, 5, 7, 11, 14, 42–8, 58, 70, 87–8, 90, 93, 119, 127, 136
  biography 8–24
  Consolation to Helvia 8, 11, 24, 34–5, 123
  Consolation to Marcia 10, 24, 34
  Consolation to Polybius 11, 24, 34, 44, 123, 136
  Hercules 7, 70, 73–5, 86–8, 93–5, 127, 143
  lost works 5, 56, 130
  Medea 68, 70, 72, 75–8, 83, 85–6, 91–2, 95, 99–102, 104, 108, 115, 122, 141–2, 148–9, 151, 154–5, 164–5, 168
  Moral Epistles 9, 19–20, 25, 27, 29, 31, 38, 40, 42, 60–4, 76, 78, 90–2, 109, 119–20, 132–4, 154
  Natural Questions 9, 24, 42, 50, 53, 56–8, 60, 123
  Oedipus 70–1, 77–8, 82, 84, 97–8, 106–9, 147
  On Anger 8, 10, 21, 24, 26, 31, 35–42, 46, 52–3, 61, 85, 91, 93, 156, 161, 164
  On the Constancy of the Wiseman 24, 128
  On Favours 20–1, 24, 49–52
  On the Happy Life 19–20, 24, 61, 118
  On Mercy 5, 11, 15, 24, 42–3, 45–8, 58, 71, 85, 87–8, 91, 124, 136, 138, 166
  On the Private Life 24, 54–7
  On Providence 24, 92, 101, 119, 149–51
  On the Shortness of Life 24, 53, 65
  On Tranquillity of Mind 24, 53
  Phaedra 70, 72, 76, 85, 91, 94, 102–6, 125, 155–6, 166–7
  Phoenician Women 70, 97–9
  Thyestes 67–72, 78, 86, 88, 110, 112–15, 123–4, 139, 141, 143, 145, 149–51, 167, 169
  Trojan Women 70, 95–7, 143
Seneca the Elder 2, 8, 13
Shakespeare, William 143–4, 147, 149, 152–6, 162–3
Shelley, Percy 165–6
slaves 3, 26, 38, 41–2, 51–2, 66, 95
Socrates 22, 24, 27, 31, 42, 53, 90, 104, 120, 159
Sophocles 71–2, 78–9, 84, 97–8, 106–8, 126–7
soul (*animus, mens*) 29–37, 63–4, 131
  and anger 36–7
  of Atreus 67–8, 114
  characters address 92
  of Clytemnestra 110
  extirpating passions 24, 26, 34
  and favours 50
  of Hercules 75
  investigation of 40
  of Medea 75–7, 85–6
  of Nero 48–9, 122
  of Phaedra's nurse 85
  philosophy doctor of 32–3, 54
  of Polyxena 96–7
  reason of 29–31, 37, 104–5, 125, 154
  and revenge 151
  of slaves 52
  studies universe 58
  survives death 64, 97
  of women 35
  writing reveals 63
Spanish Tragedy, The 144–8, 149, 156

Index

Suetonius 3, 12, 46, 118, 120–2, 136–8
suicide 3, 9–10, 21, 23–4, 47, 89, 97, 99, 102, 118–19, 155, 158
Suillius, Publius 18–20, 118

Tacitus 3–4, 10, 12–24, 42–3, 46, 51, 55–6, 80–1, 84–5, 118–19, 121, 124, 132, 135, 161
Tarantino, Quentin 168
Tarrant, Richard 72
Tertullian 131
theatres, Roman 79–80, 82
Tiberius 1, 9–10, 46, 51, 70
tyrant
　Aegisthus 112
　in *On Anger* 164
　in *Antonio's Revenge* 151
　Atreus 113
　Eteocles 98
　Ezzelino III da Romano 138–40
　Hercules rids world of 127

Lycus 93–5
　in *On Mercy* 49, 138
Nero 17
　in *Octavia* 124–5
　in Rome 38, 41–2
　Seneca teacher of 4, 42, 132, 138
　in Seneca's plays 86–7

villas 3, 21–2, 63
Virgil 2, 36, 63, 72–4, 115, 130, 148

wealth 19–21, 23, 30, 52, 62, 90, 114, 118, 120
wise man (Stoic sage) 20, 24, 30–2, 39, 51, 54–5, 113, 126–8, 133, 136

Xanthippe 22

Zeno of Citium 25–6, 29, 35, 55, 61, 131